ARISTOTLE
Nicomachean Ethics

ARISTOTLE

Nicomachean Ethics

Translation, Glossary,
and Introductory Essay

Joe Sachs
St. John's College, Annapolis

Focus Publishing
R. Pullins Company
Newburyport MA

The Focus Philosophical Library

Plato: Sophist • E. Brann, P. Kalkavage, E. Salem • 1996
Plato: Parmenides • Albert Keith Whitaker • 1996
Plato: Symposium • Avi Sharon • 1998
Plato: Phaedo • E. Brann, P. Kalkavage, E. Salem • 1998
Empire and the Ends of Politics • S. D. Collins and D. Stauffer • 1999
Four Island Utopias • D Clay, A. Purvis • 1999
Plato: Timaeus • P. Kalkavage • 2001
Aristotle:Nicomachean Ethics • Joe Sachs • 2002
Hegel: The Philosophy of Right • Alan White • 2002
Socrates and Alcibiades: Four Texts • David M. Johnson • 2003
Plato: Phaedrus • Stephen Scully • 2003
Plato: Meno • George Anastaplo and Laurence Berns • 2004
Spinoza: Theologico-Political Treatise • Martin Yaffe • 2004
Plato: Theaetetus • Joe Sachs • 2004
Aristotle: Poetics • Joe Sachs • 2005
Plato and Xenophon: Apologies • Mark Kremer • 2006
Plato: Gorgias • James Arietti and Roger Barrus • 2007
Plato: Republic • Joe Sachs • 2007
René Descartes: Discourse on Method • R. Kennington, P. Kraus and F. Hunt • 2007
Plato: Gorgias and Aristotle: Rhetoric • Joe Sachs • 2009

Cover image: representing Apollo at Olympia, drawn by Wendy Braithwaite.
Cover Designed by Josh Faigen

22 21 20 19 18 17 16 15 14 13

0714V

CONTENTS

Note: The ten books of the original text have no titles; those below are provided by the translator to indicate the general shape of the inquiry.

PREFACE TO THIS TRANSLATION

The general run of English translations of Aristotle's theoretical works (the primary such works being the *Metaphysics*, the *Physics*, and *On the Soul*) is infected by a long Latin tradition that has obscured and distorted much that it has transmitted, and has blocked access to the straightforward sources of meaning that Aristotle himself made use of and built upon in his own language. In those writings, Aristotle makes use of the most vivid and familiar contents of everyday speech to construct an explanatory vocabulary that seeks to articulate the way the world is and works. The translator who wants to connect the English reader as directly as possible with what is written must bypass the accumulated baggage of a tradition that cannot accomplish that task. But the *Nicomachean Ethics* is much less encumbered with this baggage. In it, Aristotle is writing about matters of ordinary life that have not attracted the jargon that mars the translations of his theoretical works. Why then are the available translations of the *Ethics* not adequate?

There is little or no jargon to worry about in such translations, but there are shades of meaning that connect with the whole of Aristotle's thinking, that have large consequences for understanding him. For example, in Book I of the *Ethics*, Aristotle asks what happiness would be, and that question goes around in circles until he asks what the *ergon* of a human being is (1097b 24-25). In most translations, where this word is rendered as "function," the reader and Aristotle have already begun to go separate ways, and a slight divergence of direction, over a long journey, may produce a great distance between them. A function suggests something subordinate: a stomach has a function because it contributes something necessary to the life of an animal, but what is the animal "for"? In fact, much biological theory differs from that of Aristotle by reducing an animal to a bundle of functions, self-preservative, reproductive, and so on, without recognizing that it also has a life over and above merely staying alive and leaving offspring. The word *ergon* means work, and is the root of *energeia*, being-at-work, the most important word in all of Aristotle's thinking, which turns out in Book I of the *Ethics* to begin to unlock the meaning of human happiness.

Most translations of the *Ethics* render *energeia* as "activity," which is not incorrect, but which gives no sense that this is a special word, dear to Aristotle, at the heart of his theoretical works and giving depth to everything he writes. The connection to those other works cannot be made at all, since in them the same word is traditionally translated as "actuality." But even within the *Ethics*, the word "activity" is an unfortunate choice because it goes past too smoothly and easily, giving the reader nothing to chew on, no occasion to stop and reflect, to begin to think things anew. If one regards the virtue of a translation as smoothness, and its greatest fault as awkwardness, then all philosophical writing must be lost in the translation, reduced to those ordinary choices of words that fit without a hitch into the thinking we have already done. This translation sometimes renders *energeia* as "activity," in passages in which the word is used repeatedly, but only when its special and emphatic meaning is already established for the reader. The reader is thus able to begin exploring the life of a human being in connection with the central idea of being-at-work, as Aristotle himself does in the original, and is put in a position from which the connections Aristotle has made between his theoretical and practical works can be discovered.

Two of the things that Aristotle has said are distinctive about human beings are well known: we are political animals, and we are rational animals. Both of these claims are present in the *Ethics* (1097b 11, 1098a 3-4), and they are generally translated with the two adjectives by which they are so well known. As with "activity" for *energeia*, there is nothing incorrect about using "political" for *politikon* and "rational" for *echôn logon*, but there is something inadequate about these choices. In their root senses, *politikon* means "meant for a city" and *echôn logon* means "having the power of speech." In the *Politics* (1253a 7-18), Aristotle explains that a human city is not just one more kind of herd or hive, because human speech is not just one more kind of vocal communication. Everything that is distinctively human grows out of the special character of our speech, and connects with the special character of our way of associating. These thoughts, or at least the beginnings of them, are resonating in the things Aristotle says about happiness in Book I of the *Ethics*. A translation that omits all access to them may read more smoothly, but it diminishes what Aristotle wrote, and short-changes the reader who wants to think about that. In this translation, the full meanings of these words are given once, when Aristotle begins to build arguments on them.

One more example of what a translation of the *Ethics* needs to capture is perhaps the most important word in the whole work, *hexis*. Like *energeia*, this is an uncommon word before Aristotle gets hold of it, that becomes crucial in his thinking, and the meanings of the two words are related. In everything other than human beings, being-at-work springs from nature alone, and it shapes the lives of all other living things. In human beings, our being-at-work depends on two things, the human nature we all inherit and the kinds of *hexeis* we choose to form. The name *Ethics* means "things pertaining to human character," and Aristotle understands such character to be made up of *hexeis*. We are responsible for what we turn out to be and for our own lives, because we decisively determine the *hexeis* that come to be our selves (1114b 22-24). The general run of current translations of the *Ethics* has settled on the word "state" to render the meaning of *hexis*. But what defines a *hexis* is that it is not a passive state but an active condition, a way in which we hold ourselves, having taken hold deliberately of the feelings and dispositions that are in us merely passively (1105b 25-28, 1106a 2-4). To say merely that a *hexis* is a state is like translating the word for giraffe as "animal"; it says nothing untrue, but it is not a translation at all. And when the word at stake is the one the author has chosen as the explanation of the central topic he is writing about, a translation that fails to convey its meaning has a mere void at its heart. The only thing worse than such a void would be an incorrect and misleading translation, and one recent translator has given us just that by rendering *hexis* as "habit"; this is a deadly effect of a misunderstood tradition, since it selects an English word that, while cognate with a correct Latin translation of *hexis*, is so misleading in English that it undermines everything Aristotle considers crucial in the *Ethics*.

In this translation I have aimed at accuracy above all else, with the hope of putting you in contact with Aristotle, as nearly as you can be without reading his Greek. The footnotes often go beyond supplying references and cross-references, but they are all meant to help get you closer to the original text; they contain interpretations and opinions of mine that you should not take as authoritative, but as ways to get you involved in an active reading. The introduction appeared, in a slightly different form, in the *St. John's Review*, Vol. XLIV, No. 1 (1997). It is reprinted here by permission of the editor. The glossary, in which I explain my primary translation choices, can be read through as a summary of my own interpretation, equivalent to a second introduction.

My reading of this work has grown through many years, going back to the help of such teachers as Robert Bart, when I began to read Aristotle, and J. Winfree Smith, when I began to translate some of his works for publication. For the past ten years or so, I have been part of a study group that has, through all seasons, kept meeting to read various works of Aristotle, and that spent about five years reading the *Nicomachean Ethics*. Too many people to name have been part of it at various times, but certain facts should be recorded: that the group came into being when Brother Robert Smith added casually, at the end of a dinner invitation, "if you feel like it, bring your *De Anima*"; that I have learned something new at every meeting of the group and from everyone who has been in it; and that it has embodied the genuine community of learning that is St. John's College, and benefited from considerable cross-pollination between that college's two campuses in Annapolis, Maryland, and Santa Fe, New Mexico. One loyal member of that group has been Eric Salem, whose knowledge of the *Nicomachean Ethics* matches that of any published index, and whose understanding of it surpasses that of any book; he has been kind enough to read through a draft of the entire translation, and suggest hundreds of corrections and improvements. I have had enough sense to adopt most of them. Keith Whitaker, of Focus Publishing, has also been a helpful and critical reader, and a welcoming editor and facilitator for this project.

The translation is made from the nineteenth printing of the Oxford Classical Text of the *Nicomachean Ethics*, edited by Ingram Bywater, first published in 1894. In a few places a reading given in the version edited by John Burnet in 1900 has been preferred, and Burnet's notes have been valuable sources of information of all kinds. Square brackets in the text have occasionally been used for material added for clarity, when this has gone beyond repeating the antecedent of a pronoun that is unambiguously implied. The numbers 1094a to 1181b running through the text in the margins indicate the pages and columns of the nineteenth century Bekker edition of Aristotle's works, that is used as a standard pagination; the numbers between them refer (approximately) to the lines of the Oxford Classical Text.

Enjoy Aristotle, whether you agree with him about everything or not. Even when you disagree, you may find yourself joining him in discovering that the being-at-work of thinking is an indispensable part of human happiness.

JOE SACHS
ANNAPOLIS, MARYLAND
SUMMER, 2000

INTRODUCTION
THREE LITTLE WORDS

Three words that anyone who has tried to understand the *Nicomachean Ethics* has had to wrestle with are **habit**, the **mean**, and **noble**. They might be said, very loosely, to refer to the efficient, formal, and final causes of moral virtue, but each of them is easy to misunderstand, and any misunderstanding at such a crucial place must carry one far away from Aristotle's intentions. This introduction is meant to be a preliminary approach toward uncovering those intentions. I will argue that all three words invite misunderstanding, the first because it is not habit but character that makes moral virtue possible, the second because it is not any quantitative adjustment to a mean that achieves that virtue, but a qualitative state that stands between obstacles, and the third because the word noble is simply a poor translation of a Greek word that has a much richer meaning, and a straightforward English equivalent.

PART I: HABIT

Most people, if asked to choose one word that describes the central focus of Aristotle's ethics, would be likely to say that it is habit. A faculty seminar at St. John's College some years ago got itself mired in the opinion that Aristotle must be saying that the good life is one of mindless routine, and a recent lecture there took Aristotle to task for praising habit when so much that is important in life depends upon openness and spontaneity. But is it even plausible to think that Aristotle thought the aim of a good life is to eliminate thinking and choosing?

Certainly it makes no sense to offer that opinion as a possible interpretation either of virtue or of Aristotle. But equally certainly, Aristotle says that, for the way our lives turn out, "it makes no small difference to be habituated this way or that way straight from childhood, but an enormous difference, or rather *all* the difference." (1103b, 23-5) But is this the same as saying those lives are nothing but collections of habits? We need to think about causes and effects. It may be that eating a good breakfast makes all the difference to your having a productive day, but that does not mean that the breakfast is the only cause of what you accomplish each day, or that those accomplishments are only nutritional. The habits that begin in childhood, like the nutrition that begins each morning, may be indispensable to what follows without determining it. Habits are not the only effects of habituation.

Now if you have read the *Nicomachean Ethics* in the translation of Hippocrates Apostle, you will object that Aristotle says plainly that virtues are habits. Here, though, we have run into one of the many ways in which a Latin tradition has betrayed a translator and distorted Aristotle's meaning. Aristotle says that moral virtue is a *hexis*, a word consisting of a noun ending attached to the root of the verb *echein*. The Latin *habeo* is equivalent to *echein*, and the Latin *habitus* is a perfectly good translation of *hexis*, and so, by one more easy step we get the English word "habit." But this paint-by-the-numbers approach to translation carries us so far astray that every implication of the English word is wrong. A *hexis* is not only not the same as a habit, but is almost exactly its opposite.

The meaning of the word *hexis* becomes an issue in Plato's *Theaetetus*. Socrates makes the point that knowledge can never be a mere passive possession, stored in the memory the way birds can be kept in cages. The word for that sort of possession is *ktêsis*, something that can be owned, hoarded, and locked away like money. Socrates suggests that whatever knowledge is, it must have the character of a *hexis*, an active having-and-holding that depends on the effort of concentrating or paying attention. Meno, in the dialogue named for him, speaks always from habit, but cannot begin an approach to knowledge because he will not sustain an effort to say what virtue seems to him, right now, to be. The verb *echein* means to have something in that effortful way, or to be something in an enduring and active way, and its corresponding noun is *hexis*. By choosing that word, Aristotle says that a moral virtue is an active state or condition.

Most translators do not make the mistake of turning virtues into habits, but some translate *hexis* as "disposition." But in other writings, such as the *Categories* (8b, 29) and *On The Soul* (417b 15-17), Aristotle makes it clear that the general class of dispositions includes passive states such as heat, cold, and sickness, that are easy to remove and change, as well as active states such as perceiving and knowing, that engage the soul in its depths. The general word for disposition, *diathesis*, Aristotle uses only for the passive and shallow ones; for the deep and active ones he reserves the word *hexis*. Perceiving may seem to us, as it seemed to many of Aristotle's predecessors, to be a passive state, but he is emphatic that we are only open to the world by the effort of holding ourselves ready. And if knowledge seems to be something imposed upon us by teaching or training, we are not paying sufficient attention to the kind of learning that is called recollection in the *Meno*. In Book VII of the *Physics*,

Aristotle says that children are not changed or acted upon when they begin to learn, but get straight into an active state when time or adults help them settle down out of their native condition of disorder and distraction. (247b 17-248a 6) In Plato's image we draw knowledge up out of ourselves; in Aristotle's metaphor we settle down into knowing. Think of the humble example of a child's learning its native language. If we had to tell the child what to do, the task would be hopeless. We are indispensable to them, but they do all the work. The particular language they learn comes from without, but is not imposed, but is rather something that the deepest things in them reach out to grasp. This is exactly the way Aristotle understands moral virtue; in the passage cited from the *Physics*, he says virtues no more alter what we are than putting on its roof alters a house.

It is in Book II, chapter 4, of the *Ethics* that Aristotle identifies moral virtue as an active state, distinguishing it from such passive conditions of the soul as feelings and impulses, as well as from the mere capacities that belong to us by nature. This way of arguing presupposes one of the central claims of the whole inquiry, that the virtue of an action resides in the doer, not in the deed. It may escape our notice that, if Aristotle is right, there is no point whatever in the sort of discussion that sets up hypothetical situations and asks what the right thing to do is. Would you press a button that would kill one person in China and avert nuclear war? That was once a popular dilemma that passed for ethical philosophy. A well-known book on ethics began with the plight of a pioneer woman who must kill her baby to save the rest of the family from being found by hostile natives. If this sort of talk strikes you as childish, it may be because you incline toward Aristotle's view that no action is good or right or just or courageous because of any quality of its own. Virtue manifests itself in action, but only when one acts while holding oneself in a certain way. In Greek, the phrase "holding oneself in a certain way" is *pôs echôn*, and the noun equivalent to it is *hexis*.

How must one hold oneself, if one's act is to be worthy of the name virtue? Aristotle's first and most general description of this active state is that in it one holds oneself in a stable equilibrium of the soul, in order to choose the action knowingly and for its own sake. I am translating as "in a stable equilibrium" the pair of adverbs *bebaiôs kai ametakinêtôs*. The first means "stably" or "after having taken a stand"; the second, if it didn't have the *meta* between the negative prefix and the root, would mean "immovably," and make the pair signify acting from a rigid stand. With the extra prefix, though, the second adverb means "in a condition from which one can't be moved all the way over into a different condition." A Newton's wheel in a state of stable equilibrium is like that: however one moves it, it always comes back to rest with the weight below the center. Virtue cannot, by this account, be an inflexible adherence to rules or duty or precedent.

Already, at this first step, one may see that Aristotle cannot mean by virtue what we call habit. Habitual action need not be chosen knowingly, and it does not have a flexible constancy but a mindless uniformity. Even an expert on habits can be taken unawares, as in the story told of the behavioral scientist B. F. Skinner, that a class of his once trained him always to lecture from the same corner of the room, by smiling and nodding whenever he approached it, but frowning and faintly shaking their heads when he moved away from it. Even when we deliberately impose habits on ourselves, what remains has in it nothing of the original purpose, but only a passive and mechanical response to a superficial sameness in outer circumstances. The stable equilibrium that Aristotle is talking about is not habit—*ethos* in Greek—but character: *êthos*.

In this case, the change from an epsilon to an eta carries us from the cause to its effect, since Aristotle's claim is that character is the result of habit. It should now be clear, though, that the habit is no part of that character. Our task now is to understand how an active condition of the soul can arise as a consequence of a passive one, and why the passive condition is a necessary step toward the active one. I remind you that Aristotle's main examples of active states other than the moral virtues are knowing and attentive seeing. We have only to look around us, or in the mirror, to find countless examples of the passive and mindless conditions that are our habits: biting one's nails, twisting one's hair, saying "like" between every two words. Our mindless habits seem to be at the farthest remove from conditions like knowing in which we are most alive. But in fact there is another condition in us, in which we are even farther removed from our active states.

We all start out life governed by our desires and impulses. These conditions do not last as long as habits do, but come and go, but when present they are very strong. Listen to a child who can't live without some toy that has aroused its desire in the toy store, or its greed in another child's house, or who makes you feel like a murderer for trying to leave it alone in a dark room. How can such powerful impulses be overcome? To expect a child to let go of the desire or fear that grips it may seem as hopeless as Aristotle's example of trying to train a stone to fall upward, were it not for the fact that we all know that we have somehow, for the most part, broken the power of those tyrannical feelings. We don't expel them altogether, but we do get the upper hand; an adult who has temper tantrums like those of a two-year-old has to live in an institution, and not in the adult world. But the impulses and desires don't weaken; it is rather the case that we get stronger.

Aristotle doesn't go into much detail about how this happens, but what he does say is that we get the virtues by working at them: in the give-and-take with other people, some become just, others unjust; by acting in the face of frightening things and being habituated to be fearful or confident, some become brave and others cowardly; and some become moderate and gentle, others spoiled and bad-tempered, by turning around from one thing and toward another in the midst of desires and passions. (1103b, 14-22) He sums this up by saying that when we are at work in a certain way, an active state results. This apparently unremarkable sentence seems to me to be one of the linch-pins that hold together the *Ethics*, and to mark the transition from the language of habit to the language appropriate to character. It says that a *hexis* comes into being out of an *energeia*. The latter word does not mean mere behavior, however repetitive and constant it may be. It may be translated as being-at-work, and this is the central idea in all of Aristotle's thinking. Here it ties his ethics to his whole account of nature, and to the structure of being. It is only this philosophic understanding that makes intelligible the transition out of childhood and into the moral stature that comes with character and virtue.

The moral life can be, and often is, confused with the habits approved by some society and imposed on its young. For example, the audience at every formal lecture at St. John's College stands when the lecturer enters the room. This is because the president of the college in the 1930s and 40s was a Virginia gentleman who always stood when anyone entered or left a room. What he considered good breeding became, for later generations, mere habit. This is painfully clear in these thoughtless times when some some student who stood at the beginning of a lecture gets bored and leaves in the middle of it. In such a case the politeness was just for show, and the rudeness is the truth. Why shouldn't we think that all habituation of the young is of this sort? To test this opinion, we need to look more deeply into the soul, and to realize that there is a whole layer of habituation that precedes the encounter of any child with its elders.

We all arrive on the scene of human interaction already habituated: in the habit, that is, of yielding to impulses and desires, of instantly slackening the tension of pain or fear or unfulfilled desire in any way open to us, and all this has become automatic in us before thinking and choosing are available to us at all. This is a description of what is called human nature, though in fact it is a barrier that blocks our access to our true natural state. This is why Aristotle says that "the virtues come about in us neither by nature nor apart from nature". (1103a, 24-5) What we call human nature, and Hobbes calls the state of nature, is both natural and unnatural; it is the passive part of our natures, passively reinforced by habit. Virtue has the aspect of a second nature, because it cannot develop first, nor by a continuous process out of our first condition. But it is only in the moral virtues that we possess our primary nature, that in which all our capacities can have their full development. Moral virtue does not constrain a human being but completes us as a roof completes a house. The sign of what is natural, for Aristotle, is pleasure, but we have to know how to read the signs. Things pleasant by nature, he says, have no opposite pain and no excess, because they set us free to act simply as what we are (1154b, 15-21), and it is in this sense that Aristotle calls the life of virtue pleasant in its own right, in itself. (1099a, 6-7, 16-17) A mere habit of acting contrary to our inclinations cannot be a virtue, by the infallible sign that we don't like it.

Our first or childish nature is never eradicated, though, and this is why Aristotle says that our nature is not simple, but also has in it something different that makes our happiness assailable from within, and makes us love change even when it is for the worse. (1154b 21-32) How do we move from this first nature to a more stable and satisfying condition? Parents who care about their children's happiness have no difficulty in seeing that a child sometimes has to hear the word no, even when it might easily be given one more desired thing, or allowed to avoid one more frightening thing. If the time is out of joint, a parent might even need the same sort of help from her child. I quote from *Hamlet* (III, iv, 181-9):

> Assume a virtue if you have it not,
> That monster, custom, who all sense doth eat
> Of habits evil, is angel yet in this,
> That to the use of actions fair and good
> He likewise gives a frock or livery,
> That aptly is put on. Refrain tonight,
> And that shall lend a kind of easiness
> To the next abstinence; the next more easy;
> For use almost can change the stamp of nature...

Hamlet is talking to a middle-aged woman about lust, but the pattern is universal, and expresses the common experience of human beings. What is at work here that is so effective? We are in a position to see that it is not the stamp of nature that needs to be changed, but the earliest stamp of habit. We can drop Hamlet's "almost" and rid his last quoted line of all paradox by seeing that the reason we need habit is to change the stamp of habit. A habit of yielding to impulse can be counteracted by an equal and opposite habit. This second habit is no virtue, but only a mindless inhibition, an automatic repressing of impulse. Nor do the two opposite habits together produce virtue, but rather a state of neutrality. When habit is checked and balanced by habit, something else must emerge to become responsible for action. Aristotle's use of the word *energeia* suggests that this happens on its own, with no need for anything new to be imposed. Habituation does not stifle nature, but rather lets nature make its appearance. The description from Book VII of the *Physics* of the way children begin to learn applies equally well to the way human character begins to be formed: we settle down, out of the turmoil of childishness, into what we are by nature.

We can now see how it is that habituation does not complete the progress toward virtue, but only begins it. Aristotle describes a motion from habit to being-at-work to the *hexis* or active state that can give the soul moral stature. If the human soul had no being-at-work, no inherent and indelible activity, there could be no such moral stature, but only customs. In Book I of the *Ethics*, when first trying to give content to the idea of happiness, Aristotle asks if it would make sense to think that a carpenter or shoemaker has work to do but a human being as such is inert. His reply, of course, is that nature has given us work to do, in default of which we are necessarily unhappy, and that work is to put into action the power of reason. (1097b, 24-1098a, 4) Note please that he does not say that everyone must be a philosopher, nor even that human life is constituted by the activity of reason, but that reason must come forward into our action. Later, Aristotle makes explicit that the irrational impulses are no less human than reasoning is. (1111b, 1-2) His point is that, as human beings, our desires need *not* be mindless and random, but can be transformed by thinking into choices—that is, desires informed by deliberation. (1113a, 11) The characteristic human way of being-at-work is the threefold activity of seeing an end, thinking about means to it, and choosing an action. Responsible human action depends upon the combining of all the powers of the soul: perception, imagination, reasoning, and desiring. These are all things that are at work in us all the time. Good parental training does not produce them, or mold them, or alter them, but sets them free to be effective in action. This is the way in which, according to Aristotle, despite the contributions of parents, society, and nature, we are the co-authors of the active states of our own souls. (1114b, 23-4)

PART II: THE MEAN

Now this discussion has shown that habit does make all the difference to our lives without being the only thing shaping those lives, and without being the final form they take. The same discussion also points to a way to make some sense of one of the things that has always puzzled me most in the *Ethics*, the insistence that moral virtue is always in its own nature a mean condition. Quantitative relations are so far from any serious human situation that they would seem to be present only incidentally or metaphorically, but Aristotle says that "by its thinghood and by the account that unfolds what it is for it to be, virtue is a mean." (1107a, 7-8) This invites such quantitative literalness as that in the following sentences that I quote from a recent journal article by Fred Seddon (*Ancient Philosophy* Vol. 8, pp. 101-4): "To illustrate...0 marks the mean (e.g. Courage);...Cowardice is -5 while Rashness is 3...In our number language...'Always try to lower the absolute value of your vice.'" This scholar thinks achieving courage is like tuning in a radio station on an analog dial. Those who do not go this far might still think Aristotle is praising a kind of mediocrity, like that found in people who used to go to college to get gentlemen's C's. It should be clear that no sort of courage could be found in those timid souls, whose only aim in life is to blend so well into their social surroundings that virtue would never be chosen in preference to a fashionable vice. Aristotle points out twice that every moral virtue is an extreme (1107a 8-9, 22-4), but he keeps that observation secondary to an over-riding sense in which it is a mean.

Could there be anything at all to the notion that we home in on a virtue from two sides? There is a wonderful image of this sort of thing in the novel *Nop's Trials* by Donald McCaig. The protagonist is not a human being, but a border collie named Nop. The author describes the way the dog has to find the balance point, the exact distance behind a herd of sheep from which he can drive the whole herd forward in a coherent mass. When the dog is too close, the sheep panic and run off in all directions; when he is too far back, the sheep ignore him, and turn in all directions to graze. While in motion, a good working dog keeps adjusting his pace to maintain the exact mean position that keeps the sheep stepping lively in the direction he determines. Now working border collies are brave, tireless, and determined; they have been documented as running more than a hundred miles in a day, and they love their work. There is no question that they display virtue, but it is not human virtue and not even of the same form. Some human activities do require the long sustained tension a sheep dog is always holding on to, an active state stretched to the limit, constantly and anxiously kept in balance. Running on a tightrope might capture the same flavor. But constantly maintained anxiety is not the kind of stable equilibrium that Aristotle attributes to the virtuous human soul.

We stumbled on a more stable sort of mean condition when we saw that habits are needed to counteract other habits. This way of reaching a mean also accords with the things Aristotle says about straightening warped boards, aiming away from the worse extreme, and being on guard against the seductions of pleasure. (1109a, 30-b, 9) It must be our way to the mean for each of the moral virtues, but how it works is perhaps clearest in respect to temperance. The glutton, the drunkard, the person enslaved to every sexual impulse obviously cannot ever be happy, but the opposite extremes, which Aristotle groups together as a kind of numbness or denial of the senses (1107b, 8), miss the proper relation to bodily pleasure on the other side. It may seem that temperance in relation to food, say, depends merely on determining how many ounces of cake to eat. This seems to follow from Aristotle's example of Milo the wrestler, who needs more food than the rest of us, but I think that misses the point. That example is given only to show that there is no single action that can ever be prescribed as right for every person and every circumstance, and it is not strictly analogous even to temperance with respect to food. What is at stake is not a correct quantity of food but a right relation to the pleasure that comes from eating.

Suppose that you have carefully saved a slice of cake all day for your mid-evening snack, and just as you are ready to treat yourself, a friend arrives unexpectedly to visit. If you are a glutton, you might hide the cake until the friend leaves, or gobble it down before you open the door. If you have the opposite vice, and have puritanically suppressed in yourself all indulgence in the pleasures of food, the hypothesis probably fails, and you won't have cake or any other treat to offer your visitor. If the state of your soul is in the mean in these matters, you are neither enslaved to nor shut out from the pleasure of eating treats, and can enhance the visit of a friend by sharing them. What you are sharing is incidentally the six ounces of cake; the point is that you are sharing the pleasure, which is not found on any scale of measurement. A sign that your soul is in good shape would be the fact that the pleasure is even greater when the quantity of food is less. But to discover this pleasure, you need to be free from both the tyranny of desire, and the forcible restraint of desire. The characteristically human enhancements of life open up in the middle region.

This example demonstrates that the mean that constitutes temperance is not in anything external and measureable, but only in the soul. It is also enlightening, I think, in another way. No argument seems needed about why sharing the treat is the right thing to do. We all know it is right—don't we?—and we know it more clearly and immediately than we know any principle that it might be argued from. Aristotle says that we know such things by perception, not the perception of any one of the five senses, but the sort by which we perceive that a triangle is the last kind of figure into which a polygon can be divided. (1142a, 28-30) This sort of perceiving contains thinking and imagining, but what it judges, it judges by perceiving it to be so. In matters pertaining to character, our childish habits, or any traces of them that remain in us, cloud our sight, but the effect of the liberating counter-habit is to clear that sight. That is why Aristotle says that the person of moral stature, the *spoudaios*, is the one to whom things appear as they truly are. (1113a 30-1) Once the earliest habits are neutralized, our desires are disentangled from the pressure for immediate gratification, we are calm enough to think, and most important, we can see what is in front of us in all its possibility. The mean state here is not a point on a dial that we need to fiddle up and down; it is a clearing in the midst of pleasures and pains that lets us judge what seems most truly pleasant and painful.

The other sort of mean, that which requires a constant adjustment between too much and too little indulgence, is a recognizable human condition, but not one that Aristotle will call virtue. This sheep-dog-like state of the soul is what Aristotle means by self-restraint or continence. In such people, who are perhaps most of us, the reasoning part of the soul is keeping the impulses reined in, but those impulses can slip the reins and go their own way, as parts of the body do in people with certain disorders of the nerves. (1102b, 14-22) Control in self-restrained people is an anxious, unstable equilibrium that will lapse whenever vigilance is relaxed. We sometimes think of life as a conflict between the head and the heart, but in such a situation there is no unity of the human being, but only truces, compromises, and temporary victories of parties with divergent interests. The virtuous soul, on the contrary, blends all its parts in the act of choice.

This, I think, is the best way to understand the active state of the soul that constitutes moral virtue and forms character. It is the condition in which all the powers of the soul are at work together, making it possible for action to engage the whole human being. The work of achieving character is a process of clearing away the obstacles that stand in the way of the full efficacy of the soul. Someone who is partial to food or drink, or to running away from trouble, or to looking for trouble, is a partial human being. Let the whole power of the soul have its influence, and the choices that result will have the characteristic look that we call courage or temperance or simply virtue. Now this adjective "characteristic" comes from the Greek word *charactêr*, which means the distinctive mark scratched or stamped on anything, and which is never used in the *Nicomachean Ethics*. In the sense of character of which we are speaking, the word for which is *êthos*, we see an outline of the human form itself. A person of character is someone you can count on, because there is a human nature in a deeper sense than that which refers to our early state of weakness. Someone with character has taken a stand in that fully mature nature, and cannot be moved all the way out of it.

But there is also such a thing as bad character, and this is what Aristotle means by vice, as distinct from bad habits or weakness. It is possible for someone with full responsibility and the free use of intellect to choose always to yield to bodily pleasure, or to greed, or to ambition. Virtue is a mean, first because it can only emerge out of the stand-off between pairs of opposite habits, but second because it chooses to take its stand not in any of those habits but between them. In this middle region, thinking does come into play, but it is not correct to say that virtue takes its stand in principle; Aristotle makes clear that vice is a principled choice that following some extreme path toward or away from pleasure is right. (1146b, 22-3) Principles are wonderful things, but there are too many of them, and exclusive adherence to any one of them is always a vice.

In our earlier example, the true glutton would be someone who does not just have a bad habit of always indulging the desire for food, but someone who has chosen on principle that one ought always to yield to it. In Plato's *Gorgias*, Callicles argues just that, about food, drink, and sex. He is serious, even though he is young and still open to argument. But the only principled alternative he can conceive is the denial of the body, and the choice of a life fit only for stones or corpses. (492E) This is the way most attempts to be serious about right action go astray. What, for example, is the virtue of a seminar leader? Is it to ask appropriate questions but never state an opinion? Or is it to offer everything one has learned on the subject of discussion? What principle should rule—that all learning must come from the learners, or that without prior instruction no useful learning can take place? Is there a hybrid principle? Or should one try to find the point mid-way between the opposite principles? Or is the virtue some third thing altogether?

Just as habits of indulgence always stand opposed to habits of abstinence, so too does every principle of action have its opposite principle. If good habituation ensures that we are not swept away by our strongest impulses, and the exercise of intelligence ensures that we will see two worthy sides to every question about action, what governs the choice of the mean? Aristotle gives this answer: "such things are among particulars, and the judgement is in the act of sense-perception." (1109b 23-4) But this is the calmly energetic, thought-laden perception to which we referred earlier. The origin of virtuous action is neither intellect nor appetite, but is variously described as intellect infused through-and-through with appetite, or appetite wholly infused with thinking, or appetite and reason joined for the sake of something; this unitary source is called by Aristotle simply *anthropos*. (1139a, 34, b, 5-7) But our thinking must contribute right reason (*ho orthos logos*) and our appetites must contribute *right* desire (*hê orthê orexis*) if the action is to have moral stature. (1114b, 29, 1139a, 24-6, 31-2) What makes them right can only be the something for the sake of which they unite, and this is what is said to be accessible only to sense perception. This brings us to the third word we need to think about.

PART III: THE NOBLE?

Aristotle says plainly and repeatedly what it is that moral virtue is for the sake of, but the translators are afraid to give it to you straight. Most of them say it is the noble. One of them says it is the fine. If these answers went past you without even registering, that is probably because they make so little sense. To us, the word noble probably connotes some sort of high-minded naiveté, something hopelessly impractical. But Aristotle considers moral virtue the only practical road to effective action. The word fine is of the same sort but worse, suggesting some flimsy artistic soul who couldn't endure rough treatment, while Aristotle describes moral virtue as the most stable and durable condition in which we can meet all of life's obstacles. The word the translators are afraid of is *to kalon*, the beautiful. Aristotle singles out as the distinguishing mark of courage, for example, that it is always "for the sake of the beautiful, for this is the end of virtue." (1115b, 12-13) Of magnificence, or large-scale philanthropy, he says it is "for the sake of the beautiful, for this is common to the virtues." (1122b, 7-8) What the person of good character loves with right desire and thinks of as an end with right reason must first be perceived as beautiful.

The Loeb translator explains why he does not use the word beautiful in the *Nicomachean Ethics*. He tells us *to kalon* has two different uses, and refers both to "(1) bodies well shaped and works of art...well made, and (2) actions well done." (p. 6) The latter sense is ethical, while the former is dismissed as merely "aesthetic." But we have just noticed that Aristotle says that the judgement of what is morally right belongs to sense-perception. And he explicitly compares the act that springs from moral virtue to a well-made work of art. People praise the latter by saying it would not be possible to add anything to it or take anything from it, and Aristotle says that virtue differs from art in that respect only by being more precise and better. (1106b, 10-15) An action is right in the same way that a painting might get everything just right. Antigone contemplates in her imagination the act of burying her brother, and says "it would be a beautiful thing to die doing this." (*Antigone*, line 72) This is as pure an example as I know of Aristotle's description of courage. Neoptolemus stops Philoctetes from killing Odysseus with the bow he has just returned, and says "neither for me nor for you is this a beautiful thing." (*Philoctetes*, line 1304) This is a recognition that the rightness of returning the bow would be spoiled if it were used for revenge. This is not some special usage of the Greek language, but one that speaks to us directly, if the translators let it. And it is not a kind of language that belongs only to poetic tragedy, since the tragedians find their subjects by recognizing human virtue in circumstances that are most hostile to it.

In the most ordinary circumstances, any mother might say to a misbehaving child, in plain English, "don't be so ugly." And any of us, parent, friend, or grudging enemy, might on occasion say to someone else, "that was a beautiful thing you did." Is it by some wild coincidence that twentieth-century English and fourth-century BC Greek link the same pair of uses under one word? Aristotle is always alert to the natural way that important words have more than one meaning. The inquiry in his *Metaphysics* is built around the progressive narrowing of the word *being* until its primary meaning is discovered. In the *Physics*, the various senses of motion and change are played on like the keyboard of a piano, and serve to uncover the double source of natural activity. The inquiry into ethics is not built in this fashion; Aristotle asks about the way the various meanings of the good are organized, but he immediately drops the question, as being more at home in another sort of philosophic inquiry. (1096b, 26-32) It is widely claimed that Aristotle says there is no good itself, or any other form at all of the sort spoken of in Plato's dialogues. This is a misreading of any text of Aristotle to which it is referred. Here in the study of ethics it is a failure to see that the idea of the good is not rejected simply, but only held off as a question that does not arise as first for us. Aristotle praises Plato for understanding that philosophy does not argue from first principles but toward them. (1095a, 31-3)

But while Aristotle does not make the meanings of the good an explicit theme that shapes his inquiry, he nevertheless does plainly lay out its three highest senses, and does narrow down the three into two and indirectly into one. He tells us there are three kinds of good toward which our choices look: the pleasant, the beautiful, and the beneficial or advantageous. (1104b, 31-2) The last of these is clearly subordinate to the other two, and when the same issue comes up next, it has dropped out of the list. The goods sought for their own sake are said to be of only two kinds, the pleasant and the beautiful. (1110b, 9-12) That the beautiful is the primary sense of the good is less obvious, both because the pleasant is itself resolved into a variety of senses, and because a whole side of virtue that we are not considering in this introduction aims at the true, but we can sketch out some ways in which the beautiful emerges as the end of human action.

Aristotle's first description of moral virtue required that the one acting choose an action knowingly, out of a stable equilibrium of the soul, and for its own sake. The knowing in question turned out to be perceiving things as they are, as a result of the habituation that clears our sight. The stability turned out to come from the active condition of all the powers of the soul, in the mean position opened up by that same habituation, since it neutralized an earlier, opposite, and passive habituation to self-indulgence. In the accounts of the particular moral virtues, an action's being chosen for it own sake is again and again specified as meaning chosen for no reason other than that it is beautiful. In Book III, chapter 8, Aristotle refuses to call courageous anyone who acts bravely for the sake of honor, out of shame, from experience that the danger is not as great as it seems, out of spiritedness or anger or the desire for revenge, or from optimism or ignorance. Genuinely courageous action is in no obvious way pleasant, and is not chosen for that reason, but there is according to Aristotle a truer pleasure inherent in it. It doesn't need pleasure dangled in front of it as an extra added attraction. Lasting and satisfying pleasure never comes to those who seek pleasure, but only to the *philokalos*, who looks past pleasure to the beautiful. (1099a, 15-17, 13)

In our earlier example of temperance, I think most of us would readily agree that the one who had his eye only on the slice of cake found less pleasure than the one who saw that it would be a better thing to share it. And Aristotle does say explicitly that the target the temperate person looks to is the beautiful. (1119b, 15-17) But since there are three primary moral virtues—courage, temperance, and justice—it is surprising that in the whole of Book V, which discusses justice, Aristotle never mentions the beautiful. It must somehow be applicable, since he says it is common to all the moral virtues, but in that case the account of justice seems to be incomplete, unless it is completed in some later part of the *Ethics* by being brought into relation to the beautiful. This is exactly what does happen, although I read the book dozens of times before I grasped it.

Justice seems to be not only *a* moral virtue, but in some pre-eminent way *the* moral virtue. Aristotle says that there is a sense of the word in which the one we call just is the person who has all moral virtue, insofar as it affects other people. (1129b, 26-7) He even quotes a line from Euripides, that "neither sunset nor sunrise is so wonderful" as justice. In spite of all this, I believe that Aristotle treats justice as something inherently inadequate, a condition of the soul that cannot ever achieve the end at which it aims. Justice concerns itself with the right distribution of rewards and punishments within a community. This would seem to be the chief aim of the lawmakers, but Aristotle says that they do not take justice as seriously as friendship. They accord friendship a higher moral stature that justice. (1155a, 23-4) It seems to me now that Aristotle does too, and that the discussion of friendship in Books VIII and IX replaces that of justice.

What is the purpose of reward and punishment? I take Aristotle's answer to be *homonoia*, the like-mindedness that allows a community to act in concord. For the sake of this end, he says, it is not good enough that people be just, while if they are friends they have no need to be just. (1155a, 24-9) So far, this sounds as though friendship is merely something advantageous for the social or political good, but Aristotle immediately adds that it is also beautiful. The whole account of friendship, you will recall, is structured around the three-fold meaning of the good. Friendships are distinguished as being for use, for pleasure, or for love of the friend's character.

Repeatedly, after raising questions about the highest kind of friendship, Aristotle resolves them by looking to the beautiful: it is a beautiful thing to do favors for someone freely, without expecting a return (1163a, 1, 1168a, 10-13); even in cases of urgent necessity, when there is a choice about whom to benefit, one should first decide whether the scale tips toward the necessary or the beautiful thing (1165a, 4-5); to use money to support our parents is always more beautiful than to use it for ourselves (1165a, 22-4); someone who strives to achieve the beautiful in action would never be accused of being selfish (1168b, 25-8). These observations culminate in the claim that "if all people competed for the beautiful, and strained to do the most beautiful things, everything people need in common, and the greatest good for each in particular, would be achieved... for the person of moral stature will forego money, honor, and all the good things people fight over to achieve the beautiful for himself." (1169a, 8-11, 20-22) This does not mean that people can do without such things as money and honor, but that the distribution of such things takes care of itself when people look to the good that is highest by nature. Justice, by contrast, Aristotle says in the *Politics*, looks only to what is necessary, and has only the sort of beauty that necessary things can have. (1332a, 11-15)

The description of the role of the beautiful in moral virtue is most explicit in the discussion of courage, where the emphasis is on the great variety of things that resemble courage but fail to achieve it because they are not solely for the sake of the beautiful. That discussion is therefore mostly negative. There is also something of a tragic feeling to it, with its ever-present paradigm of the extreme situation of war, in which nothing might be left to choose but a beautiful death. We can now see that the discussion of justice was also of a negative character, since justice itself resembles the moral virtue of friendship without achieving it, again because it does not govern its action by looking to the beautiful. The largest collection of positive examples of beautiful actions in the *Ethics* is in the discussion of friendship, which points to the healthy community in which civil war and other conflicts are driven away by the choice of what is beautiful in life. (1155a, 24-7) By the end of the ninth book, there is no doubt that Aristotle does indeed believe in a primary sense of the good, at least in the human realm, and that the name of this good is the beautiful.

And it should be noticed that the beautiful is at work not only in the human realm. In *On The Soul*, Aristotle argues that while the soul moves itself in the act of choice, the ultimate source of its motion is the practical good toward which it looks, which causes motion while it is itself motionless. (433a, 29-30, b, 11-13) This structure of the motionless first mover is taken up in Book XII of the *Metaphysics*, where Aristotle argues that the order of the cosmos depends on such a source, which causes motion in the manner of something loved; he calls this source, as one of its names, the beautiful, and says it is that which is beautiful not in seeming but in being. (1072a, 26-b, 4) Like Diotima in Plato's *Symposium*, Aristotle makes the beautiful the good itself.

Before ending this introduction, I want to comment on the fact that the beautiful in the *Ethics* is not an object of contemplation simply, but the source of action. In a lecture on the *Poetics* I discussed the intimate connection of beauty with the experience of wonder. The sense of wonder seems to me to be the way of seeing which allows things to appear as what they are, since it holds off our tendencies to make things fit into the theories or opinions we already hold, or to use things for purposes that have nothing to do with them. That is why philosophy begins in wonder, as does the whole of the contemplative life. But the way I have just described the experience of wonder in a theoretical context is exactly the same as what Aristotle repeatedly says is the ultimate effect of moral virtue: that the one who has it sees truly and judges rightly, since only to someone of good character do the things that are beautiful appear as they truly are (1113a, 29-35), that practical wisdom depends on moral virtue to make its aim right (1144a, 7-9), and that the eye of the soul that sees what is beautiful as the end or highest good of action gains its active state only with moral virtue (1144a, 26-33). That is why both right desire and right reason make their appearance only in the middle ground between habits of acting and between opposite principles of action. The experience of wonder brings thinking to a stop, but also lets it begin; similarly, the contemplation of things as they are stands apart from action, but also lets action find its aim. The true and the good stem from one source, and converge in the beautiful.

ARISTOTLE
NICOMACHEAN ETHICS

BOOK I

Chapter 1. Every art and every inquiry, and likewise every action 1094a and choice, seems to aim at some good, and hence it has been beautifully said that the good is that at which all things aim. But a certain difference is apparent among ends, since some are ways of being at work, while others are certain kinds of works produced, over and above the being-at-work. And in those cases in which there are ends of any kind beyond the actions, the works produced are by nature better things than the activities. And since there are many actions and arts and kinds of knowledge, the ends also turn out to be many: of medical knowledge the end is health, of shipbuilding skill it is a boat, of strategic art it is victory, of household management it is wealth. But in as many such 10 pursuits as are under some one capacity—in the way that bridle making and all the other skills involved with implements pertaining to horses come under horsemanship, while this and every action pertaining to war come under strategic art, and in the same way other pursuits are under other capacities—in all of them the ends of all the master arts are more worthy of choice than are the ends of the pursuits that come under them, since these latter are pursued for the sake of those arts. And it makes no difference whether the ends of the actions are the ways of being at work themselves, or something else beyond these, as they are with the kinds of knowledge mentioned.

Chapter 2. If, then, there is some end of the things we do that we want on account of itself, and the rest on account of this one, and we do not choose everything on account of something else (for in that way 20 the choices would go beyond all bounds, so that desire would be empty and pointless), it is clear that this would be the good, and in fact the highest good. Then would not an awareness of it have great weight in one's life, so that, like archers who have a target, we would be more apt to hit on what is needed? But if this is so, one ought to try to get a

1

grasp, at least in outline, of what it is and to what kind of knowledge or capacity it belongs.

And it would seem to belong to the one that is most governing and most a master art, and politics[1] appears to be of this sort, since it prescribes which kinds of knowledge ought to be in the cities, and what sorts each person ought to learn and to what extent; also, we see that the most honored capacities, such as generalship, household economics, and rhetorical skill, are under this one. Since this capacity makes use of the rest of the kinds of knowledge, and also lays down the law about what one ought to do and from what one ought to refrain, the end of this capacity should include the ends of the other pursuits, so that this end would be the human good. For even if the good is the same for one person and for a city, that of the city appears to be greater, at least, and more complete both to achieve and to preserve; for even if it is achieved for only one person that is something to be satisfied with, but for a people or for cities it is something more beautiful and more divine. So our pursuit aims at this, and is in a certain way political.

Chapter 3. One would speak adequately if one were to attain the clarity that goes along with the underlying material, for precision ought not to be sought in the same way in all kinds of discourse, any more than in things made by the various kinds of craftsmen. The things that are beautiful and just, about which politics investigates, involve great disagreement and inconsistency, so that they are thought to belong only to convention and not to nature. And the things that are good also involve some inconsistency of this sort, because harm results from them for many people, for before now some people have been ruined by wealth, and others by courage. So one ought to be content, when speaking about such things and reasoning from such things, to point out the truth roughly and in outline, and when speaking about things that are so for the most part, and reasoning from things of that sort, to reach conclusions that are also of that sort. And it is necessary also to take each of the things that are said in the same way, for it belongs to an educated person to look for just so much precision in each kind of discourse as the nature of the thing one is concerned with admits; for to demand demonstrations from a rhetorician seems about like accepting probable conclusions from a mathematician.

All people are good at making distinctions about the things they are

---

[1]   Aristotle does not specify the noun implicit in the substantive adjective "the political..." (*hê politikê*), so "politics" here, from its context, means either the knowledge, the art, or some other capacity that is devoted to the things of the city. The word art (*technê*) applies to the skilled know-how involved in making or producing anything, from shoes to health to laws to good citizens. The city (*polis*) is the self-sufficient political community, large enough to feed and defend all its members but small enough for them all to have active dealings with one another.

acquainted with, and each is a good judge of those things. Therefore,   1095a
good judgment goes along with the way each one is educated, and the
one who has been educated about everything has it in an unqualified
way. For this reason, it is not appropriate for a young person to be a student of politics, since the young are inexperienced in the actions of life,
while these are the things about which politics speaks and from which
it reasons. Also, since the young are apt to follow their impulses, they
would hear such discourses without purpose or benefit, since their end
is not knowing but action. And it makes no difference whether one is
young in age or immature in character, for the deficiency doesn't come
from the time, but from living in accord with feeling and following every
impulse. For knowledge comes to such people without profit, as it does
to those who lack self-restraint; but to those who keep their desires in   10
proportion² and act in that way, knowing about these things would be
of great benefit.

   About the one who is to hear this discourse, and how it ought
to be received, and what task we have set before ourselves, let these
things serve as a prelude.

   Chapter 4. Now taking up the thread again, since every kind of
knowing and every choice reach toward some good, let us say what it
is that we claim politics aims at, and what, of all the goods aimed at
by action, is the highest. In name, this is pretty much agreed about by
the majority of people, for most people, as well as those who are more
refined, say it is happiness, and assume that living well and doing
well are the same thing as being happy. But about happiness—what it   20
is—they are in dispute, and most people do not give the same account
of it as the wise. Some people take it to be something visible and
obvious, such as pleasure or wealth or honor, and different ones say
different things, and even the same person often says different things;
when sick one thinks it is health, but when poor, that it is wealth, and
when they are conscious of ignorance in themselves, people marvel
at those who say it is something grand and above them. And some
people believe that, besides these many good things, there is some
other good, by itself, which is also responsible for the being good of
all these other things.

   Now to review all the opinions is perhaps rather pointless, and it
would be sufficient to review the ones that come most to prominence or   30
seem to have some account to give. And let it not escape our notice that

---

² This phrase (*kata logon*) might be translated "in accord with reason," and the
word *logos* is sometimes even translated as "principle," but these renderings
mistakenly suggest that desire must be secondary to thought, or that action
should be deduced from rules. At 1139b 4-5, Aristotle puts thought and desire
on a perfectly equal footing in human choice, and this chapter is the first of
many explanations he gives of why the precision of formulated principles
and deductive conclusions cannot govern human action.

arguments from first principles differ from those that go up toward first principles. For Plato rightly raised this question, and used to inquire whether the road is from first principles or up to first principles, just as, on a race course, the run is either from the judges to the boundary or back again. One must begin from what is known, but this has two meanings, the things known to us and the things that are known simply.[3] Perhaps then we, at any rate, ought to begin from the things that are known to us. This is why one who is going to listen adequately to discourse about things that are beautiful and just, and generally about things that pertain to political matters, needs to have been beautifully brought up by means of habits. For the primary thing is that something is so, and if this is sufficiently evident, there is no additional need for the reason why. And such a person either has or easily gets hold of the things that come first. If one neither has them nor has it in him to get hold of them, let him harken to Hesiod:

10
> Altogether best is he who himself has insight into all things,
> But good in his turn is he who trusts one who speaks well.
> But whoever neither himself discerns, nor, harkening to another,
> Lays to heart what he says, that one for his part is a useless man.

Chapter 5. For our part, let us speak from the point where we digressed. Most people and the crudest people seem, not without reason, to assume from people's lives that pleasure is the good and is happiness. For this reason they are content with a life devoted to enjoyment. For there are three ways of life especially that hold prominence: the one just now mentioned, and the political life, and third, the contemplative life. Now most people show themselves to 20 be completely slavish by choosing a life that belongs to fatted cattle, but they happen to get listened to because most people who have power share the feeling of Sardanapalus.[4] But refined and active people choose honor, for this is pretty much the goal of political life. Now this appears to be too superficial to be what is sought, for it seems to be in the ones who give honor rather than in the one who is honored, but we divine that the good is something of one's own and hard to take away. Also, people seem to pursue honor in order to be

---

3   In Bk. I, Chap. 1 of the *Physics* and at 1029b 3-12 of the *Metaphysics*, Aristotle discusses this distinction at more length. What is "known to us" is first for us because it is familiar, but it hardly deserves the name of knowledge; what is "known" in the simple or proper sense comes last in the order of our inquiry, but is first in the order of things, making everything else known. Dialectical inquiry begins where we are, rather than attempting prematurely to reason from clear and distinct first principles.

4   An Assyrian king of the 9th century BC, credited with saying "Eat, drink, and be merry, since the other things are not worth this snap of the fingers."

convinced that they themselves are good. At any rate they seek to be honored by the wise and by those who know them, and for virtue; it is clear, then, that at least according to these people, virtue is something greater,[5] and one might perhaps assume that this, rather than honor, is the end of the political life.

But even this seems too incomplete, since it seems possible, while having virtue, even to be asleep or to be inactive throughout life, and on top of these things, to suffer evils and the greatest misfortunes. No one would consider one who lived in that way to be happy, except when defending a hypothesis.[6] And this is enough about these things, since they are spoken of sufficiently in the current popular writings. And the third way of life is the contemplative one, about which we shall make an investigation in what follows. The life of money making is a type of compulsory activity, and it is clear that wealth is not the good being sought, since it is instrumental and for the sake of something else. For this reason one might suppose that the things spoken of before are more properly ends, since they provide contentment on account of themselves, though it appears that even they are not what is sought, even though many arguments connected with them are tossed around. So let these things be put aside.

Chapter 6. No doubt the better thing to do is to examine the universal good and go through the difficulties in the way it is spoken of, and yet such an inquiry becomes like trudging uphill because the men who introduced the forms were my friends.[7] But no doubt it would be admitted to be better, indeed to be necessary when keeping the truth safe is at stake, even to abandon the things that are one's own, both

30

1096a

10

---

5   Virtue (*aretê*) means the excellence that makes anything an outstanding specimen of its kind, especially well fitted to its ends. In itself it has no moral implications. It carries them conventionally when it is applied to human beings, and this is its primary use, but the word by no means excludes amoral or immoral conceptions of human superiority. Meno, in the Platonic dialogue of that name, believes that virtue is nothing but money and power, however acquired, but he repeatedly finds it impossible to deny that it involves temperance and justice (*Meno* 73A-B, 78D-E). This mixture of incompatible attitudes is part of the ordinary human heritage, out of which dialectic may begin. The English word "virtue" has something of this same fruitful ambiguity; compare "she defended her virtue" with "the virtue of this tax-avoidance scheme is..."

6   In the *Topics* (104b 19-23) Aristotle uses the word hypothesis for three paradoxes that thinkers have defended: that contradiction is impossible (Antisthenes), that everything is in motion (Heracleitus), and that there is only one being (Melissus). In Plato's *Gorgias*, starting at 470E, Socrates defends the hypothesis mentioned here, that a just person is happy even while unjustly suffering the greatest afflictions.

7   This exemplary act of finding the mean in departing from one's teacher out of respect for that teacher's own highest aims has given rise to a proverb: a friend to Plato but a greater friend to the truth. A fragment of a verse eulogy

for other reasons and because we are philosophers; for while both [the truth and one's friends] are loved, it is a sacred thing to give the higher honor to the truth.

Now those who brought in this opinion did not make forms within which a primary and a derivative instance were spoken of (which is why they did not construct a form of number), but the good is attributed to what something is and also to the sort of thing it is and to a relation it has, while the thinghood of something, which is something on its own, by nature has priority over a relation it has (for this is like an offshoot and incidental attribute of what is), so that there could not be any form common to these.[8] Further, since *good* is meant in just as many ways as *being* is (for in the sense of what something is, the good is spoken of as, for instance, the god or the intellect; in the sense of being of a certain sort, it is spoken of as the excellences; in the sense of being a certain amount, it is spoken of as the proper limit; in the sense of being related to something, it is spoken of as the useful; in the sense of being some time, it is spoken of as an opportune moment; and in the sense of place, it is spoken of as a dwelling or other things of that sort),[9] it is clear that there could not be any common good that is one and universal, for if there were it could not have been meant in all the ways of attributing being but only in one.

---

attributed to Aristotle called Plato "a man whom the wicked have no right even to praise,/ who, alone or the first of mortals, showed clearly/ by his own life and by the course of his arguments/ that a man becomes good and happy at the same time." [Quoted by Olympiodorus: see Barnes, *The Complete Works of Aristotle* (Princeton University Press, 1985), Vol. II, p. 2463, and Jaeger, *Aristotle* (Oxford University Press, 1967), p. 107.]

8   The form (*eidos* or *idea*) was treated in discussions in Plato's Academy and in his dialogues as some element common to things that bear the same name, identical in them all, and hence universal to them. In the *Meno* (72B-D), Socrates asks, about bees, virtues, and health, what it is in each kind that doesn't differ at all but makes every instance *be* a bee, a virtue, or health. Aristotle's point here is that this question doesn't always have an unequivocal answer; in particular, it doesn't work when asked of all good things. A good diet is a secondary or derivative notion, that makes sense only in relation to good health, and in turn to the good of some species of animal. In this cluster of instances, there is a primary sort of good that determines different kinds of good derivative from it.

9   The examples given are six of the eight ways being is meant, or is attributed to things. When something is said to *be* a tree, the verb does not have an unequivocal meaning that can be plugged in when something is said to *be* red, etc. Aristotle would call redness a being, but not an independent thing. In the *Metaphysics*, at 1017a 23-27, Aristotle adds acting and being acted upon to the six senses of being, sometimes called "categories," given here. (Yet another two are given in the book called the *Categories*, but they are easily reducible to two of the eight, while the whole point of distinguishing these highest classes of things is that they are irreducibly many.)

Further, since, of the things that come under one form, there is also   30
one kind of knowledge, there would also be some one kind of knowledge
of all things that are good, but as it is there are many, even of the good
things that come under one way of attributing being; for example, of
the opportune moment, in war, the knowledge of it is the general's art,
while in disease it is the physician's art, and of the proper limit in food,
the knowledge is the physician's art, while in exercises it is the art of
the gymnastic trainer. And one might raise the question even of what
in the world they mean by speaking of each whatever-itself, seeing as
how there is one and the same meaning for both a human being and the   1096b
human-being-itself, namely the meaning of human-ness. For insofar as
something is a human being, there will be no difference, and if that is the
way it is, there will be no difference either insofar as something is good.
Surely it will not be any more good by being everlasting, inasmuch as
a long-lasting thing is no more white than one that lasts only a day. The
Pythagoreans seem to speak in a more credible way about the good,
when they place one-ness in the column of good things,[10] and Speusippus seems to have followed them. But about these things let there be
some other discussion.

But a certain debatable point in the things that have been said
comes to light, on the grounds that the arguments were not meant to
be about every sort of good, but that the goods spoken of as coming   10
under one form are those that are pursued, and with which people
are satisfied, for their own sake, while the things that tend to produce
these, or to preserve them in some way, or to prevent their opposites
are spoken of as good by derivation from these and in a different way.
It is clear, then, that good things would be meant in two ways, some on
account of themselves and others derived from these. Then separating
the things that are good in themselves from the useful things, let us
examine whether the former are meant in accordance with one form.
But what sort of things should one set down as good in themselves?
Are they not those things that one pursues even when they are isolated
from everything else, such as having good sense, or seeing, or certain

---

[10] Instead, that is, of making it the source of all good; the good itself, mentioned
in Plato's *Republic*, is identified in his teachings in the Academy with the one
itself, discussed in his *Parmenides*. A version of the Pythagorean column of
goods, along with a column of corresponding opposites, is given in 986a of
the *Metaphysics*. Beginning at 1072b 30 of that work, Speusippus is linked
with the Pythagoreans as believing that the highest good is not a source of
things but something that develops, perhaps what is now called an "emergent
property," but Aristotle certainly does not treat that opinion as credible. The
Pythagoreans taught that all things are numbers, and Aristotle is quick to
point out the absurdities that follow from that (e.g., at 990a 18-29), but since
it implied that numbers are not separate from perceptible things, he found
it on that score preferable to the technical opinions of Plato and some of his
disciples (see 1090a 16-35).

pleasures and honors? For even if we pursue these things by reason of some other thing, one would still place them among things good in themselves. Or is there nothing else except the form that is good in itself? But then the form would be of no use. But if the things mentioned are among things good on account of themselves, the meaning of the good in all of these would have to show itself as the same, just as the meaning of whiteness is the same in snow and in lead paint. But of honor and good sense and pleasure there are distinct and divergent meanings of that by which they are good. Therefore there is not any good that is shared and comes under one form.[11]

But then in what way is good meant? For these things certainly do not seem to have the same name by chance. But do they have the same name by being derived from one thing, or by all adding up together into one thing, or rather by analogy?[12] For as sight is in relation to the body, intellect is in relation to the soul, and some other thing is in relation to something else. But perhaps these things ought to be let go for now, since to be precise about them would be more at home in another kind of philosophic inquiry. And it is similar with the form, for even if there is some one good that is attributed in common, or is something separate itself by itself, it is clear that it is not a thing done or possessed by a human being, and something of that sort is being

---

[11] The argument is about as tight as could be: either the good itself has no instances, or all the instances of it that are good in themselves must be good in the same way. But note that the conclusion depends on accepting the common opinions that honor and pleasure are good in themselves, while Aristotle has already questioned whether honor is dependent on a higher good and whether pleasure, in the sense of bodily enjoyment, is good at all in any way that could satisfy a human being. The discussion here is a dialectical beginning, and one must ask how it holds up at the end of the whole ten books of inquiry, especially since a different and better threefold distinction of goods is made at 1104b 30-31.

[12] A tree and a dog are each said to have a bark, but it is only by chance that the same name is used. A knife and a human being are both called medical, by derivation from one thing: the medical art. A human being and a society are both called healthy by analogy, since they have in common only a similar relation of the parts to the whole. A human being and a dog are both animals, by sharing a common universal in an unequivocal way, and hence come under one form in the broad sense the word "form" has in this discussion. The remaining possibility, that each thing called by a certain name is partial, and is only so called because all of them together add up to that meaning, is what was referred to in Plato's Academy as an eidetic number, a form composed of unlike forms. Aristotle drops that possibility here, and addresses it elsewhere only where he attacks it, in the *Metaphysics*, Book XIII, Chapters 6-9. Two excellent reconstructions of this notion, of very different kinds, are made by Jacob Klein, in *Greek Mathematical Thought and the Origin of Algebra* (M.I.T. Press, 1968), Chapter 7C, and Robert Williamson, in "*Eidos* and *Agathon* in Plato's *Republic*," in The St. John's Review, Vol. XXXIX, Nos. 1 and 2 (1989-90).

looked for now. But perhaps it might seem to someone that it would be better to be acquainted with it with a view to those good things that can be possessed or done; for having this as a sort of pattern, we would   1097a also know the things that are good for us better, and if we know them, we will hit upon them.

Now while the argument has a certain plausibility, it seems to be discordant with the kinds of knowledge we have, for all of them leave aside an acquaintance with the good itself in order to aim at some particular good and hunt for what they lack. And surely it is not reasonable that all those skilled in arts should be ignorant of, and not even look for, something of such great assistance. And it is impossible to say in what respect a weaver or a carpenter will be benefitted in relation to his art by knowing this good itself, or how one who has beheld the form itself will be a better doctor or general. For it appears that the doctor does not   10 consider health in that way, but the health of a human being, or perhaps rather that of this particular person, since he heals them each by each. So let these things have been spoken of just this much.

Chapter 7. And let us go back again to the good that is being sought, whatever it may be. For it seems to be a different thing in each different action and art, since it is a different thing in the medical art and the general's art, and similarly with the rest. What then is the good in each of them? Or is it that for the sake of which they do everything else? In the medical art this is health, in the general's art it is victory, in the housebuilder's art it is a house, and in a different art it is something   20 else, and in every action and choice it is the end, since everyone does everything else for the sake of this. And so, if there is some end for all actions, this would be the good that belongs to action, and if there is more than one such end, these would constitute that good. So the argument, in transforming itself, has reached the same place;[13] and one must try to make this still more clear.

Now since the ends seem to be more than one, while we choose some of them on account of something else, such as wealth, flutes, and instrumental things generally, it is clear that they are not all complete,[14]

---

[13] The same place is the question formulated at the beginning of Chapter Two and again at the beginning of Chapter Four, with each circular digression giving it more content.

[14] "Complete" here translates *teleion*, the adjective derived from *telos*, the word translated as "end" in Chapter One above, and used interchangeably by Aristotle with the phrase *hou heneka*, "that for the sake of which." The root sense of *telos* is wholeness or completion, and Aristotle's "teleology" is his teaching that all natural events aim at producing or maintaining the wholeness of natural beings, understood not only in a bodily and biological sense but also as the wholeness of being-at-work that constitutes their lives. In human beings, the achievement of this wholeness of life requires choices carried out in action; hence the end appears as a purpose, the accomplish-

but it is manifest that the highest good is something complete. So if there is some one thing alone that is complete, this would be what is being sought, but if there are more than one of them, it would be the most complete of these. And we say that a thing that is pursued on account of itself is more complete than a thing pursued on account of something else, and that what is never chosen on account of anything else is more complete than things chosen both for themselves and on account of something else, and hence that, in an unqualified sense, the complete is what is chosen always for itself and never on account of anything else. And happiness seems to be of this sort most of all, since we choose this always on account of itself and never on account of anything else, while we choose honor and pleasure and intelligence and every virtue indeed on account of themselves (for even if nothing resulted from them we would choose each of them), but we choose them also for the sake of happiness, supposing that we will be happy by these means. But no one chooses happiness for the sake of these things, nor for the sake of anything else at all.

And the same thing appears to follow from its self-sufficiency, for the complete good seems to be self-sufficient. And by the self-sufficient we mean not what suffices for oneself alone, living one's life as a hermit, but also with parents and children and a wife, and friends and fellow citizens generally, since a human being is by nature meant for a city. But one must take some limit for these connections, since by stretching out to ancestors and descendants and friends of one's friends they go beyond all bounds; but this must be examined later.[15] But we set down as self-sufficient that which, by itself, makes life choiceworthy and lacking in nothing, and such a thing we suppose happiness to be. What's more, we suppose happiness to be the most choiceworthy of all things while not counting it as one of those things, since if it were counted among them it is clear that it would be more choiceworthy together with the tiniest amount of additional good, for the thing added becomes a preeminence of good, and of good things, the greater is always more worthy of choice. So happiness appears to be something complete and self-sufficient, and is, therefore, the end of actions.

But perhaps to say that the highest good is happiness is obviously something undisputed, while it still begs to be said in a more clear and distinct way what happiness is. Now this might come about readily if one were to grasp the work of a human being. For just as with a flute player or sculptor or any artisan, and generally with those to whom some work or action belongs, the good and the doing it well seem to be in the work, so too it would seem to be the case with a human being, if

---

ment of which completes the action. The purpose behind all other purposes would be the human end that is complete simply.

[15] This comes up in relation to descendants and ancestors in Bk. I, Ch. 11, and in relation to friends in Bk. IX, Ch. 10

indeed there is some work that belongs to one. But is there some sort of work for a carpenter or a leather worker, while for a human being there is none? Is a human being by nature idle? Or, just as for an eye or a hand or a foot or generally for each of the parts, there seems to be some sort of work, ought one also to set down some work beyond all these for the human being? But then what in the world would this be? For living seems to be something shared in even by plants, but something peculiarly human is being sought. Therefore, one must divide off the life that consists in nutrition and growth. Following this would be some sort of life that consists in perceiving, but this seems to be shared in by a horse and a cow and by every animal. So what remains is some sort of life that puts into action that in us that has articulate speech; of this capacity, one aspect is what is able to be persuaded by reason, while the other is what has reason and thinks things through. And since this is still meant in two ways, one must set it down as a life in a state of being-at-work, since this seems to be the more governing meaning.

And if the work of a human being is a being-at-work of the soul in accordance with reason, or not without reason, while we say that the work of a certain sort of person is the same in kind as that of a serious person of that sort, as in the case of a harpist and of a serious harpist, and this is simply because in all cases the superiority in excellence is attached to the work, since the work of a harpist is to play the harp and the work of a serious harpist is to play the harp well—if this is so and we set down that the work of a human being is a certain sort of life, while this life consists of a being-at-work of the soul and actions that go along with reason, and it belongs to a man of serious stature to do these things well and beautifully,[16] while each thing is accomplished

---

[16] Two notions important to the *Ethics* as a whole begin to be made use of here. The word serious (*spoudaios*) is usually translated as "good" or "excellent," as though it were simply an idiom of ancient Greek that had lost its root meaning. But the meaning of the word belongs to the primary evidence from which ethics argues. We all consider some people more worthy of respect than others, and if we disagree about who they are we can begin a discussion. A serious harpist is not just one who is highly skilled technically, but one who chooses well the uses worthy of that skill. The serious person is not one who displays a sense of urgency and cannot relax, but one who recognizes the few things that are worth being serious about. (Compare 1025a 9-16.)

The beautiful (*to kalon*) is often translated as "noble" or "fine," on the grounds that the Greek word applied to admirable actions as well as to things well shaped or formed. But again, this is not a use of language peculiar to any place or time, but a word that intends something that belongs to the primary evidence that all ethical discussion must have in common. Just recall the last time you said "that was a beautiful thing you did," and reflect on what you meant. It may be that such judgments are fluctuating or conventional (1094b 14-16), but even to raise the question whether they always are, one must be open to the possibility of judging on a more stable basis.

well as a result of the virtue appropriate to it—if this is so, the human good comes to be disclosed as a being-at-work of the soul in accordance with virtue, and if the virtues are more than one, in accordance with the best and most complete virtue. But also, this must be in a complete life, for one swallow does not make a Spring, nor one day, and in the same way one day or a short time does not make a person blessed and happy.

So let the good have been sketched in outline in this way, for presumably one needs to rough it in first and then inscribe the details later. And it would seem to be in the power of anyone to carry forward and articulate things that are in good shape in the outline, and that time is a good discoverer of such things, or makes the work easier; in fact the advances in the arts have come from this, since it is in anyone's power to add what is left out. But it behooves one to remember the things that were said before, and not to look for precision in the same way in all things, but in accordance with the underlying material in each case, and to the extent that it is appropriate to that course of inquiry. For both a carpenter and a geometrician look for a right angle, but in different ways, for the one seeks it to the extent that it is useful to the work, while the other seeks for what it is or what it is a property of, since he is someone who beholds the truth. So one ought to do the same in other things, so that side issues do not become greater than the work being done. [17]

And one ought not to demand a reason in all things alike, either, but it is sufficient in some cases for it to be shown beautifully that something is so, in particular such things as concern first principles; that something is so comes first and is a first principle. And of first principles, some are beheld by way of examples, others by sense perception, others by becoming experienced in some habit, and others in other ways. So one must try to go after each of them by the means that belong to its nature, and be serious about distinguishing them rightly, since this has great weight in what follows. For the beginning seems to be more than half of the whole, and many of the things that are inquired after become illuminated along with it.

Chapter 8. And, in connection with the beginning, one must examine it not only from its conclusion and the things on the basis of which the statement was made, but also from the things that are said about it; for when something is true, everything that pertains to it is consonant with it, but when something is false, the truth quickly

---

[17]   The dismissal of any discussion of the good itself, in Chapter 6 above, is an example of this. Aristotle believes there are forms, and that there is a highest good separate from perceptible things, but these topics require long and complex inquiry, in Books VII-IX and XII of the *Metaphysics* especially. As he says at 1096b 30-31, these questions are at home in a different sort of philosophizing.

shows itself dissonant with it. Now since good things have been parceled out into three kinds, some being called external while the others are associated with the soul or the body, we speak of the ones that are associated with the soul as the most governing and as especially good, and it is the actions and ways of being at work that belong to the soul that we set down as associated with the soul. Therefore our beginning is well stated, at least according to this opinion, which is an ancient one and agreed to by the philosophers. And it is right, too, that certain actions and ways of being at work should be said to be the end, since in that way the end comes to be among the goods associated   20
with the soul and not among the external goods. It is also consonant with our statement that the one who is happy is said to live well and do well, since the end was just about said to be some way of living well and acting well.

And it appears that all the things that are looked for concerning happiness are present in what was said. For to some people it seems to be virtue, to others practical judgment, and to others some sort of wisdom, while to others it seems to be all or some of these combined with pleasure, or not without pleasure, while others include external abundance alongside these. Some of these things are said by many people and from ancient times, others by a few well-reputed men, and it is reasonable that neither of these groups would be wholly mistaken, and that they would be right in some one point at least or even in most of them. Now our statement is consonant with the ones who say that   30
happiness is virtue or a certain virtue, since being at work in accordance with it is part of virtue. But presumably it makes no small difference whether one supposes the highest good to consist in possession or in use, that is, in an actively maintained condition or in a way of being at work. For even if the actively maintained condition is present it is   1099a
possible for it to accomplish no good thing, for instance in someone who is asleep or in someone who is incapacitated in some other way, but if the being-at-work is present this is not possible, for necessarily the one who is at work in accordance with virtue will act and act well. Just as, with those at the Olympic games, it is not the most beautiful or the strongest who are crowned, but those who compete (for it is some of these who are victors), so too among those who in life are well favored and well mannered[18] it is the ones who act rightly who become accomplished people.

And the life they lead is also pleasant in itself. For feeling pleasure is one of the things that belong to the soul, and to each person, that to which he is said to be passionately devoted is pleasant, for example, a horse to one who is passionately devoted to horses, a show to one who   10

---

18   Literally "the beautiful and good," the phrase, sometimes run together as one word, by which the Athenian aristocracy referred to itself.

is passionately devoted to shows; and in the same way acts of justice are pleasant to one who is passionately devoted to justice and generally things in accord with virtue to one who is passionately devoted to virtue. In most people, then, the things that are pleasant to them are in conflict with one another, since they are not pleasant by nature, but the things that are pleasant to those who are passionately devoted to what is beautiful are the things that are pleasant by nature, and of this sort are actions in accordance with virtue, so that they are pleasant both to these people and in themselves. So the life these people lead has no additional need of pleasure as a sort of appendage, but has its pleasure in itself. For in addition to what has been said, one who does not delight in beautiful actions is not even a good person, for no one would call anyone just who did not delight in acting justly, nor call anyone generous who did not delight in generous actions, and similarly in the other cases. And if this is so, actions in accordance with virtue would be pleasant in themselves.

But certainly they are also good and beautiful, and each of these in the highest degree, if the one who judges rightly about them is the serious person, who judges them the way we said. Therefore happiness is best and most beautiful and most pleasant, and these are not separated in the manner of the epigram at Delos:

> Most beautiful is what is most just, and most desirable is to be healthy;
> But most pleasant by nature is to get exactly what one yearns for.

All of these are present in the best ways of being at work, and it is these, or the one of these which is best, that we declare to be happiness. Nevertheless, it appears that there is an additional need of external goods, as we said, since it is impossible, or not easy, to engage in beautiful actions if one is not equipped for them. For many things are done, as if by instruments, by means of friends and wealth and political power, and those who lack certain things, such as good ancestry, good children, and good looks, disfigure their blessedness; for someone who is completely ugly in appearance, or of bad descent, or solitary and childless is not very apt to be happy, and is still less so perhaps if he were to have utterly corrupt children or friends, or good ones who had died. So as we said, there seems to be an additional need of this sort of prosperity, which is why some people rank good fortune on the same level as happiness, while others give that rank to virtue.

Chapter 9. This is also why there is an impasse about whether happiness comes by learning or habit or training of some other kind, or else comes to one's side by some divine lot or even by chance. Now if there is anything else that is a gift of the gods to human beings, it is reasonable that happiness too should be god-given, and it most of all human things, in the measure by which it is the best of them. But perhaps this would be more at home in another sort of investigation, though it appears that even if happiness is not god-sent but comes to one by means of virtue and some sort of learning or training, it is still one of the most divine things, for the prize for virtue also seems to be the highest end and something divine and blessed. And it should also be widely shared, since it admits of belonging to all those who are not incapacitated for virtue, by means of some sort of learning and taking pains. And if it is better for it to be this way, rather than for one to be happy by chance, it is reasonable that this is the way it stands, if indeed things in accordance with nature occur naturally in the most beautiful possible way, as similarly is the case with things that result from art or from any sort of cause, and especially from the highest sort of cause. But for what is greatest and most beautiful to be left to chance would be too discordant.

And what is being sought is further illuminated by our formulation, for happiness was said to be a certain sort of being-at-work of the soul in accordance with virtue, while all the other good things are either conditions that need to be present for happiness or else things that naturally assist the work and are useful as tools. And these things would also be in agreement with what was said in the beginning, for we set down that the highest good is the end of politics, while it takes the greatest part of its pains to produce citizens of a certain sort, namely, ones that are good and inclined to perform beautiful actions.[19] It is reasonable, then, that we do not speak of a cow or horse or any other animal as happy, since none of them is able to share in being at work in such a way. And for this reason a child is not happy either, since he is not yet capable of performing such actions on account of age; children who are called happy are pronounced blessed on account of our hope.[20] For there is need, as we said, of both complete virtue and a complete life, for many changes and all sorts of chances come about in the course of a life, and it is possible for the most thriving person to fall into great misfortunes in old age, just as the story is told of Priam

20

30

1100a

---

[19] These would include, in any community, a willingness to sacrifice comfort or property, or to risk injury or death, if such actions were necessary means to something manifestly worthwhile.

[20] To some extent, the Greek word *eudaimonia* differs from our word happiness, but Aristotle's interest is not in words and their use. Sardanapalus, referred to in Chapter 5 above as a spokesman for most people, would have to say that no one is in a better condition than a child or animal completely wrapped up in pleasure and play. Aristotle's criterion here for happiness amounts to the same thing as the criterion by which he says below, at 1111b 8-9, that children and animals do not make choices: his opinion that they cannot distance themselves from what is immediate in order to give preference to something remote that is recommended only by reason or beauty.

in the epics about Troy; no one calls happy the one who suffers such fortunes and dies in misery.

10   **Chapter 10.** But then ought one to call no other human being happy either who is still alive, and is it necessary, as Solon said, to look at the end? But if one ought really to lay down this rule, is anyone happy once he is dead? Or is this completely absurd, both for other reasons and especially for us who say that happiness is some way of being at work? But if we do not say that someone who is dead is happy, and Solon did not mean that, but that only at that time may one safely pronounce a human being blessed, as being then beyond evils and misfortunes, this too has in it something disputable, since there seem to be things that are good or evil for one who has died, if indeed there also are for someone

20 who is alive but not aware of them, such as honors and dishonors and good actions and misfortunes of children and of descendants generally. But this also contains an impasse, for it is possible for many reverses of fortune concerning descendants to befall someone who has lived blessedly until old age and died proportionately to that, and for there to be some among their descendants who are good and happen to have lives in accord with what they deserve, while others have lives of an opposite sort. And it is evident that they admit of having every possible degree of separation from their ancestors, so that it would become absurd if the one who is dead were to change along with them, and become at one time happy but then miserable again; but it would be absurd as well if

30 the fortunes of the descendants did not pertain at all to their ancestors over some length of time.

But one ought to go back again to the thing that produced the earlier impasse, for perhaps what is now being inquired about might also be seen into from that direction. If in fact one ought to look to the end and at that time judge each person blessed, not as being blessed but as having been so before, how is it not absurd if, when someone is happy, what belongs to him cannot be truly judged as his because one does

1100b not want to call the living happy on account of reverses and because one assumes that happiness is something durable and not at all easily changed, while fortunes often come back around again for the same people? For it is clear that, if we were to follow along with the fortunes, we would often call the same person happy and miserable in turns, making the happy person out to be a kind of chameleon or a structure built on rotten foundations.

So is following up these fortunes not right at all? For what goes well or badly does not lie in them, but a human life has need of them

10 as something added, as we said, while the things that govern happiness are ways of being at work in accordance with virtue, while opposite ways of being at work determine an opposite condition. And what is now producing an impasse bears witness to this formulation, since in none of the acts of human beings is stability present in the same way

it is present in ways of being at work in accordance with virtue; for these seem to be more durable even than the kinds of knowledge. And among these themselves, the most honored are the ones that are more enduring because those who are blessed pass their lives in them most of all and most continuously, since this seems to be the reason that forgetfulness does not encroach upon them. So what is sought will belong to the happy person, who will be happy throughout life, for such a person will always, or most of all people, be acting and contemplating the things that go along with virtue, and will bear what fortune brings   20 most beautifully and in complete harmony in every instance, being in the true sense good and flawlessly squarely centered.

But since many things happen by chance, going all the way from the great to the small, the small bits of good fortune, and similarly those of the opposite sort, are clearly not of decisive weight in one's life, but if great ones come along, and many of them, they will readily make one's life more blessed (for it is the nature of them to contribute to adorning life and also for the use of them to become beautiful and serious), and if it turns out the opposite way this limits what is blessed and mars its dignity, since it imposes pains and hinders many ways of being at   30 work. Nevertheless, even in these circumstances something beautiful shines through when one bears many and great misfortunes calmly, not through insensitivity, but through good breeding and greatness of soul. If, as we said, it is ways of being at work that govern life, no one who is among the blessed could become miserable, since such a one will never do base or hateful things; for we suppose that one who is   1101a truly good and sensible will bear all fortunes gracefully and will always act in the most beautiful way the circumstances permit, just as a good general will make the best use for war of the terrain that is at hand and a shoemaker will make the most beautiful shoe out of the leather that is given, and the same way with all other artisans as well. And if it is this way, one who is happy could never become miserable, though surely one would not be blessed if he were to fall into fortunes like those of Priam. But neither would such a one be changeable and easily thrown off balance, since one will not be easily dislodged from happiness, even   10 by the misfortunes of fortune, unless they are many and great, and from such misfortunes such a person would not become happy again in a short time, but, if at all, in the fullness of some long time in which one had come to devote oneself to great and beautiful causes.

What then prevents our calling happy the person who is at work in accordance with complete virtue and supplied with a sufficient stock of external goods, not for any chance amount of time but for a complete life? Or ought one to add, when he shall have both lived in that way and died in a proportionate way, since the future is unclear to us, and we set it down that happiness is final in every sense and complete in every way? And if this is so, we shall call blessed those among the living to   20 whom the things mentioned belong and go on belonging, but blessed as human beings. And let the distinctions be made to this extent about these things.[21]

Chapter 11. That the fortunes of one's descendants and all one's friends have no influence at all seems too unfeeling and contrary to people's opinions, but since the things that come to pass are many and have all sorts of differences, with some of them more relevant and others less, to distinguish each of them would seem a long if not endless task, but to sketch what is said in a general outline would perhaps be sufficient. Now if, just as among the misfortunes that surround oneself, some have a certain weight and power to tip the scale of one's life while others seem more lightweight, so too is the same thing the case with the things that relate to all one's friends, and it makes a difference whether each experience happens to concern those who are living or those who are dead, much more even than whether the lawless and terrible things in the tragedies are presupposed or enacted on stage, and so one ought to reckon in this difference and more, perhaps, the impasse about whether those who have done their part and departed this life have any share in anything good or the reverse. For it seems from these considerations that if anything at all gets through to them, whether good or the reverse, it would be something faint and small, either simply or as it relates to them, or if not, at any rate so little and of such a kind as not to make happy those who are not, or to take away the blessedness of those who are. So it appears that when the friends of the departed fare well, and likewise when they fare badly, this has an influence on those who are departed, but of such a kind and amount as neither to make the happy not be happy nor anything else of the sort.[22]

Chapter 12. Now that these distinctions have been made, let us

---

[21] The beginning outline formulation of what happiness is, arrived at in Chapter 7, has now been tested in Chapters 8-10 and found to imply that happiness is an inner condition manifested in outward acts, pleasant in itself, and, to the extent possible with human things, in one's own power and durable. Perhaps even more important, the arguments by which it was tested have turned up a series of crucial pieces of evidence: (1) We recognize some actions as beautiful things to do (1099a 5-7). (2) A political community always has a stake in the inclination its citizens have toward doing what is beautiful (1099b 29-32). (3) Happiness is possible only to mature human beings, who can choose what is beautiful in preference to what is immediately gratifying (1099b 32-1100a 4). (4) Among things recognized as beautiful are greatness of soul amid misfortunes (1100b 30-33) and an acceptance of death that preserves its proportion to one's life (1101a 17).

[22] An incidental remark in the middle of this chapter stands out, and seems to carry meaning poetically, as well as logically. A playwright keeps horrendous deeds, like the blinding of Oedipus, offstage as a matter of tact. Aristotle too, in this chapter, may be speaking the truth in a way that will be tactful to listeners or readers who try to make their lives do credit to their dead loved ones.

consider whether happiness belongs among things that are praised or rather among things that are honored, for it is clear that it does not belong among capacities.[23] Everything that is praised seems to be praised for being some sort of attribute or for holding itself in a certain condition, since we praise someone who is just or courageous or generally good, as we also praise virtue, on account of actions and works, and we praise someone who is strong or a good runner, and so on, for being naturally possessed of some attribute and standing in some relation toward something good and serious. This is clear also from praise that concerns the gods, since it is obviously ridiculous to hold them up against ourselves, but this is what happens, because praise comes about   20
by holding things up to some standard, as we said. But if praise is for things of that sort, it is clear that there is no praise for the highest goods, but something greater and better, as is also evident since we pronounce the gods, as well as the most godlike among men, blessed and happy. And it is the same with good things, for no one praises happiness as one would praise justice, but rather blesses it as something better and more divine. And Eudoxus also seems to have been a good advocate for pleasure's title to the medal of highest honor because he believed its not being praised, though it is something good, indicates that it is something more powerful than the good things that are praised, and   30
is of the same sort as the god and the good, for to these as well other things are held up as to a standard.

Praise belongs to virtue, for from this, people become apt at performing beautiful actions, and honorific speeches are similarly for deeds, whether of the body or of the soul. But perhaps to be precise about these things is more appropriate to those have taken pains over honorific speeches, but for us it is clear from what has been said that happiness   1102a
belongs among things that are honored and among ends. And it seems to be this way because it is also a source, since every one of us does everything else for the sake of this, and we set down the source and cause of good things as something honored and divine.

Chapter 13. And since happiness is a certain way of being at work in accordance with complete virtue, something one would have to examine would be virtue, for perhaps in this way we might get a better insight into happiness. And it seems that the one skilled in politics in the true sense has taken pains about this especially, for such a one wants to make the citizens good and obedient to the laws. We have,   10
as a pattern in these matters, those who gave laws to the people of Crete and Sparta, and any others of that sort there might have been. And if this investigation belongs to politics, it is clear that the inquiry would be in accord with the project we chose at the beginning. And it is clear that one ought to examine virtue of a human sort, since we

---

[23] We post-Nietzscheans might say "it is clearly not something value-free."

were looking for the human good and a human happiness, and by human excellence we mean the kind that belongs not to the body but to the soul, and we assert that happiness is a being-at-work of the soul. Now if this is the way it is, it is clear that one who is skilled in politics needs to know in some way the things that concern the soul, just as one who is going to cure the eyes must also know about the whole body, and even more so, to the extent that politics is more honorable and elevated than medicine; and the more refined among medical doctors do busy themselves in many ways with knowing about the body. So the one skilled in politics must study the soul, but must study it for the sake of political concerns and to the extent that is sufficient for what is sought, for to be more precise than that is perhaps too much trouble for the things proposed.

Now some things about the soul are said in an adequate way even in popular writings, and one ought to make use of them, for example, that there is an irrational part of the soul and a part having reason. Whether these are distinct in the same manner as the parts of the body, or of any divisible thing, or else are two in meaning while they are inseparable in nature, as are the convex and the concave in the circumference of a circle, makes no difference for the present concern. And within the irrational part, one part seems to be common to living things and vegetative—I mean the part responsible for nutrition and growth—for one would attribute such a power of the soul to all things that take nourishment, and even to embryos, and attribute the very same power to fully developed living things, since this is more reasonable than supposing some other one. So the excellence of this would seem to be something common and not human, for this part or this power seems to be most at work during sleep, while a good and a bad person are least distinguishable in sleep. (This is why people say that for half their lives the happy do not differ at all from the miserable, and this follows reasonably, since sleep is an inactivity of that in the soul by which it is said to be serious or contemptible.) There is an exception if in some way some motions penetrate a little bit, and in this way the dreams of decent people become better than those of people at random. But this is enough about these things, and one ought to leave the nutritive part alone, since by its nature it has no allotment of the human sort of excellence.

But a certain other nature belonging to the soul seems to be without reason and yet to share in reason in some way. For we praise the reason that belongs to people who are self-restrained or unrestrained, and the part of the soul in them that has reason, since it exhorts them in the right way and to what is best, but there seems also to be naturally present in them something else besides reason, which does battle with and strains against reason. For exactly as in the case of parts of the body subject to muscular spasms, when one has chosen to move them

to the right they are on the contrary turned away to the left, so too is   20
it with the soul, for the impulses of unrestrained people are contrarily
directed. But while in the body we see the part that swerves, with the
soul we do not see it. Nevertheless one must presumably consider
there to be something in the soul as well contrary to reason, which
opposes it and stands in its way, though it makes no difference in what
way it is distinct. But this seems to have a share in reason, as we said;
in a self-restrained person at any rate it is obedient to reason, and
presumably in a temperate and brave person it is still more amenable
to reason, since in such a person all parts of the soul are in harmony
with reason.[24]

So it appears that the irrational part of the soul is twofold, since
the vegetative part of it has no share at all in reason, while the desiring   30
and generally appetitive part does share in it in some way, insofar as
it listens to and can obey reason. In the same way too we call listening to one's father or friends "being rational," though not of course
in the way mathematicians mean that. And that the irrational part is
in some way persuaded by reason, is indicated by admonition and by
every sort of chastisement and encouragement. But if one ought to say   1103a
that this part of the soul has reason, then having reason will also be
twofold, namely having it in the governing sense and in itself, or in
the sense of something that can listen to a father. And virtue as well
is divided in accordance with the same distinction, for we speak of
virtues as pertaining either to thinking or to character, and speak of
wisdom, astuteness, and practical judgment as intellectual virtues, and
generosity and temperance as virtues of character. For in speaking of
character we do not mean that someone is wise or astute, but gentle
or temperate, but we also praise someone who is wise for an active
condition of the soul, and among active conditions of the soul, we call
the ones that are praised virtues.   10

BOOK II

Chapter 1. Now since virtue is of two sorts, one pertaining to
thinking and the other to character, excellence of thinking is for the
most part, both in its coming to be and in its growth, a result of
teaching, for which reason it has need of experience and time, while
excellence of character comes into being as a consequence of habit,
on account of which it even gets its name by a small inflection from

---

24   This overcoming of inner conflict will become an important mark of a true
virtue. The temperate person does not have to restrain an impulse toward
every chocolate bar, but has outgrown the subjection to such feelings that
characterizes a child or an adult of weak character. Similarly, in Plato's
Republic (443D), Socrates says that a just person "himself rules himself and
organizes and becomes a friend to himself, being a harmony of the three
parts of the soul."

habit.[25] It is also clear from this that none of the virtues of character
20 comes to be present in us by nature, since none of the things that are by
nature can be habituated to be otherwise; for example, a stone, which
by nature falls downward, could not be habituated to fall upward,
not even if one were to train it by throwing it upward ten thousand
times, nor could fire be habituated to move downward, nor could
any of the things that happen by nature in one way be habituated
to happen in another way. Therefore the virtues come to be present
neither by nature nor contrary to nature, but in us who are of such a
nature as to take them on, and to be brought to completion in them
by means of habit.

Also, with those things that come to belong to us by nature, we
are provided with the potencies for these beforehand, and we produce
the being-at-work of them in return. (This very thing is obvious in the
case of the senses, for it was not from repeatedly seeing or repeatedly
30 hearing that we took on the senses, but on the contrary, having them,
we used them—we did not get them by using them.) But we do take on
the virtues by first being at work in them, just as also in other things,
namely the arts; the things that one who has learned them needs to do,
we learn by doing, and people become, say, housebuilders by build-
1103b ing houses or harpists by playing the harp. So too, we become just by
doing things that are just, temperate by doing things that are temperate,
and courageous by doing things that are courageous. What happens
in cities gives evidence of this, for lawmakers make the citizens good
by habituating them, and since this is the intention of every lawmaker,
those that do not do it well are failures, and one regime differs from
another in this respect as a good one from a worthless one.

Also, it is from and by means of the same things that every virtue
both comes into being and is destroyed, and similarly every art, for
people become both good harpists and bad harpists from harp playing,
10 and it is analogous with housebuilders and all the rest; from building
houses well people will be good housebuilders and from building them
badly they will be bad ones. If it were not that way, there would have
been no need of a teacher, but everyone would have been born good

---

[25] The word character (*êthos*) derives from habit (*ethos*) by a mere lengthening of
the initial vowel from epsilon to eta. How the condition meant by character
derives from habit is more complex. Ethical virtue is by no means simply a set
of socially approved habits. It requires a pre-existent natural capacity meant to
be completed properly in a certain way, as the following discussion explains;
an appropriate habit, which might be imposed by parents or by other social
training, is a second necessary condition for its development. But there is a
third and crucial necessary factor that brings a virtue into being, that is the
deliberate contribution of the person who comes to have it, the *hexis* or active
condition that enters the discussion in Chap. 5 below, as a result of which
Aristotle considers us to be responsible for our own characters (1114b 22-24).

or bad at the arts. And it is the same way in the case of the virtues, for by acting in our dealings with people some of us become just, others unjust, and by acting in frightening situations and getting habituated to be afraid or to be confident, some of us become courageous and others become cowards. And it is similar with the things that are involved with desires and with angry impulses, for some people become temperate and gentle, while others become spoiled and irritable, the ones from   20
turning themselves this way in these situations, the others from turning themselves that way. In a word, active states come into being from being at work in similar ways. Hence it is necessary to make our ways of being at work be of certain sorts, for our active states follow in accordance with the distinctions among these. It makes no small difference, then, to be habituated in this way or in that straight from childhood, but an enormous difference, or rather all the difference.

Chapter 2. Now since our present occupation is not for the sake of contemplation, as the other kinds of study are (for we are investigating not in order that we might know what virtue is, but in order that we might become good, since otherwise there would be no benefit from it), it is necessary to investigate, with respect to the things involved in   30
actions, how one ought to perform them, since these actions also deter- mine the sorts of active states that come into being, as we have said. Now the phrase "acting in accordance with right reason" is commonly accepted, and let it be set down—there will be a discussion of it later, both what right reason is and how it is related to the other virtues.[26]
But let this be acknowledged in advance—that every discourse that   1104a
concerns actions is obliged to speak in outline and not precisely—just as we said also at the beginning that one ought to demand that discourses be in accord with their material, while matters that are involved in actions and are advantageous have nothing rigidly fixed about them, any more than do matters of health. And since the general discourse is of this sort, still more does the discourse that concerns particulars lack precision, for it falls under no art nor under any skill that has been handed down, but it is always necessary for those who are acting to look at the circumstances surrounding the occasion themselves, just as is the case also with the medical art or the art of steering a ship. But even though the present discourse is of this sort, one ought to try to   10
help it along.

First, then, one must recognize this, that things such as virtues are of such a nature as to be destroyed by deficiency and by excess, as we see (since one must use visible examples as evidence for invisible things) in the case of strength and health; for excessive gymnastic exercises, as well as deficient ones, destroy one's strength, and similarly drink and food, when they come to be too much or too little, destroy one's

---

[26]   See Book VI, Chapters 5-13, where the final formulation at 1144b 26-28 identi- fies right reason in matters of action with practical judgment.

health, while proportionate amounts produce, increase, and preserve these. And it is the same way also with temperance and courage and the other virtues. Someone who runs away from and fears everything and endures nothing becomes a coward, while someone who fears nothing at all but goes out to confront everything becomes rash; similarly, someone who indulges in every pleasure and refrains from none becomes spoiled, while someone who shuns them all, like a boorish bumpkin, becomes in a certain way insensible. So temperance and courage are destroyed by excess and by deficiency, but are preserved by an intermediate condition.

But it is not only the case that the same things from which and by the action of which their coming into being and increase comes about, produce their destruction as well, but it is also in these same things that the being-at-work of the virtues will consist. For it is that way also in the more visible cases, such as that of strength, since strength comes about from taking in a lot of food and enduring a lot of labor, while it is especially the strong person who would be capable of doing these very things. And so it is in the case of the virtues as well, for by refraining from pleasures we become temperate, and once having become temperate we are most capable of refraining from them; and it is similar in the case of courage, for by habituating ourselves to disdain frightening things, and by enduring them, we become courageous, and having become courageous we shall be most capable of enduring frightening things.

Chapter 3. As a sign of the active states of one's soul, one must consider the pleasure or pain that accompanies one's deeds, for someone who refrains from bodily pleasures and delights in this very thing is temperate, but someone who does so while feeling burdened by it is spoiled, and someone who endures terrifying things and delights in them, or is at any rate not pained by them, is courageous, but someone who does so while being pained is a coward. For the sort of virtue that belongs to character is concerned with pleasures and pains, since it is on account of pleasure that we perform base actions, and on account of pain that we refrain from beautiful actions. Hence it is necessary to be brought up in some way straight from childhood, as Plato says, so as to take delight and feel pain in those things in which one ought, for this is the right education.[27]

Also, if the virtues are concerned with actions and feelings, while

[27] This is what is called an education in music in Plato's *Republic*, and is discussed from 376E to 403C. Aristotle's reference is to 402A, where Socrates gives the reason for what contemporary readers call "censorship" of the stories and music children are allowed to hear. The point is not whether depictions of sex and violence, or music without grace, will make children act in certain ways, but that it will coarsen their sensibilities before they are able to make choices on their own.

pleasure or pain follows upon every feeling and every action, for this reason too virtue would be concerned with pleasures and pains. Punishments indicate this too, since they come about by means of these, for they are a certain kind of medicines, and medicines by their nature work through opposites. Also, as we said just now, every active condition of the soul is in its nature related to and concerned with the sorts   20 of things by the action of which it naturally becomes worse or better, and it is by means of pleasures and pains that people become base, through pursuing and avoiding them, either the ones one ought not, or when one ought not, or in a way one ought not, or in as many other ways as such distinctions are articulated. This is also why people define the virtues as certain states of freedom from passion, and of calmness, but they do not define them well, because they say this simply but do not add "as one ought" and "as one ought not" and "when" and the rest.

Therefore, it is established that virtue of this sort is an aptitude productive of the best actions that concern pleasures and pains, and that vice is the opposite. And this might become evident to us from the following considerations that concern the same things. For since   30 there are three things that lead to choices and three that lead to avoidance, the former being what is beautiful, what is advantageous, and what is pleasant, and the contraries being what is ugly, what is harmful, and what is painful, the good person is apt to go right and the bad person is apt to go astray concerning all of these, but especially concerning pleasure, for this is shared with the animals, and follows along with everything that comes by choice, since even the beautiful   1105a and the advantageous seem pleasant.[28] Also, this has grown up with us all from infancy, and for this reason it is difficult to scrub away this feeling, since it is ingrained in our life. And we measure our actions, some of us more, others less, against the yardstick of pleasure and pain. On account of this, then, it is necessary that our whole concern be about these things, for to be delighted or pained well or badly plays no small role in our actions. And it is even harder to fight against pleasure than Heracleitus says it is to fight against anger,[29] but artfulness and

---

[28]   The word used here for choice has a reduced meaning that can apply to an animal-like act guided exclusively by imagination and aimed solely at pleasure. Note too, by the way, that Aristotle includes some of his most important observations in subordinate clauses within throw-away arguments; a spectacular example has occurred here, with the meaning of *good* being distinguished into its three primary senses. This picks up the question that was dismissed at 1096b 30, not with the precision that would carry it outside the inquiry about ethics, but with a definite dialectical step forward, and later observations will continue the upward motion from the evidence of human action toward a single governing meaning of the good.

[29]   "It is hard to fight against anger, for what it wants to happen, it purchases

10   virtue always come to be concerned with what is more difficult, for it is better to do well at this. And so for this reason the whole concern both of virtue and of politics is about pleasures and pains, since one who deals with these well will be a good person, and one who deals with them badly will be bad.

Let it stand as stated, then, that virtue is concerned with pleasures and pains, that it grows by the action of those things out of which it comes into being, or is destroyed by them when they do not happen in the same way, and that it is at work in connection with those things out of which it has come into being.

Chapter 4. One might raise as an impasse, though, how we mean that it is necessary to become just by performing just actions and temperate by performing temperate actions, for if people do things that are just or temperate they already are just or temperate people, just as, if they do the things that have to do with writing or with music, they are literate or musical people. Or is it not even this way in the case of the arts? For it is possible to produce something literate by chance or by being advised by someone else. One will be literate, then, only when one produces something literate and does so in a literate way, that is, in accordance with the art of writing within oneself. Anyway, it is not the same in the case of the arts as with the virtues, for the things that come into being by means of the arts have their being-well-made in themselves; it is sufficient for these to come into being in a certain condition. But with the things that come about as a result of the virtues, just because they themselves are a certain way it is not the case that one does them justly or temperately, but only if the one doing them also does them being a certain way: if one does them first of all knowingly, and next, having chosen them and chosen them for their own sake, and third, being in a stable condition and not able to be moved all the way out of it.[30]

1105b   For having the other kinds of artfulness, these things do not count, except the mere knowing, but for having the virtues, the knowing is of little or no strength, while the other conditions have not a little but

---

in exchange for life" (Fragment 85 in the Diels numbering). Exactly what Heracleitus meant by *thumos*, translated here as "anger," is uncertain. In Plato's *Republic* (439E-441C), Socrates distinguishes it as the middle, spirited part of the soul, that can ally itself with either reason or desire to control the third part. The "musical" education Socrates prescribes, which Aristotle has called the right education at 1104b 13 above, is aimed at taming and winning over this irrationally spirited element straight from childhood.

[30]   The last eleven words of the sentence translate Aristotle's marvelous adverb *ametakinêtôs*; *akinêtôs* would mean in the manner of someone immovable or rigid, but the added prefix makes it convey the condition of those toys that can be knocked over but always come back upright on their own, a flexible stability or equilibrium.

all the power, and they are the very ones which arise from repeatedly performing just or temperate actions. Thus, while the actions are called just or temperate whenever they are the sorts of things that a just or temperate person would do, the one who does them is not just or temperate unless he also does them in the way that just and temperate people do them. It is well said, then, that by performing just actions one becomes a just person and by performing temperate actions one   10 becomes a temperate person, and no one is going to become good by not performing these actions. But most people do not perform them, but believe that by taking refuge in talk[31] they are philosophizing and in that way will be people of serious stature, doing something similar to those sick people who listen to the doctors carefully but do none of the things they order. So just as they will be in no good condition in body if they treat themselves in this way, neither will those who philosophize in this way be in any good condition in soul.

Chapter 5. After these things, one must examine what virtue is. Now since there are three kinds of things that come to be present in the   20 soul— feelings, predispositions, and active conditions—virtue would be one of these. And by feelings I mean desire, anger, fear, confidence, envy, joy, affection, hatred, yearning, jealousy, pity, and generally those things which are accompanied by pleasure or pain. It is the predispositions in accordance with which we are said to be apt to feel these, such as those by which we are predisposed to be angry or to be annoyed or to feel pity. And it is the active conditions in accordance with which we bear ourselves well or badly toward the feelings; for example, in relation to being angry, if we are that way violently or slackly, we bear ourselves badly, but if in a measured way, we bear ourselves well, and similarly in relation to other feelings.

Now neither virtues nor vices are feelings, because we are not said to be of serious or trifling moral stature as a result of our feelings, but   30 we are said to be so as a result of our virtues and vices, and because we are neither praised nor blamed as a result of our feelings (for one is not praised for being afraid or for being angry, nor is one blamed simply for being angry, but for being so in a certain way), but we are praised   1106a or blamed as a result of our virtues and vices. Also, we are angry and frightened without choice, but the virtues are certain kinds of choices, or not present without choice. And on top of these things, as a result of the feelings we are said to be moved, but as a result of the virtues and vices we are said not to be moved but to be disposed in a certain way.

And for these reasons, the virtues and vices are not predispositions either, since we are not called good or bad, nor are we praised or

---

[31] Aristotle's words here allude to something Socrates says in Plato's *Phaedo* at 99E, but are in no way intended to apply to him; Socrates ends that dialogue by accepting death in accordance with his philosophic talk, knowingly, by deliberate choice, and from a firm conviction.

blamed, simply for being predisposed to feel something. Also, we are
10   predisposed by nature, but we do not become good or bad by nature;
but we spoke about this before.[32] So if the virtues are neither feelings
nor predispositions, what remains is that they are active conditions.
Therefore what virtue is, in the sense of the general class to which it
belongs, has been said.

Chapter 6. But it is necessary to say not only this, that it is an active
condition, but also what sort of active condition it is. And something one
ought to state is that every virtue, as well as bringing that of which it is
the virtue to completion in a good condition, also makes it yield work
of a good kind, as the excellence of the eye makes both the eye and its
work first-rate, since by means of the excellence of the eye we see well.
20   Similarly, the excellence of a horse both makes it a first-rate horse, and
makes it good at running, at carrying its rider, and at holding still in
the face of enemies. So if this is the way things are in all cases, then also
the virtue of a human being would be the active condition from which
one becomes a good human being and from which one will yield up
one's own work well.

How this will be, we have already spoken of, but it will be clear in
the following manner as well, if we examine what sort of nature virtue
has. Now in everything continuous and divisible it is possible to take a
greater amount, a lesser amount, or an equal measure, and these either
on account of the thing itself or in relation to us, and the equal measure
is a certain kind of mean between excess and deficiency. By a mean that
30   belongs to the thing, I am speaking of what holds a position equally
apart from either of the extremes, which is one and the same thing for
everyone, but the mean in relation to us is what neither goes too far nor
falls short, and this is not one thing nor the same thing for everyone. For
example, if ten are a lot and two are few, then six are a mean amount
for those who take it according to the thing, since it both exceeds and
is exceeded by an equal amount, and this is a mean according to the
arithmetic proportion. But the mean in relation to us is not something
1106b   one needs to take in this way, for it is not the case, if ten pounds is a lot
for someone to eat and two pounds a little, that the gymnastic trainer
will prescribe six pounds, for perhaps even this is a lot for the one who
is going to take it, or a little. For it is a little to Milo,[33] but to someone
beginning gymnastic training it is a lot. And it is similar with running
and wrestling.

Now in this way everyone who has knowledge avoids excess and
deficiency, but seeks the mean and chooses this, but not the mean that
belongs to the thing but the mean in relation to us. So if every kind
of knowledge accomplishes its work well in this way, by looking to

---

[32] See 1103a18-32.

[33] Milo of Croton was the Olympic champion wrestler six times. Reports credited him with being able both to carry and to eat a whole ox.

the mean and guiding its works toward this (which is why people are   10
accustomed to remark about works that are in a good condition that it
is not possible either to take anything away from or to add anything to
them, on the grounds that excess and deficiency destroy what is well
made, but the mean condition preserves it; and good craftsmen, as we
are saying, do their work looking toward this), while virtue is something
more precise and better than any art, just as nature is, then virtue would
be something apt to hit the mean.

I am speaking of virtue of character, for this is concerned with feelings and actions, and among these there is excess and deficiency, and
the mean. For instance, it is possible to be afraid or be confident or to
desire or be angry or feel pity, or in general to feel pleasure or feel pain   20
both more and less, and on both sides not in the right way; but to feel
them when one ought, and in the cases in which, and toward the people
whom, and for the reasons for the sake of which, and in the manner one
ought is both a mean and the best thing, which is what belongs to virtue.
And similarly, concerning actions also, there is excess and deficiency,
and the mean. And virtue is concerned with feelings and actions, in
which excess and deficiency go astray, while the mean is praised and
gets them right, and both of these belong to virtue. Therefore, virtue is
a certain kind of mean condition, since it is, at any rate, something that
makes one apt to hit the mean. Also, it is possible to go wrong in many
ways (for what is bad belongs to what is unlimited, as the Pythagoreans
conjectured, and what is good belongs among what is limited), but there   30
is only one way to get something right (which is why the one is easy
and the other is difficult, it being easy to miss the target and difficult to
hit it); so for these reasons excess and deficiency belong to vice and the
mean condition belongs to virtue,

> For the good are good simply, but the bad are bad in every sort
> of way.

Therefore, virtue is an active condition that makes one apt at
choosing, consisting in a mean condition in relation to us, which is   1107a
determined by a proportion and by the means by which a person
with practical judgment would determine it. And it is a mean condition between two vices, one resulting from excess and the other from
deficiency, and is also a mean in the sense that the vices of the one sort
fall short and those of the other sort go beyond what is appropriate
both in feelings and in actions, while virtue both discovers and chooses
the mean. Hence, in terms of its thinghood and the articulation that
spells out what it is for it to be, virtue is a mean condition, but in terms
of what is best and what is done well, it is an extreme. But not every
action admits of a mean condition, nor does every feeling, for some
of them as soon as they are named are understood as having baseness   10
involved with them, such as joy at others' misfortunes, shamelessness,

and envy, and in the case of actions, adultery, stealing, and murder; for with all these things and things like them what is meant is that the things themselves are base, and not the excesses or deficiencies of them. There is, then, never any possibility of getting anything right about them, but one always goes astray, nor is there any doing well or not well about such things by committing adultery with the right woman and when and in the way one ought, but simply doing any of these things is to go wrong. It would be like believing that there was also a mean condition and an excess and deficiency concerned with

20   being unjust or a coward or dissipated, for at that rate there would be a mean condition in excess and in deficiency, and an excess in excess and a deficiency in deficiency. But just as there is no excess or deficiency of temperance or courage, because the mean is in a certain way an extreme, so there is no mean condition or excess and deficiency of those other things, but however one does them one is in the wrong; in general there is no mean in excess and in deficiency, nor any excess or deficiency of the mean condition.[34]

Chapter 7. But it is necessary not just to speak of this universally,
30   but also to apply it to the particulars, for in discourses about actions, those that are universal are common to more instances, but those that are about parts of the topic are more truthful, since actions are concerned with particulars, and discourse needs to harmonize with them. So one should take these from the list.[35] Now concerning fear and confidence,
1107b   the mean condition is courage; of people who go to excess, the one who

---

[34] Failure to pay attention to this argument causes serious misunderstandings of what Aristotle intends by a mean. Since there cannot be too much courage, the mean is not a synonym for playing it safe; since there cannot be too little courage, it is a condition that, when present at all, is all-sufficient. A virtue such as courage is not a limited thing but the thing that confers limit on something else. It is in fear and confidence, and in the actions they lead to, that there can be excess and deficiency, but courage is not a position on the scale of fear and confidence. It is a condition of the soul in which one holds oneself, in which actions can be clearly envisioned and freely chosen without being determined by fear or confidence. These things gradually become more evident as the inquiry proceeds, but it should be clear at this point that a virtue, while it occupies a mean between vices and hits a mean in making choices, is not itself any kind of quantity.

[35] In 1220b-1221a of the *Eudemian Ethics*, there is a list of fourteen virtues of character alongside their corresponding vices of excess and deficiency. In the present chapter thirteen virtues (or quasi-virtues) of character, with their corresponding vices, are mentioned, but not displayed in a diagram. There are two minor virtues in each work that do not appear in the other (proper passion for honor and charm here, dignity and patience there), and one virtue taken in the *Eudemian Ethics* list as belonging to character (practical judgment) is treated in this work as an intellectual virtue. The avoidance of a diagram here seems deliberate, as Aristotle's stated purpose of attending to the particular virtues would be undermined by forcing them into too rigid an application of a general scheme.

exceeds in fearlessness is without a name (and many of these things are nameless), the one who exceeds in confidence is rash, and the one who exceeds in fearing but falls short in being confident is a coward.[36] Concerning pleasures and pains—though not all of them and less so concerning pains—the mean condition is temperance and the excess is dissipation. Those who fall short concerning pleasure don't turn up very often, for which reason they and their sort have not happened on a name, but let them be termed "insensible." Concerning giving and taking money, the mean condition is generosity, the excess and deficiency being wastefulness and stinginess. In the latter, people exceed and fall short in contrary ways, for the wasteful person exceeds in letting go of things but falls short in getting them, while the stingy person exceeds in getting and falls short in letting go. Though we are speaking now in outline and under headings, content with just this, more precise distinctions will be made later about these topics.

There are also other dispositions concerned with money, the mean condition being magnificence (for a magnificent person is different from a generous one, since the former is concerned with great things and the latter with small ones), the excess being gaudiness or vulgarity, and the deficiency being chintziness; and these differ from those that concern generosity, but in what way they differ will be said later. And concerning honor and dishonor, the mean condition is greatness of soul, the excess is spoken of as a certain sort of vanity, and the deficiency is smallness of soul, and as we were saying generosity was related to magnificence, differing by being concerned with small things, so too, related in that way to greatness of soul, which is concerned with great honor, there is a certain disposition which is concerned with small honor, for it is possible to have an appetite for honor in the way one ought and also more or less than one ought; the person who exceeds in such appetites is called passionate for honor, the one who falls short is said to be lacking the passion for honor, and the person at the mean is without a name. The dispositions too are without names, except that of the person passionate for honor, which is called the passion for honor, which shows that the people at the extremes claim the right to the mean territory, and we do the same; there are times when we call the person at the mean passionate for honor and times when we speak of such a person as lacking the passion for honor, and times when we praise the person who is passionate for honor, but times when we praise the person who lacks the passion for honor. The reason why we do this will be stated in what follows, but for now let us mention the rest of the virtues in the

10

20

30

1108a

---

[36] We might call the nameless type incautious. The threefold distinction suggests that we recognize someone as a coward whether he gets that way from too much fear or too little confidence, while we see rashness as overconfidence rather than under-cautiousness. See 1115b 24-1116a 9.

way we have been led along.[37]

Concerning anger, there are also excess, deficiency, and a mean condition, and while they are pretty much without names, since we speak of the person at the mean as gentle, let us call the mean condition gentleness; of the extremes, let the person who exceeds be irritable and the vice irritability, and let the one who falls short be slow to anger and the deficiency slowness to anger. And there are three other mean conditions, that have some likeness to each other but differ from one another, for while they are all concerned with communal life in words and actions, they differ because one is concerned with what is true in them and the others with what is pleasant; of the latter, one sort occurs in playfulness and the other in all things in the course of life. So one ought to speak about these also, in order that we might see more clearly that the mean condition is praised in everything, while the extremes are neither praised nor are they right, but they are blamed. Now most of these are also without names, but we ought to try, as in the other cases, to make up names ourselves for the sake of clarity and to make it easy to follow.

Concerning truth, then, one who is at the mean is a truthful person, and let the mean condition be called truthfulness; pretence in the direction of exaggeration is bragging and the one who has it is a braggart, while pretence in the direction of understatement is irony and the one who has it is ironic. Concerning what is pleasant in playfulness, the person at the mean is charming and the disposition is charm, the excess is buffoonery and one who has it is a buffoon, and the one who falls short is a certain sort of boor and the active condition is boorishness. Concerning the remaining sort of pleasantness in life, the one who is pleasant in the way one ought to be is friendly and the mean condition is friendliness,[38] the one who goes to excess, if it is for no purpose, is

---

[37] This phrase implies following the "beaten path" of popular or conventional opinion, though commentators often twist it to mean Aristotle's own "usual method." In the *Politics* (1256a 2, b 15-22), the beaten path of opinion is Aristotle's warrant for accepting a kind of teleology at variance from his own opinions, as these are developed in all his theoretical works. Political inquiry does not impose philosophic conclusions on human communities, but studies people who have certain ineradicable opinions. In the *Parts of Animals* (643b 11), the beaten path is Aristotle's guide to the natural, though not neatly logical, classification of animals. Here in the study of ethics, the recognition that excellence of character is always a mean between opposite vices is like the popular classification of animals as birds, fish, and so on; Aristotle takes it as deeply revealing, not the whole story, and not to be taken as having logical precision or pushed to extremes.

[38] In Bk. IV, Chap. 6, this is said to be a nameless virtue that resembles friendship. The full treatment of friendship and its relation to action, character, and feeling occupies Bks. VIII and IX.

obsequious, but if it is for his own advantage, he is a flatterer, and the one who falls short and is unpleasant in everything is a certain sort of contrary person and hard to get along with.

And there are also mean conditions among and involving the feelings, for while a sense of shame is not a virtue, the person with a sense of shame is also praised, since even in these matters one sort of person is spoken of as a mean, and another sort as going to excess, as the shy person is ashamed about everything; the one who falls short, or is ashamed about nothing at all, is shameless, while the one at the mean is the person with a sense of shame. Righteous indignation is a mean condition between joy at the misfortunes of others and envy, which are concerned with pain and pleasure at what occurs among those who happen to be one's neighbors, for the person inclined toward righteous indignation is pained at those who fare well without deserving it, while the envious person, exceeding that, is pained at all those who fare well, and the one who takes joy in others' misfortune falls so far short of being pained as to be delighted. But there will be a fitting occasion concerning these things in another place; and concerning justice, since it is not meant in a single sense, after distinguishing these we will speak about the way in which both its kinds are mean conditions.[39]

Chapter 8. Since there are three dispositions, two of them vices, one resulting from excess and the other from deficiency, and one of them a virtue, the mean condition, they are all in some way opposite to all; for the extremes are opposite both to the mean and to one another, while the mean is opposite to the extremes. Just as the equal amount is greater in relation to the lesser and less in relation to the greater, so too the mean active conditions exceed in relation to the deficiencies and fall short in relation to the excesses in both feelings and actions. For the courageous person appears rash in relation to the coward and cowardly in relation to the rash person, and similarly the temperate person appears dissipated in relation to the insensible person and insensible in relation to the dissolute person, and the generous person appears wasteful in relation to the stingy person and stingy in relation to the wasteful person. Hence the people at each of the extremes push the person at the mean away toward the other extreme, and the coward calls the courageous person rash while the rash person calls him a coward, and analogously

30

1108b

10

20

---

[39] The two sorts of mean mentioned in this paragraph are only quasi-virtues, mere habits or predispositions of feeling. Righteous indignation (*nemesis*) is the natural basis of justice, evident in the child's heartfelt protest "that's not fair," but it is not a developed state of character that disposes one toward right choices. It is not mentioned again, but is superseded by the discussion of justice in Bk. V. A sense of shame is discussed again in Bk. IV, Chap. 9, but as a temporary stage of development that people need to grow out of. All the other active states identified in this chapter as virtues are discussed at greater length in Bks. III and IV.

in the other cases.[40] But while these are opposed to one another in this way, the greatest contrariety belongs to the extremes in relation to one another rather than to the mean, for these stand farther apart from one another than from the mean, just as the great is farther from the small and the small from the great than the two of them are from the equal. Also, a certain likeness to the mean shows up in some of the extremes, as in rashness in relation to courage or in wastefulness in relation to generosity, while in the extremes in relation to one another there is the greatest unlikeness; but things standing at the greatest remove from one another are defined as contraries, so that the things standing at the greater remove would be the more contrary.

In comparison with the mean it is in some cases the deficiency that is more opposite, but in other cases the excess; for example, in relation to courage it is not rashness, which is the excess, that is more opposite, but cowardice, which is the deficiency, but in relation to temperance it is not insensibility, which is the lack, that is more opposite, but dissipation, which is the excess. This turns out to be the case for two reasons, one of which comes from the thing itself, for on account of one extreme's being nearer to and more like the mean, we do not place this but its contrary as more opposite to the mean; for example, since rashness seems to be more like courage and nearer to it, while cowardice seems more unlike it, we set the latter down as more opposite, since the things that stand at a greater remove from the mean seem to be more contrary to it. This, then, is one reason, coming from the thing itself, but the other reason comes from us ourselves, for those things toward which we ourselves tend more by nature in any way appear more contrary to the mean. For example, we ourselves tend more by nature toward pleasures, on account of which we are more easily carried away toward dissipation than toward orderliness. So we more so call those things contrary toward which the extra tendency occurs more, and for this reason dissipation, which is the excess, is more contrary to temperance.

Chapter 9. It has been said sufficiently, then, that virtue of character is a mean condition, and in what way, namely because it is a mean between two kinds of vice, the one resulting from excess and the other from deficiency, and that it is such a mean condition on account of being apt to hit the mean in feelings and actions. And this is why it is work to be of serious moral stature, since in each kind of thing it is work to get hold of the mean; for instance, to take the center of a circle belongs not to everyone but to one who knows something, and so too, while getting angry, or giving and spending money, belong to everyone and are easy, to whom and how much and when and for what purpose and in what way to do these things are no longer in everyone's power, nor

---

40   A powerful historical example of this may be found in Thucydides's account of a civil war in Corcyra, in Bk. III, Chap. 82 of *The Peloponnesian War*.

are they easy; for this reason what is done well is rare and praiseworthy and beautiful.   30

Hence the one who aims at the mean ought first to pull back from what is more contrary to it, just as Calypso advises,[41]

Keep the ship out beyond that thick spray and swell,

for of the extremes the one is a greater error, the other a lesser. Since then, to hit the mean with extreme precision is a difficult thing, as the second best way to sail,[42] as people say, one ought to take the least of the evils, and this will be most the case in the way which we are speaking of. Also,   1109b one ought to consider what we ourselves are carried away toward, since different people are of a nature to incline toward different things, and this will be recognizable from the pleasure or pain that comes about in our own case. We ought then to drag ourselves over toward the opposite side, for by pulling far away from going wrong we will come to the mean, the very thing that people do who straighten warped pieces of lumber. And in everything one must guard most against the pleasant thing and against pleasure, for we do not judge it without bribes. So exactly the way the town elders felt toward Helen, we ought to feel toward pleasure,   10 and to think over in every instance what they said, for by sending it off in that way we shall go astray less.[43]

By doing these things, then, to say it in summary, we shall be most able to hit the mean. But this no doubt is difficult, and especially in

---

[41] The line is spoken by Odysseus to his men at XII, 219 of the *Odyssey*, as a result of Circe's advice to him in lines 106-110 that he would lose six men near Scylla but lose everyone near Charybdis. (Calypso's advice to him to keep the North star always on his left when he sailed from Ogygia is at V, 276-7. The order and location of events in the first half of the *Odyssey* are notoriously difficult to keep straight.)

[42] This is generally taken to mean that, when the wind fails, one sails in the second best way by rowing. A famous occurrence of this metaphor is in Plato's *Phaedo*, at 99D.

[43] At III, 156-160 of the *Iliad*, the old men of Troy say, in effect, let her beauty exert its power somewhere else. At 398A of the *Republic*, Plato elaborates the same message toward Homer himself, that a poet so holy, wondrous, and pleasant must be sent off, crowned and anointed, to some other city.
The three pieces of general advice in this paragraph are extensively referred to in the secondary literature as "rules." This goes back at least to the footnotes in John Burnet's 1900 text of this work, creeps even into the translation in the Loeb edition, and then turns up in later commentary as though it had been Aristotle's own word. But Aristotle uses the word rule (*kanôn*) only in two places in this work, and only in order to say that there can be no such thing in ethics; the only rule is the judgment of a good human being (1113a 33), because a rule applied to particulars would need to be flexible (1137b 29-32), that is, not a straightedge at all. In the course of this inquiry, as the understanding of pleasure is progressively deepened, major exceptions to the second and third of the generalizations given here will emerge.

particular cases, for it is not easy to determine how and with whom and on what sort of grounds and for how much time one ought to be angry, and we sometimes praise those who underdo it and call them gentle, while at other times we praise those who are severe by proclaiming them manly. But the person who deviates a little from what is done well is not blamed, whether the deviation is toward the more or toward the less, but someone who deviates more is blamed for it, since this person does not escape notice. But at what point and for how much of a deviation one is to be blamed is not easy to determine by a formulation, for no other perceptible thing is either; such things are in the particulars, and the judgment is in the perceiving. Therefore this much is clear: that while the mean active condition is praised in all things, one ought to incline away from it sometimes toward the excess and sometimes toward the deficiency, for in that way we shall most easily hit the mark of the mean and of what is done well.

BOOK III

Chapter 1. Now since virtue is concerned with feelings and actions, and praise and blame come about for willing actions, but for unwilling actions there is forgiveness and sometimes even pity, it is no doubt a necessary thing for those who inquire about virtue to distinguish what is a willing act and what is an unwilling act, and it is a useful thing for lawmakers as well, with a view to honors and punishments. Now it seems that unwilling acts are the ones that happen by force or through ignorance, a forced act being one of which the source is external, and an act is of this sort in which the person acting, or acted upon, contributes nothing, for instance if a wind carries one off somewhere, or people do who are in control. But with respect to those things that are done through fear of greater evils, or for the sake of something beautiful—for instance if a tyrant who was in control of one's parents and children were to order one to do some shameful thing, and in the case of one's doing it they would be saved but as a result of one's not doing it they would be killed—there is some dispute whether they are willing or unwilling.

Something of this sort happens also in connection with things thrown overboard in a storm, for no one simply throws them away willingly, but all those who have any sense do so for their own safety and that of the rest of the people aboard. Such actions then are mixed, but they are more like willing acts, since at the time when they are done they are preferred, and the end for which an action takes place is in accordance with its occasion. So one has to say what is willing or unwilling at the time when someone does it; and one does things of this sort willingly, for the source of the moving of the parts that are instrumental in such actions is in oneself, and anything of which the source is in oneself is also up to oneself either to do or not. So things of this sort are willing acts, though in an unqualified sense they would perhaps be unwilling acts, since no one would choose any such thing for itself.

Sometimes people are even praised for actions of this sort, when   20
they endure something shameful or painful in return for things that are great and beautiful, and conversely they might be blamed, since enduring things that are exceedingly shameful for no beautiful object, or for one only moderately beautiful, belongs to a person of low moral stature. For some things, while no praise is forthcoming, there is forgiveness, when one does what one ought not to do on account of motives of this sort, when they strain human nature too far, and no one could endure them.[44] Yet some things perhaps it is not possible to be forced to do, but one ought instead to die suffering the most terrible things, for the things that force the Alcmaeon of Euripides to kill his mother seem ridiculous.[45] But it is difficult sometimes to distinguish what   30
sort of thing should be chosen in return for what, and what should be endured for what, and still more difficult for those who have discerned it to abide by what they have chosen, since for the most part the things one anticipates are painful and the things they force one to do are shameful, which is why praise and blame come about according as people are or are not forced.   1110b

So what sort of thing ought one to say is forced? In an unqualified sense, is it not what is done whenever the cause is in external things and the one acting contributes nothing? But with those things that are in themselves unwilling acts, but are chosen in the present circumstances and in return for these particular ends, and their source is in the one acting, while they are unwilling acts in themselves, in the present circumstances and in return for these particular ends they are willing acts. But they are more like willing acts, since actions are in the particulars, and with respect to these they are willing acts. But it is not easy to give an account of what sort of things one ought to choose in return for what sort of ends, since there are many differences among the particular circumstances.

But if someone claims that things that are pleasant or beautiful are sources of compulsion (for they exert force while being external),   10

---

[44] These conditions amount to a definition of forgiveness (sun-gnômê): it is a judgment, made by putting oneself in another's place in imagination, that the other person's action was wrong, but only for reasons no human being could be expected to overcome.

[45] The play is lost, but fragments indicate the following chain of reasons for the killing: his father's command, accompanied by curses, when he was dying at Thebes, where he fought as one of the seven allies because his wife persuaded him to, because in turn she was bribed with a necklace. One might contrast this with the several strong reasons that converge to drive the Orestes of Aeschylus to the same act (*Libation Bearers*, 299-305).

everything would be forced according to that person, since everyone does everything for the sake of these ends.[46] Also, those who act by force and are unwilling act with pain, while those who act on account of what is pleasant and beautiful do so with pleasure. And it is ridiculous to blame external things but not oneself, for being easily caught by such things, and to take credit oneself for beautiful deeds but blame the pleasant things for one's shameful deeds. So it appears that what is forced is that of which the source is from outside, while the one who is forced contributes nothing.

What is done on account of ignorance is in every instance not a willing act, but it is unwilling by its painfulness and in one's regretting it,[47] for while someone who does a thing on account of ignorance without being in any way distressed by the action has not acted willingly, since he did not even know what he was doing, he has not acted unwillingly either, since he is not pained by it. So since the unwilling person seems to be in repentance for what was done on account of ignorance, let the one who is not repentant, since he is different, be nonwilling, since it is better for one who differs to have a special name. But acting on account of ignorance seems different from acting while being ignorant, since someone who is drunk or angry does not seem to act on account of ignorance but on account of one of the states mentioned, and while not knowing but being ignorant. Now every bad person is ignorant of what one ought to do and what one ought to keep away from, and on account of being in error in such a way people come to be unjust and generally bad; but unwillingness is not meant to be applied because someone is ignorant of what is advantageous, for the ignorance that is involved in choice is the cause not of something unwilling but of depravity, nor is it a general kind of ignorance that makes an act unwilling (since people are certainly blamed for that), but an ignorance of the particulars in which the action occurs and with which it is concerned, for in these cases there is pity and forgiveness, since the one who is ignorant of any of these acts unwillingly.

Perhaps, then, it would not be a bad idea to distinguish what these circumstances are and how many of them there are. And so they are:

---

[46] Comparison with 1104b 30-31 shows that a dialectical step has been taken toward the primary meaning of the good. The advantageous has dropped out of the earlier threefold division of goods sought by human action, since it can never be an end but is always a means to something else. The beautiful and the pleasant remain.

[47] In this context, pain is a synonym for remorse, an effect the act has on one's feelings, and regret is a synonym for repentance, an effect the act has to change one's thinking. Neither of these notions belongs exclusively to a Christian context, nor does that of forgiveness, explicated above at 1110a 24. All three of these things are decisive criteria for ethical conclusions within any view of the world.

who is acting, what the act is, what it is concerned with or consists in, and sometimes also with what (such as an instrument), for the sake of what (such as saving a life), and in what manner (such as gently or violently) it is done. Now no one could be ignorant of all these without being insane, since it is clear that one could not be ignorant of who is acting, for how could one not know at least that this is oneself? But someone might be ignorant of what he is doing, as people say that while they were talking things slipped out, or that they didn't know the things were forbidden to speak of, as Aeschylus said about the   10 mysteries,[48] or that they set it off while meaning to show it, as the person said about the catapult. Or someone might suppose that her son was an enemy, as Merope did,[49] or that the spear that came to hand was rounded at the end, or the stone was pumice; or by giving some-one something to drink to save his life, one might kill him; or when meaning just to touch, the way sparring partners do, one might land a punch. So since ignorance is possible about all these circumstances in which the action takes place, the person who was ignorant of any of them seems to have acted unwillingly, and espccially in the case of the most controlling circumstances; and the most controlling ones seem to be the things in which the action consists and for the sake of which it is done. And if an action is to be called unwilling as a result of this sort of ignorance, it is also necessary that it be painful to the one who   20 does it and held in regret.

Since an unwilling act is one that is done by force or on account of ignorance, a willing act would seem to be one of which the source is in oneself, when one knows the particular circumstances in which the action takes place. For things done on account of spiritedness or desire are probably not rightly called unwilling acts. In the first place, none of the other animals would any longer do anything willingly, nor would children. And then, of the things that result from desire and spirited-ness, do we do none of them willingly, or do we do the beautiful ones willingly and the shameful ones unwillingly? Or is this ridiculous when one thing is responsible for them? And perhaps it is absurd   30 to call things toward which one ought to extend oneself unwilling, and one ought to get angry at some things and to desire some things, such as health and knowledge. And while unwilling acts seem to be painful, those that result from desire seem to be pleasant. Also, what difference does it make to whether things that are wrong are unwilling

[48] Aeschylus was brought to trial for revealing secret religious rituals in some of his plays (now lost), but was acquitted. His remark, "I said what came to my mouth," became a proverbial excuse.

[49] In Euripides's lost play *Cresphontes* she recognizes her son just in time to avoid killing him. In Aristotle's *Poetics*, 1153b 31-1154a 10, this is one example of how acting with or without knowledge affects the impact of tragedy.

acts, that they result from reasoning or from spiritedness? Both kinds
of error are to be avoided, and irrational feelings seem to be no less
human than reasoning is, so that actions that come from spiritedness
and desire belong to the human being too.[50] So it is absurd to set these
down as unwilling acts.

Chapter 2. Now that willing and unwilling acts have been distinguished, it follows next to go through what concerns choice, for this
seems to be what belongs most properly to virtue and to determine
one's character more than one's actions do. A choice is obviously
something willing, but they are not the same thing, as what is willing covers a wider range, since children and the other animals share
in willing acts but not in choice, and we speak of things done on the
spur of the moment as willing acts, but not as things done as a result
of choice. Those who say that choice is desire, or spiritedness, or wishing, or some sort of opinion do not seem to speak rightly. For choice
is not shared by irrational beings, while desire and spiritedness are.
And a person lacking self-control acts while desiring something but
not choosing it, while a person with self-control conversely acts while
choosing something but not desiring it. And while desire sets itself
against choice, desire does not set itself against desire.[51] And desire is
for what is pleasant or painful, while choice is of something neither
painful nor pleasant.

Still less is it spiritedness, for things done out of spiritedness seem to
be the ones least in accord with choice. But it is surely not wishing either,
even though that appears a close approximation to it, since there can be
no choice of impossible things, and if anyone were to claim to choose
something impossible, that person would seem to be foolish; but there
is wishing even for impossible things, such as deathlessness. And there
is also wishing for things that can in no way be done by oneself, such
as for a certain actor to win an award, or for an athlete to win a contest,

---

[50] In Plato's *Republic*, the soul is divided into three parts, the reasoning, spirited,
and desiring parts. In an image in 588B, Socrates likens the whole soul, and
the reasoning part, to the look of a human being, while the other two parts
have the look of an animal and a monster. A misreading of this image might
make spiritedness and desire seem alien presences in us, though Socrates is
clear that the human being is responsible for taming and uniting everything in
the soul. In Plato's *Laws*, beginning in 863A, the Athenian Stranger prescribes
different and lesser penalties for crimes of passion that are unpremeditated
results of the desire for pleasure or an unbridled temper, but still holds the
person who acts in those ways responsible. The present paragraph seems to
be addressed not to Plato, but to his superficial readers.

[51] In the context of the preceding sentence, this must mean that once an object
is fixed on by desire, it is not desire that can oppose it but only a different
capacity. Two different desires may obviously conflict. In such a case, Aristotle says in Bk. III, Chap. 11, of *On the Soul*, now one of them, now the other,
knocks its rival out of the way like a ball.

1111b

10

20

but no one chooses such things, but only those things one believes could come about by one's own act. Also, wishing is rather for an end, while choice is of things that are related to the end; for example, we wish to be healthy, but we choose those things by means of which we will become healthy, and we wish to be happy and say so, while it would not fit the meaning to say we choose to be happy, since, universally, choice seems   30
to be concerned with things that are up to us.

So it could not be opinion either, since there seems to be opinion about all things, and no less about things that are everlasting or things that are impossible than about things that are up to us; and opinion is divided into the false and the true, not into the bad and the good, while choice instead is divided into the latter two kinds. Now no doubt no   1112a
one even claims that choice is the same as opinion as a whole, but it is not even the same as some particular opinion, for by choosing good or bad things we *are* certain kinds of people, but not by having opinions. And we choose to take or avoid something from among those alterna- tives, but we have an opinion about what it is or whom it benefits or in what way, while taking or avoiding is not at all what we have as an opinion. And choice is praised for being a choice of what it ought to be, more than for being rightly made, while opinion is praised for being as something truly is. And we choose what we most of all know to be good, but we have opinions about things we do not know very well, and it seems not to be the same people who choose best who also have the best opinions, but rather some people seem to have better opinions   10
but to choose what they ought not, on account of vice. And if an opinion comes before a choice or comes along with it, that makes no difference, for we are not considering this, but whether it is the same as any sort of opinion.

What then is choice, or what sort of thing is it, since it is none of the things mentioned? It is obviously something willing, but not everything that is willing is something chosen. But might it just be one that has been deliberated about first? For choice is involved with reason and thinking things through. And even its name seems to give a hint that it is something taken before other things.[52]

Chapter 3. But do people deliberate about all things, and is every- thing a thing to be deliberated about, or about some things is deliberation not possible? Perhaps one ought to mean by a thing to be deliberated   20
about, not what some fool or insane person might deliberate about, but those things that people with sense would deliberate about. Now no

---

[52] Choice is *proairesis*. Without the prefix *pro* it would mean taking one thing out of some array, as a child or animal might, but that prefix could mean merely taking in preference, implying no temporal structure. Aristotle construes it as meaning taking in advance, beforehand in one's thinking.

one deliberates about everlasting things, such as the cosmos, or about the diagonal and side of a square, that they are incommensurable; but neither does one deliberate about things that are in motion but always happen according to the same pattern, whether by necessity or else by nature or by means of some other cause, such as solstices and the risings of stars; nor about things that are sometimes one way and sometimes another such as drought and rain; nor about things that are by chance, such as finding a treasure; but not about all human things either, as no

30   Spartan deliberates about how the Scythians should best be governed, for none of these things could happen through us. We deliberate about things that are up to us and are matters of action, and these are the ones that are left. For the causes responsible for things seem to be nature, necessity, and chance, and also intelligence and everything that is due to a human being. And among human beings, each sort deliberates about the things to be done by its own acts.

1112b   And there is no deliberation about the precise and self-contained kinds of knowledge, such as about letters (for we are not in doubt about how something ought to be spelled), but as many things as come about by our act, but not always in the same way, about these we do deliberate, for example about the things done by medical skill or skill in business, and more so about piloting a ship than about gymnastic training, to the extent that the former is less precisely formulated, and similarly also about the rest of the skills but more about those that are arts than those that are kinds of knowledge, since we are more in doubt in connection with the former. Deliberating is present in things that happen in a certain way for the most part, but are unclear as to how they will

10   turn out, and in which this is undetermined. And we take others as fellow deliberators for large issues, not trusting that we ourselves are adequate to decide them. We deliberate not about ends but about the things that are related to the ends, for a doctor does not deliberate about whether he will cure someone, nor a rhetorician about whether he will persuade, nor someone holding political office about whether he will produce good order, nor does anyone else deliberate about ends, but having set down the end, they consider in what way and by what means it would be the case.

When it appears that the end would come about by more than one means, people examine through which of them it will come about most easily and most beautifully, but if the end will be accomplished by only one means, they examine how it will come to be through this means, and this in turn through some other, until they come to the first thing that will be responsible for the end, which is the last thing in the pro-

20   cess of discovery. The one who deliberates in the way described seems to be inquiring and analyzing just as one would with a geometrical diagram (and it is evident that, while not all inquiry is deliberation, as mathematical inquiries are not, all deliberation is inquiry), and what

comes last in an analysis is what comes first in the synthesis.[53] And if people come up against something impossible, they back off, for instance if the thing requires money and it is not possible for this to be procured; but if it seems to be possible they get started with acting. And things are possible which could come about by our own act, for those that are done by the help of friends are in a certain sense by our own act, since the source is in us. Sometimes one is looking for instruments and at other times for how to use them, and similarly in other cases, sometimes for that by means of which and sometimes for how or by whose help.

30

So it seems, as was said, that a human being is the source of actions and that deliberation is about the things to be done by oneself, while the actions are for the sake of something else. For the end could not be deliberated upon, but the things that are related to the end are; and deliberation is not about particulars either, such as whether this is a loaf of bread and whether it has baked long enough, for these things belong to sense perception. And if they would always be deliberated upon it would go to infinity. What is deliberated and what is chosen are the same thing, except that the thing chosen is already determined, since the thing chosen is what is decided out of the deliberation. For each person stops searching for how he will act when he traces the source of it back to himself, and to the part of himself that leads the way, for this is what chooses. And this is clear also from the ancient regimes that Homer depicted, for the kings used to report what they had chosen to their people. Since, among the things that are up to us, the desired thing that has been deliberated upon is what is chosen, choice would be the deliberate desire of things that are up to us, for having decided as a result of deliberating, we desire in accordance with our deliberation.[54] So let this have been a description of choice in outline, and of what sort of things it concerns, and that they are means to ends.

1113a

10

---

[53] The great examples of ancient Greek geometry that we possess, Euclid's *Elements* and Apollonius's *Conics*, demonstrate their propositions synthetically, but a few instances of analysis have survived in Apollonius's Propositions II, 44, 46, 47, and 49-51, and in manuscript additions to Euclid's Propositions XIII, 1-5. The synthesis starts with something admitted and deduces what is sought; the analysis assumes what is sought and deduces other things until it reaches one that is already admitted, then reverses the steps, so long as they are all logically convertible, to produce a synthetic demonstration. Rene Descartes, in the fourth of his *Rules for the Direction of the Mind*, blamed the ancient geometers for concealing their method of discovery and begrudging it to posterity, but it was no secret. Descartes, who invented a geometrical algebra, was primarily interested in the power to solve problems, while his ancient predecessors seemed interested, instead, in contemplating theorems in the full complexity of their derivation from self-evident beginnings.

[54] This discussion of moral responsibility has shown it to be dependent on a certain kind of thinking, so choice will be addressed again in connection

Chapter 4. But it was said that wishing is for the end, and it seems to some that it is for the good, to others that it is for the apparent good. But for those who say that what is wished for is the good, it turns out that what someone wishes for who does not select it rightly is not wished for at all (for if it is to be something wished for, it is also good, but if it were to happen as assumed, it would be bad),[55] while for those in turn who say that what is wished for is the apparent good, it follows that there would not be anything that is by nature wished for, but only what seems good to each person, but different things appear good to different people, and even, if it so happens, contrary things. But then if these results are not satisfactory, must one not say that what is wished for simply and truly is the good, but for each person the apparent good? Then to the person of serious moral stature, what is wished for would be what is truly good, but to a flighty sort of person it would be any random thing, just as, in the case of bodies, for the ones that are in good condition those things are healthy that truly are so, while for the ones that are sickly different things might be healthy, and similarly in the case of what is bitter or sweet or hot or heavy or of any other sort. For the person of serious moral stature discerns each thing correctly,[56] and in each kind of thing, the true instance shows itself to such a person. For in accordance with each sort of active condition there are special things that are beautiful and pleasant, and the person of serious moral stature is distinguished most of all, perhaps, for seeing what is truly so in each kind, since such a person is like a rule and measure of what is beautiful and pleasant. In most people, a distortion seems to come about by the action of pleasure, since it appears good when it is not. So people choose the pleasant as good, and avoid the painful as bad.

Chapter 5. Since then what is wished for is the end, while the things related to the end are deliberated about and chosen, the actions involving these things would be results of choice and willing acts. And the ways of being at work that belong to the virtues are concerned with these

---

with the intellectual virtues at 1139a 31-b 5. The direction of the inquiry here emphasizes a refinement of desire as it is transformed into choice by the thinking involved in deliberation; there a mirror image of the same conclusion will show that the rationality characteristic of human beings is fused with desire. This has been called the central teaching of Aristotle's ethics.

55 This paradox is argued by Socrates in Plato's *Gorgias* (466E-468E): those who have the power and resources to do as they please at any moment, but have not thought through the interconnections and consequences of their acts, do not do what they wish to do, since they haven't even thought through what that is.

56 Again, as in the previous chapter, dialectical reasoning from our primary ethical experience leads to a conclusion about knowing, and once more the point will come up again in the discussion of the intellectual virtues, at 1144a 34-36, where the mutual dependence of the two kinds of excellence becomes evident.

acts. Therefore virtue is up to us, and likewise also vice. For in those cases in which acting is up to us, not acting is also up to us, and where it is up to us to say no, it is also up to us to say yes; so if it is up to us to act when this is a beautiful thing, it will also be up to us to refrain from acting when this would be an ugly thing to do, and if it is up to us not to act when this would be a beautiful thing, it is also up to us to act when it is an ugly thing. But if doing the things that are beautiful or ugly is up to us, and likewise refraining from doing them, and this is what it is to be good or bad people, therefore being decent or base is up to us. To say that no one is willingly wretched or unwillingly happy seems to be partly false and partly true, for no one is happy unwillingly, but baseness is something willing; either that or one ought to dispute the things that were just now said and assert that a human being is not a source and begetter of actions just as much as of children. But if these things seem correct, and we are not able to trace our actions back to any other sources besides those that are in us, then those things of which the sources are in us are also up to us and willing acts.

What is done by each person privately and by the lawmakers themselves seems to bear witness to these conclusions, for they punish and take vengeance on people who do vicious things—all those who do not do them by being forced or as a result of ignorance for which they are not themselves responsible—and honor those who do beautiful things, so as to encourage the ones and deter the others. And yet no one encourages us to do things that are neither up to us nor willing acts, since it would be no use to be persuaded not to feel heat or pain or hunger or anything else of that sort, since we shall feel them none the less. In fact people apply punishment for ignorance itself if the one who is ignorant seems to be responsible for it, as when the penalties are doubled for people who are drunk, for the source is in oneself, since one has the power not to get drunk, which is the cause of the ignorance.[57] And they also punish those who are ignorant of anything in the laws which one ought to know and which is not difficult to know, and similarly in other cases in which people seem to be ignorant through carelessness, on the grounds that it is up to people themselves not to be ignorant, since they are in control of how much care they take.

But perhaps one is not the sort of person who takes any care. Still, people are themselves responsible for having become that sort by living carelessly, and for being unjust or dissipated, in the one case by acting dishonestly or, in the other, by passing their time in drinking and things of that sort, for it is the ways of being at work involved in each way of acting that produce such people. And this is clear from the kinds of

---

[57]   This refers to a decree of Pittacus, one of the Seven Sages of early Greek times. He was a commoner in Mytilene who was elected dictator during a civil war in 589 BC. Aristotle mentions this law also in the *Politics* (1274b 18-23) and the *Rhetoric* (1402b 11-15).

training there are for any sort of competition or performance, for people perfect themselves by being at work. So in order to be unaware that it is
10   from one's being at work involved in each way of acting that one's active conditions come about, one would have to be completely unconscious. Also it is unreasonable for the person who is unjust to wish not to be unjust, or for the person who is dissipated to wish not to be dissipated. If someone who is not ignorant does things as a result of which one will be an unjust person, that person would be unjust willingly, and will not stop being unjust and be just simply because he wishes to, any more than a person who is sick will be healthy by wishing to. It may so happen that one got sick willingly, by living without self-restraint and disobeying one's doctors; in that case it was in one's power at one time not to get sick, but that is no longer possible for one who has given up one's health, just as it is not possible for someone who has thrown a rock to take it back again. Nevertheless, to have thrown and launched
20   it was up to oneself since the source was in oneself. In that way too it was in the power of an unjust or dissipated person at the beginning not to have come to be that way, which is why they are that way willingly, but once they have become so it is no longer possible not to be so.

And it is not only the vices of the soul that come about willingly, but also, in some people, corruptions of the body,[58] and we censure them for these also. For while no one blames those who are ill-formed by nature, people do censure those who are that way through lack of exercise and neglect. And it is similar also with sickliness and disability, for no one would reproach a person who was blind by nature or from disease or from an injury, but instead would feel pity, but everyone would censure a person who goes blind from drunkenness or other dissipation. So of the corruptions involving the body, the ones that are up to us are censured, but the ones that are not up to us are not, and if it is this way
30   with them, then also in the case of the other sorts of corruption, the ones that are censured must be up to us.

But suppose someone were to say that all people aim at the apparent good, but they are not in control of how things appear, but rather
1114b   whatever sort of person each one is, of that sort too does the end appear to anyone. So if each one were in some way responsible for one's own active condition, then each would be in some way responsible oneself for how things appear, but if not, no one is responsible for wrongdoing

---

58   "Vices" and "corruptions" here translate the same Greek word (*kakiai*) that applies in general to all kinds of badness. As it applies to character and action, Aristotle narrows its meaning (and that of its near-synonyms *ponêria* and *mochthêria*) to the particular kind of deliberately chosen badness that is usually meant by the word vice. In the next sentence, "ill-formed" translates *aischros*, which has the primary meaning "ugly" and is most often used in this work for actions, where it is most often translated as "shameful."

by oneself, but does these things through ignorance of the end, believing that by these means one will secure the highest good for oneself. But the targeting of the end is not self-chosen; instead one needs to be born having something like vision,[59] by which to discern rightly and choose what is truly good, and one in whom this is naturally right is of a fortunate nature, for with respect to what is greatest and most beautiful, and which is impossible to get or to learn from anyone else,   10 but which one will have in such a condition as one was born with—to be well and beautifully born in this respect would be the complete and true blessing of nature.

But if these things are true, in what way would virtue be any more willing than vice? For to both the good person and the bad, the end appears and is laid down in the same way, by nature or in whatever manner, and they act in whatever way they act by referring everything else to this end. So whether the end does not appear by nature to each person as whatever sort of thing it is, but in some respect is dependent on oneself, or whether the end is natural but virtue is something willing because a serious person does everything else willingly, vice would be no less willing, for what is done by one's own means is present in the   20 actions of the bad person even if not in the end. If, then, as was said, the virtues are willing things (since we ourselves are in a certain way jointly responsible for our active conditions, and by being people of a certain sort, we set down the end as being of that sort), then the vices must be willing things too, since they come about in a similar way.

About the virtues in common, then, the general class to which they belong has been stated by us, that they are mean conditions and that they are active conditions, and that on account of themselves they make one apt to do those things by which they come about, and that they are up to us and willing things, and that they make one do things in the way that right reason would dictate. But our actions and   30 our active conditions are not willing in the same way, since we are in control of our actions from beginning to end, so long as we know the particulars, while of our active conditions we are in control of their   1115a beginnings, but the process by which they add to themselves is not known in particular, any more than in the advance of a disease; but because it was up to us to make use of them in a certain way or not, for that reason they are willing things. But taking up again what concerns

---

[59]   This idea of an innate moral vision is so tempting, and Aristotle's argument for this hypothetical assumption is so vigorously developed, that readers sometimes mistake it for his own opinion. Aristotle does say that habituation has to work on a natural capacity already present (1103a 23-26), but only effort of a kind that each person is solely responsible for making can develop that capacity. To see what is morally relevant requires not a special sense, but an active condition that counteracts distortions (1113a 33-b 2).

each of the virtues, let us say what they are and what sort of things they are involved with, and how. How many of them there are will also be clear at the same time.

Chapter 6. First let us speak of courage. That it is a mean condition concerned with fear and confidence has already become evident. And it is clear that we fear things that are frightening, and that these are, to put it simply, bad things, and hence fear is defined as an expectation of something bad. And we do fear all bad things, such as loss of reputation, poverty, disease, loss of friends, and death, but a courageous person seems not to be concerned with all of these; some things one ought to fear and it is even a beautiful thing to fear them and a shameful thing not to, such as loss of reputation, for the one who fears it is decent and has a sense of shame, while the one who does not fear it is shameless. But he may be called courageous by some people in a sense altered from its proper meaning, since he has some likeness to a courageous person, for a courageous person is someone fearless. Also, one ought not, perhaps, to fear poverty or disease, or generally any of those things that do not result from vice and are not caused by oneself; even so, the one who is without fear of these things is not courageous either, though we say even this on account of a likeness, since some people who are cowards when there is danger of war are generous and bear up confidently to the loss of money. And neither is someone a coward if he fears insolence toward his children and wife, or envy, or anything of the sort, nor is someone courageous who is defiant when he is about to be punished by a whipping.

In connection with what sort of frightening things, then, is someone courageous? Or is it in connection with the greatest of them? For no one is more apt to endure terrifying things. But the most frightening thing is death, for it is a limit, and it seems that there is nothing beyond it to be good or bad for the one who is dead. But it would seem that the courageous person is not concerned with death in every situation, such as at sea or by disease. In what situations then? Or is it in the ones that are the most beautiful? But these are the ones that occur in war, for they occur in the midst of the greatest and most beautiful sort of danger. And the honors given in cities and by kings are in agreement with these conclusions. In the governing sense,[60] then, one would call

---

[60] There may be cases in which disobeying an order requires more courage than standing up to the enemy, or facing a disease is more what courage demands than going to war would be, but even such cases are measured by the standard of courage in war. Aristotle's step-by-step argument, that clears the way to this paradigm case, continues in the next two chapters to clear away everything that resembles battlefield courage but misses the mark. This makes the examination of courage itself a paradigm for all the virtues of character, and a dialectical confirmation of what most purely characterizes all of them. Aristotle is always in search of the primary instance of whatever he studies, rather than the most comprehensive definition of it.

courageous a person who is unafraid in the face of a beautiful death, and in whatever circumstances make death be close at hand, and such most of all are the things involved in war. It is not that a courageous person is not also unafraid at sea and in diseases, but it is not in the same way that sailors are, for those who are courageous have given up hope of safety and are disdainful of such a death, while the sailors are full of good hope on account of their experience. The courageous show courage at once in situations in which there is a defence, or in which dying is a beautiful thing, but in those other types of destruction neither possibility is present. **1115b**

Chapter 7. While the same things are not frightening to all people, we speak of some things as beyond a human being. These, then, are frightening to everyone, or at least to anyone with any sense, but frightening things that are on a human scale differ in magnitude and as greater or lesser, and similarly with things that inspire confidence. **10** But the courageous person is as undaunted as a human being can be, and while such a person will be frightened even of such things as vary in magnitude, he will endure them in the way one ought and keeping them in proportion, for the sake of the beautiful, since this is the end that belongs to virtue.[61] But it is possible to fear these things more or less, and also to fear things that are not frightening as though they were. One way of going wrong comes from fearing something one ought not to fear, another from fearing something in a way one ought not to fear it, another from fearing something when one ought not, or anything of that sort, and it is similar with things that inspire confidence. So one who endures or fears what one ought, for the reason one ought, as one ought, when one ought, and is confident in similar ways, is courageous, since the courageous person undergoes things and acts in accordance with what is worthy and in a way that is proportionate. **20** Now the end of any way of being at work is what corresponds to the active condition it comes from, and to a courageous person, courage is a beautiful thing, and so its end is something beautiful as well, since each thing is determined by its end. So it is for the sake of the beautiful that the courageous person endures and does the things that are in accord with courage.

---

[61] This has been implicit from the beginning of Aristotle's discussion of the mean, as one might gather from the comparison of right action to a work of art that the artisan gets just right (1106b 9-16) and from the warning that the mean in matters of action is judged and decided not by reasoning or rules but by sense-perception (1109b 22-23). The mean provided a sufficient criterion by which to speak about virtue, but the beautiful, as its end, is its deeper and more governing cause, since, as Aristotle points out below, it is the end that determines anything. In any dialectical inquiry, what emerges later is nearer to what is being sought, and in an inquiry into ethics, it is when the discussion comes closest to particular examples that it gets to the heart of its topic.

Among those who are excessive, the sort who exceed in fearlessness are without a name (and it was mentioned by us in what preceded that many of these things are without names), though one would have to be insane or incapable of feeling pain if one were to fear nothing, not even an earthquake or a flood, as people say about the Celts;[62] and the sort who exceed in confidence about frightening things are rash. The

30   rash person seems to be a braggart who makes a pretence of courage; at any rate he wants to appear to be the way the courageous person *is* in relation to frightening things, and he mimics courage in those situations in which he can. Hence most of these people are brash cowards, for though they make a show of boldness where they can, they do not stand up to frightening things. The person who is excessive in fearing is a coward, and all such qualifications as fearing things one ought not to fear and in a way one ought not to fear them apply to such a person;

1116a   he is also deficient in feeling confident, but is more apparent for being excessive in his pains. A coward is someone with faint hope, since such a person is afraid of everything, and a courageous person is the opposite, since confidence belongs to someone full of hope. So the coward, the rash person, and the courageous person are concerned with the same things, but they bear themselves differently toward them, since the former kinds exceed and fall short, while the latter is in a mean condition and is as one ought to be. Also, rash people are impulsive, and are eager prior to the dangerous occasions but hold back in the midst of them, while courageous people are sharply intent in the midst of deeds

10   but calm beforehand.

So as was said, courage is a mean condition concerning things that are confidence-inspiring or frightening in the circumstances stated; it chooses something and endures it because it is a beautiful thing, or because not to do so would be a shameful thing. But to die as a way of running away from poverty or love or anything painful does not belong to a courageous person, but rather to a coward, for to run away from distressing things is softness, and such a person does not endure death because it is a beautiful thing, but as a way of escaping something bad.

Chapter 8. Courage, then, is a thing of this sort, but there are also other things that are called courage, in five ways. First, there is an active

---

62   Later called the Gauls by the Romans, the Celts were the dominant inhabitants of Europe, with scattered tribes stretching from present-day Spain and Ireland in the west all the way to Asia minor. They are taken as standing for the incautious type of overbold people, as distinct from the overconfident type, described next, who overreact to situations that permit confidence as a way of covering up their fearfulness. One modern equivalent of the Celtic type was the Israeli hero Moshe Dayan, who said he thought he was given credit for courage when really he just lacked some chemical that makes the rest of us afraid when bombs go off around us.

condition that comes from citizenship, since it is most like courage. For
citizens seem to endure dangers on account of the penalties that come
from the laws, and reproaches, and on account of honors; and because of   20
this, those peoples seem to be most courageous among whom cowards
are dishonored and courageous people are honored. Homer fashions
people of this sort, such as Diomedes and Hector[63]:

> Polydamas will be the first to lay censure upon me,

and

> For Hector one day will say in public address to the Trojans,
> "Tydeus's son under fear of me..."

and this most closely resembles the courage described above, because
it comes about by means of a virtue, since it is on account of a sense of
shame and a craving for something beautiful (since it is for honor), and
to escape reproach, which is something shameful.

One might also assign to the same group those who are forced by   30
their rulers, but they are inferior, to the extent that they act not from
a sense of shame but from fear, and by avoiding not what is shameful
but what is painful, since those who are in charge force them, as Hector
does[64]:

> And if I see anyone covering up away from the battle,
> It will be a sure thing that he won't escape the dogs.

And those who assign positions and beat the men who draw back do the
same thing, as do those who position men alongside trenches or things   1116b
of that sort, for they all force them. But one ought not to be brave by
compulsion, but because it is a beautiful thing.

And experience in connection with each kind of situation also seems
to be courage, which is why Socrates believed that courage is knowledge.[65] But different people are experienced in different things, and in
what pertains to war it is the professional soldiers, since there seem to
be many empty threats belonging to war, and these people most of all
have seen them all; so these appear courageous, because the others do
not know what sort of situations are present. Then too, they are most
able, as a result of their experience, to do unto others and not be done
to, being competent to use armor and having on whatever sort would   10
be most effective for giving and for not taking damage; so they are

---

[63] The first line is Hector's at *Iliad* XXII, 100 and the next line and a half are
spoken by Diomedes at VIII, 148-9.
[64] It is Agamemnon who uses (approximately) these words at *Iliad* II, 391-3.
[65] This is the definition of courage given by Nicias in Plato's *Laches*, at 194E-
195A. Socrates accepts it only if it is expanded to mean that courage requires
the possession of all knowledge. A famous saying of Socrates was "virtue is
knowledge."

like armed men fighting unarmed ones or athletes fighting untrained people, for in athletic contests too, it is not the most courageous people who are the most effective fighters, but those who are strongest and whose bodies are in the best shape. But professional soldiers become cowards whenever the danger strains them too far and they are left behind in numbers and equipment, for they are the first to run away, while the citizen forces die holding their ground, the very thing that happened at the temple of Hermes.[66] For to the latter it is a shameful thing to run away, and death is to be chosen over that sort of safety, while the former from the beginning were braving the danger on the grounds that they were more powerful, and once they have determined otherwise they run away, fearing death more than disgrace; but the courageous person is not that way.

Also, people extend spiritedness to mean courage, for those who, on account of spiritedness, are like wild animals carried away onto people who have wounded them, seem to be courageous, because courageous people too are of a spirited kind. For spiritedness is most impulsive toward dangers, which is why Homer says "he hurled strength into their spirits," and "he roused their strength and spiritedness," and "a sharp passion flared his nostrils," and "his blood seethed"[67]; for all such words seem to refer to the rousing and stirring of spiritedness. So while courageous people act on account of the beautiful, spiritedness works along with it in them; but wild animals react to pain, since their spiritedness comes from being hit or from being frightened, for if they are in the woods they do not rush forward. So hurrying on toward danger on account of being driven out by pain and spiritedness, while foreseeing none of its terrors, is not courage, since at that rate even donkeys would be courageous when they are hungry, for being beaten will not hold them back from their food; even adulterers do many daring things on account of lust. But the sort of bravery that comes from spiritedness seems to be the most natural, and when it includes in addition choice and something for the sake of which it acts, it seems to be courage. But people also feel pain when they are angered and feel pleasure when they take revenge, but those who fight for these reasons, while they are effective fighters, are not courageous, since they do not act on account of the beautiful

---

[66] A note in one of the manuscripts identifies this as a reference to a battle in 353 BC at Coronea in Boeotia.

[67] The first two quotations are from the *Iliad*, the first a mixture of XIV, 151 and XVI, 529 and the second similar to V, 470; the third is from XXIV, 318-19 of the *Odyssey*. The third doesn't involve battlefield dangers, but Odysseus's inability to hold back his feelings for his father. The fourth is not from Homer, but is used by the poet Theocritus, and is cited in *On the Soul* (403a 31) as a materialist's definition of anger. Aristotle's point is not dependent on exact quotation; he is borrowing poetic language that evokes the look shared by courage and spiritedness.

or as reason determines, but from passion; but they have something very close to courage.

Nor are those who are full of hope courageous, since it is on account of having been victorious often over many people that they are confident in dangerous situations; but they are much like courageous people, since both are confident, but while courageous people are confident on account of what was said above, these people are so from believing they will be the strongest and will suffer nothing. Those who get drunk do something of this sort, since they become full of hope. But whenever things do not turn out for them in such a way as they expect, they run away, but it belongs to the courageous person to endure things that are and appear frightening to a human being, because it is a beautiful thing and not to do so would be a shameful thing. Hence also, it seems to be characteristic of a more courageous person to be fearless and undisturbed in sudden frights than in those that are evident in advance, for it would come more from an active condition of the soul since it would be less a result of preparation; for one might choose things that are evident in advance from calculation and reason, but things that are sudden are chosen in accordance with one's active state.

Those who are ignorant also appear to be courageous, and are not far from those who are full of hope, but they are worse to the extent that they have nothing they consider worth facing, while the others do. This is why the hopeful hold their ground for a certain time, but those who are deceived run away if they recognize that something is different, or suspect it, which is what the Argives had happen to them when they fell among the Spartans they took for Sicyonians.[68]

So what sort of people are courageous has been said, as well as what sorts of people seem to be courageous.

Chapter 9. And courage, though it is concerned with confidence and fear, is not concerned with both to a similar degree, but is concerned more with frightening things, since it is one who is undisturbed in these situations and bears oneself toward them as one ought who is courageous, rather than one who is that way in occasions of confidence. So it is for enduring painful things, as was said, that people are called courageous. Hence courage too is painful, and it is justly praised, since it is more difficult to endure painful things than to refrain from pleasant ones. Nevertheless, it would seem that the end that goes with courage is pleasant, but is blocked from sight by the things that encircle it[69]; such a thing also happens in gymnastic contests, for to boxers, the end for

10

20

30

1117b

---

68   This incident at Corinth in 392 BC is described in Xenophon's *Hellenica*, IV, 4.

69   See 1113a 31-b 2, where pleasure is said to distort one's view of what is good; it may be also that pleasure (of an obvious and familiar kind) distorts one's view of what is pleasant (more fully and genuinely). Pleasure will be repeatedly re-examined in the course of the inquiry.

the sake of which they fight is something pleasant, the crown of leaves and the honors that come with it, but being hit is painful, since boxers are made of flesh, and burdensome, as is all the hard labor, and because these pains are many, that for the sake of which they are endured, since it is a small thing, appears to be nothing pleasant at all.[70]

So if what is involved in courage is also of this sort, death and injuries will be painful to the courageous person, who will undergo them unwillingly, but will endure them because it is a beautiful thing,
10   and not to do so would be a shameful thing. And to the extent that one more nearly has all virtue and is happier, the more will one be pained at the possibility of death, for to such a person living is most worthwhile, and this person will be deprived of the greatest goods knowingly, and this is painful. Still, such a person is courageous none the less, and perhaps even more so, because he prefers what is beautiful in war above those other things. So being at work pleasantly is not present within all the virtues, except to the extent that one fixes one's attention upon the end. This does not, perhaps, imply that such people would be the most effective professional soldiers,[71] but those who are less courageous and have nothing else good in their lives would be,
20   since these people are ready to face dangers and they put up their lives in exchange for small gains.

So let courage have been discussed to this extent; it is not difficult to comprehend what it is, in outline at least, from what has been said.

Chapter 10. And after this, let us speak about temperance, since these seem to be the virtues of the irrational parts of the soul. Now it was said by us that temperance is a mean condition concerning pleasures, for it is less concerned with pains, and not in a similar way, while dis-

---

[70] In Herodotus's *History*, VIII, 26, a Persian, who learns that the only prize at the Olympic games was a crown of olive leaves, wonders how his army can hope to defeat men who compete not over money but over virtue. In Herodotus's depiction of the battle of Thermopylae (VII, 219-238), a deliberate suicidal stand by 300 Spartans, it is apparent that the Spartan king Leonidas was pleased to have such an opportunity, and that the Persian emperor Xerxes was enraged to have an enemy who was entirely beyond his power.

[71] While battlefield courage is the primary instance by which all courage is measured, it cannot be the only sort worthy of the name. Chapter 6 clears away all other sorts of danger as lesser, Chapter 7 clears away rash and cowardly acts on the battlefield that may seem courageous, and Chapter 8 clears away five ways people might be brave on the battlefield that do not come from a stable condition of the soul that leads to a deliberate choice of an action for its own sake. What results is a pattern taken from rare situations that would seldom arise more than once in any lifetime. That pattern not only measures other ways of being in war as less courageous; it also illuminates the innumerable everyday occasions in which the better choice requires confronting and enduring frightening things, and can only be made rightly by someone with a stable character and clear sight.

sipation manifests itself in the same situations. Let us now distinguish, then, what sorts of pleasures it is concerned with. And these are divided into those that pertain to the soul and those that are bodily; examples are the passion for honor and the passion for learning, for someone who is passionately devoted to either of these takes delight in it, even   30
though the body experiences nothing, but rather one's thinking does, and those who are concerned with pleasures of this sort are not spoken of as either temperate or dissipated. And likewise, neither are those who are concerned with any other pleasures that are not bodily; for people who love talking and tend to go on at length and pass whole days talking about anything that occurs to them are loquacious, but we don't speak of them as dissipated, nor say this of people who are grieving   1118a
over possessions or friends.

So temperance would be concerned with bodily pleasures, but not even with all of these, for people who delight in things that come by way of sight, such as colors, shapes, and paintings, are not spoken of as either temperate or dissipated, even though it would seem to be possible to delight in these things too either as one ought or to excess or deficiently; and it is similar with the things connected with hearing, for no one speaks of people who delight excessively in music and acting as dissipated, or of those who do so as one ought as temperate. Nor do we speak that way of those concerned with smell, except incidentally,   10
for we do not call people who delight in the smells of fruit or roses or incense dissipated, but rather those who delight in perfumes or sauces, since it is dissipated people who take delight in these, because by means of them recollection comes to them of the things they yearn for. One might view others too, when they are hungry, as taking delight in the smells of food, but delighting in such things belongs to the dissipated person, since it is to such a person that these are objects of yearning. Nor is there any pleasure from these senses in the other animals, except incidentally. For dogs delight not in the smells of rabbits but in eating meat—the smell brought about the perception; nor does the lion delight   20
in the sound of the cow, but in its meat, but it perceived that the cow was nearby through its sound, and seems to delight in that, and likewise not in seeing "a deer or a wild goat,"[72] but because it will have meat.

Temperance and dissipation are concerned with pleasures of this sort, which the rest of the animals share in, which is why these pleasures have a slavish and animal-like look, and they are touch and taste. But these pleasures seem to make use of taste only a little or not at all, for what belongs to taste is distinguishing flavors, which people do when they test wines or prepare sauces, and they don't especially take delight in these acts, or at least dissipated people don't, but rather in   30

---

[72]   In *Iliad* III, 24, that is what Paris looks like to Menelaus when he spots him. In these examples, Aristotle uses three different vivid words for meat.

the enjoyment which comes about entirely through touch, in both foods and drinks as well as in the acts said to be devoted to Aphrodite. And this is why a certain person who was a gourmet prayed for his gullet to become longer than that of a crane, since the pleasure was in the

1118b   contact. So it is the most widely shared of the senses that dissipation applies to, and it would seem justly to be the most reproached vice, because it is present not insofar as we are human beings but insofar as we are animals. And to delight in such things and love them most of all is animal-like. The pleasures from touch that most belong to free people[73] are set aside as distinct, such as those that come about in the gymnasium from massage or heat, since the sort of touch that is characteristic of a dissipated person doesn't involve the whole body but only certain parts of it.

Chapter 11. Some desires seem to be shared in common, while others seem to be confined to certain people and cultivated; for

10   example, the desire for food is natural, since every being that needs it desires dry or moist nourishment, and sometimes both, and one that is young and reaching its peak desires sex, as Homer says[74]; but not everyone has a desire for this or that particular sort of food, or for the same sorts, and hence what is desired seems to be our own preference. Nevertheless, it also has something natural in it, since different things are pleasant to different sorts of people, and some things are more pleasant to everyone than any random thing would be. So in the natural desires, few people go wrong, and in one direction, toward too much, since eating or drinking whatever it may be until one is overfull is to exceed what is natural in amount, for the natural desire

20   is to fulfill one's need. Hence these people are called greedyguts, since they fill the belly beyond need, and those who come to be that way are people who are too slavish. But many people go wrong, and in many ways, in connection with the pleasures that are confined to certain people, for those who are said to be passionately devoted to such pleasures are so called either for delighting in things they ought not to delight in, or more than most people do, or in a way that they ought not, and dissipated people go to excess in all these ways; for they too delight in some things they ought not (when they are despicable things), and if one ought to delight in some such things, they delight in them either more than one ought or more than most people do. It is clear, then, that excess in connection with pleasures is dissipation and is to be blamed.

---

[73] Such people are free in two senses, as having the leisure to exercise in a gymnasium, and as opposed to those who are enslaved (see 1118b 21) to their desires.

[74] Several times in the *Iliad* (e.g., IX, 133-4) Homer uses the word "bed", which is the word Aristotle uses here, as a euphemism for sex, with an added phrase about its naturalness.

But concerning pains, it is not the same way as with courage; one is not called temperate for enduring pains or dissipated for not enduring them, but rather the dissipated person is so called for being more pained than one ought to be because one does not happen upon pleasant things (and so pleasure even causes pain to such a person), and the temperate person is so called for not being pained at the absence of or abstention from what is pleasant. So the dissipated person desires all things that are pleasant, or those that are most pleasant, and is led so much by desire as to choose these things in preference to all others; and this is why a dissipated person is pained both by missing out on pleasures and by desiring them, since desire involves pain, though it seems absurd to be pained on account of pleasure.

People who fall short in things concerned with pleasures and delight in them less than one ought don't turn up very often, for such insensitivity is not human. Even the rest of the animals discriminate among foods, and delight in some but not in others, and if there is any for which no food is pleasant, or no food differs in pleasure from any other, that animal would be a long way from what it is to be human. Since they do not turn up very often, such a person has not gotten a name.

The temperate person is in a mean condition concerning these things, and is not pleased by the things that a dissipated person takes most pleasure in, but instead has disdain for them,[75] and in general is not pleased by things one ought not to take pleasure in, and is not greatly pleased by anything of the sort, and feels neither pain nor desire when they are absent, or only moderately so, and not more than one ought or when one ought not, or anything at all of that sort. But those things that are pleasant and lead to health and to being in good condition, the temperate person will desire moderately and in the way one ought, as he will desire the other pleasant things that are not impediments to health and good condition, and are not contrary to what is beautiful, and not beyond his resources. One who would go that far loves such pleasures more than they deserve, but the temperate person is not that sort, but is one who loves them in the way right reason judges.

Chapter 12. Dissipation seems like something more willing than cowardice, since one is for pleasure while the other is on account of pain, of which the former is chosen while the latter is avoided. Also,

---

[75] The virtue of temperance is not an effort of self-control, nor is it a natural condition of being born without strong desires; it is an active state of character acquired by good upbringing, that lets one see clearly, and feel comfortably, that one doesn't really want to gorge oneself on bodily pleasures that one will regret later. As courage was the exemplary and purest virtue of character, temperance is the most fundamental, acquired by overcoming the strongest impulses of childhood.

pain deranges one, and ruins the nature of the person who has it, while pleasure does nothing of the sort, and so is more willing. For this reason too, dissipation is more reproached, for it is easier to habituate oneself in connection with pleasures, since there are many such things in the course of life, and the process of habituation is without dangers, but the opposite is the case with frightening things. But cowardice, unlike its particular instances, might seem to be something willing, since the condition itself is painless, while the occasions of it make one so

30   deranged by pain that one even throws down one's arms and disgraces oneself in other ways, and hence they seem to be things one is forced to do. But with a dissipated person, conversely, the particular instances are willing acts (for they are done by someone desiring and yearning to do them), but the whole condition is less so, since no one desires to be dissipated.

We also apply the word for dissipation[76] to the misbehavior of chil-

1119b   dren, since it has some likeness. Which is named after which makes no difference to the things now being explored, but it is clear that the later condition is named after the earlier one. And the meaning seems to have been transferred not badly, for anything that has a lot of growth while stretching out toward ugly things needs to be kept back, and of this sort most of all are desire and a child. For children too live in accordance with desire, and the desire for what is pleasant is greatest in them. If, then, the desire will not be obedient and come under a ruler, it will have come to great strength, for in someone without understanding, the desire for pleasure is insatiable and comes from all sides, and the being-at-work of desire makes its innate strength grow; if desires are great and vehe-

10   ment they even knock the reasoning power out of commision. Hence it is necessary for desires to be moderate and few, and not opposed to reason—such a condition as we call obedient and disciplined—and just as a child needs to live by the instructions of a tutor, so too is the desiring part of the soul related to reason. This is why the desiring part of a temperate person needs to be in harmony with reason, for the aim to which both look is the beautiful, and the temperate person desires what one ought, as one ought, when one ought, which is what reason also prescribes. Let these things, then, have been said about temperance.

---

[76] In Greek, the same word means "spoiled" as in the case of an overindulged child, and "dissipated" as in a fully formed adult state of character; its root sense is "unpruned," extending to mean "unpunished," "uncorrected," or "undisciplined." This paragraph makes clear that the habituation that forms character is not conditioning or programming, but a counterweight applied against desires when people are too young to have understanding. It is thus a setting free of one's nature, rather than an imposition upon it.

BOOK IV

Chapter 1. Let us speak next about generosity. It seems to be the mean condition that concerns money, since the generous person is praised not in situations that pertain to war, nor in those in which a temperate person is, nor again in legal judgments, but in connection with giving and getting money, and more so with the giving. By money we mean all those things of which the worth is measured in monetary terms. And wastefulness and stinginess are excesses and deficiencies in connection with money; we apply stinginess always to those who take money more seriously than one ought, but we carry wastefulness over 30 sometimes, intertwining it with other things, since we call unrestrained people and those who spend money on dissipation wasteful. Hence such people seem to be of the lowest sort, for they have many vices at the same time, but the word is not being applied to them appropriately, for a wasteful person means someone who has one vice, that of destroying 1120a one's property. For a wasteful person is someone who is ruined by his own act, and the destruction of one's property seems to be a kind of self-destruction, since the living of one's life depends on these means. We take wastefulness, then, in that sense.

Now with those things that have a use, it is possible to use them either well or badly, and wealth consists of things to be used. And for each kind of thing, the person who has the virtue connected with it uses it best; so the person who will use wealth best is the one who has the virtue that is connected with money, and this is the generous person. But the using of money seems to be spending and giving, while the getting and preserving of it are acquisition rather than use. Hence it is 10 more characteristic of a generous person to give money to whom one ought than to get it from whom one ought and not get it from whom one ought not. For it is more characteristic of virtue to act well than to be acted upon well, and to do beautiful things rather than not do shameful ones, and it is not unclear that acting well and doing beautiful things go with giving, while being acted upon well or not doing what is shameful goes with getting. And gratitude goes to one who gives, not to one who does not take, and praise even more so. And not to take is an easier thing than giving, for people let go of what is their own too little, more so than they take what is someone else's. And those who give are called generous, but those who do not take are not praised for 20 generosity, though nonetheless they are praised for justice, while those who take are not praised at all. And generous people are loved practically the most of those who are recognized for virtue, since they confer benefits, and this consists in giving.

Actions in accord with virtue are beautiful and are for the sake of the beautiful; the generous person, then, will give for the sake of the beautiful, and in the right way, for it goes along with right giving that it be to whom and as much as and when one ought, and as many other qualifications as apply. And it involves doing these things with pleasure, or without pain, for what comes from virtue is pleasant, or painless—least of all things is it painful. But one who gives to whom one ought not, or not for the sake of the beautiful but for some other reason, would not be called generous but some other name; nor would one who gives with pain be called generous, since such a person would choose the money rather than the beautiful action, and this is not what characterizes a generous person. Nor will a generous person take money from anywhere one ought not, for getting it in such a way does not belong to someone who does not place a high value on money, and such a person would not even be apt to ask for things, since it is not characteristic of someone who does good for others to have a ready hand for taking benefits from them. Such a person will take money from where one ought, such as out of his own possessions, not as something beautiful, but as a necessary thing in order to have it to give. But he will not be careless of what belongs to him, since he wants to assist some people by means of it. And such a person will not give to any random people, in order to be able to give to whom one ought, when and where that would be a beautiful thing. But it is most definitely characteristic of a generous person to go to excess in the giving,[77] so that less is left for himself, for not looking out for oneself is part of being generous.

But generosity is meant in relation to one's means, for the generosity is not in the amount of what is given, but in the active condition of the giver, and this depends on one's means. So nothing prevents someone who gives less from being the more generous, if one is giving out of a smaller supply. It seems that those who have not acquired but inherited their property are more generous, for they are without experience of need; also, all people have greater love for the results of their own efforts, as parents and poets do. But it is not easy for a generous person to be rich, who is not apt either to get or to preserve money, but is apt to give it away and values it not for itself but for the sake of giving it. Hence people complain about fortune because those most worthy of being so are least often rich. But this does not happen without reason, for it is not possible to have money, just as it is not possible to have other things, without taking trouble to have it. But a generous person will certainly not give to whom one ought not, nor when one ought not, nor any other

---

[77] This makes it clear that hitting the mean is not a question of giving exactly the right amount of money, even with the qualification in the next paragraph. It is rather a question of recognizing the right people to help, and the right occasions to do so. Virtues of character confer limits on actions and feelings, but do not calculate or consist in quantities. It was said at 1107a 6-8 and 22-23 that virtues are extremes in one sense as well as being means between opposite kinds of vice, and leading one to see beautiful possibilities that lie between the misguided acts those vices would lead to.

such thing, for this would no longer be to act in accord with generosity, and one who used up money on these things would not have it for things one ought to spend it on. For just as was said, it is the one who spends in accord with one's means and for what one ought who is generous, while it is the one who is excessive who is wasteful. That is why we do not call tyrants wasteful, since it does not seem to be easy to exceed the amount of their property by giving and spending.

Now since generosity is a mean condition concerned with giving and getting money, the generous person will give it and spend it for what one ought and everything one ought, in small and large matters alike, and do these things with pleasure, and also will take every- thing one ought from where one ought. For since the virtue is a mean condition concerning both, the person who has it will do both in the way one ought; for a decent sort of taking goes along with the same sort of giving, but taking that is not of that sort is contrary to decent giving. So the kinds that go together come into being together in the same person, while the kinds that are contrary to one another clearly cannot. And if it happens to a generous person to spend money in a way counter to what is right and beautiful, he will be pained by it, but moderately and as one ought, since it belongs to virtue also to be pleased and pained at what one ought and as one ought. Also, a generous person is easy to deal with about money, and is capable of being cheated, since such a person does not value money highly and is more bothered about not having spent what one ought than pained about having spent what one ought not, not accepting the opinion of Simonides.[78] But a wasteful person goes astray in these matters, for such a person is neither pleased nor pained at the things one ought to be or in the way one ought to be; this will be clearer to those who follow on.

It was said by us that wastefulness and stinginess are excesses and deficiencies, and in two things, in giving and getting, since we put spending in with giving. Wastefulness goes to excess in giving and not getting, but falls short in getting, while stinginess falls short in giving and goes to excess in getting, though only in small ways. Now the kinds of wastefulness are not very often coupled together, since it is not easy to give to everyone while taking from nowhere, for the resources quickly run out for those who give away their pri- vate property, and it is just such people who seem to be wasteful. However, such a person might seem in no small way to be better off

30

1121a

10

20

---

[78] Simonides was a popular lyric poet who spent much of his life in Athens. His epitaph for the Athenians who died at Marathon was chosen over one written by Aeschylus, and one he wrote for the Spartans at Thermopylae was preserved by Herodotus (VII, 228). He was considered to be the first person who wrote poems for money, and was famous for saying it is better to be rich than wise.

than a stingy person, for he is easily cured by both age and lack of means, and is able to come to the mean. For such a person has the things that belong to a generous person, since he gives and does not take, though in neither respect in the way one ought or well. So if he could be habituated in this, or could change in some other manner, he would be generous, since he would give to whom one ought and not take from where one ought not. And this is why such a person does not seem to be base in character, for to go to excess in giving and not getting is a sign neither of a vicious person nor of bad breeding but of someone foolish. The person who is wasteful in this manner seems to be much better than a stingy person both for the reasons mentioned
30   and because the former benefits many people, while the latter benefits no one, not even himself.

But most wasteful people, as was said, also take from where they ought not, and are in that respect stingy. But they come to be inclined to take on account of wanting to spend, while not being able to do this readily, since they quickly use up what belongs to them. So they are
1121b   driven to provide for themselves from other sources. At the same time, on account of giving no consideration to what is beautiful, they take money carelessly and from everywhere, for they yearn to give, but the how or from where of it makes no difference to them. It is for this very reason that their acts of giving are not generous, for they are not beautiful, nor for the sake of the beautiful, nor given as one ought to give; sometimes those whom they make rich ought to be poor, while they would give nothing to others who are of moderate character, but much to flatterers or people who provide them some other pleasure. Hence most of them are also dissipated, for by spending readily they are lavish also in dissipations, and on account of having no leaning toward living
10   beautifully, they fall away toward pleasures.

So the wasteful person who has not come under guidance passes over into dissipated acts, but if such a person happens to have care taken over him, he might arrive at the mean and at what one ought to do. But stinginess is both incurable (for old age and every sort of incapacity seem to make people stingy), and more innate in human beings than wastefulness, for most people are lovers of money more than they are givers of it. Also it extends far, and is of many forms, for many ways of being stingy seem possible. For since it is present in two modes, deficiency in giving and excess of taking, it does not come about
20   as complete in everyone, but is sometimes divided, and some people go to excess in taking while others fall short in giving. Those who fall into such designations as thrifty, tight-fisted, and miserly all fall short in giving, but do not yearn after the possessions of others nor wish to take them, in some cases on account of a certain decency and caution about shameful acts. (For some people seem, or at least claim, to watch over their money in order that they might not ever be forced to do anything

shameful, and among these are the skinflint[79] and everyone of that sort, who are named from an excess of not giving.) In other cases in turn, people keep away from the possessions of others out of fear that it is not easy to take what belongs to others and not have others take what is one's own; it contents them neither to take nor to give.   30

But yet other people go to excess in getting, by taking everything from everywhere, such as those who work at jobs not fit for free[80] souls, pimps and all people of that sort, and loan sharks at high interest on small amounts. All these people take money where one ought not and   1122a at a rate one ought not to take. Profiting from shameful things seems to be common to them, since they all endure reproach for the sake of gain, and a small gain at that. For stingy is not what we call those who take large amounts where one ought not, and that one ought not to take, such as tyrants who plunder cities and rob temples, but instead we call them corrupt and sacrilegious and unjust. But certainly a gambler or a pilferer, and also a thief, are counted among the stingy, since they profit from shameful things, for both sorts engage in their activities for the sake of gain and endure reproach, the one sort taking the greatest risks for the   10 sake of an income, while the other sort make a profit from their friends, to whom they ought to give. So both sorts, wishing to make gains where they ought not, profit from shameful things, and thus all such ways of getting money are stingy. And stinginess is reasonably called opposite to generosity, both because it is a greater evil than wastefulness, and because people go wrong more with it than from the sort of wastefulness described. So let what concerns generosity and its opposite vices have been discussed to this extent.

Chapter 2. And the next thing would seem to be to go through what concerns magnificence, since this too seems to be a virtue connected with money, but it does not extend, as generosity does, to all   20 actions involving money but only concerns lavish expenditures. In these cases, it surpasses generosity in magnitude, for as the name itself indicates, it is expenditure on something great that is conspicuous.[81] But great magnitude is relative, since the expense is not the same for the patron of a warship as for the patron of a civic delegation, so what is fitting is relative to the person, and to that on which and for which the money is spent. But one who spends money in small or moderate

---

[79] Literally, someone who splits cumin seeds.

[80] Aristotle is playing on the root of the word for generosity, which means "free with one's property" or "free in manner." Some stingy souls pursue occupations more appropriate to slaves. Similarly, the pleasures of a dissipated person are called slavish (1118b 4-6, 21).

[81] The word is literally "conspicuous greatness," but its use in Athens was especially for public benefactions, such as funding dramatic festivals, military equipment, or civic delegations to other cities. Aristotle will emphasize the common connotation of the part of the word that originally meant "conspicuous" as implying appropriateness.

outlays in proportion to their worth, such as the one "often giving to a wandering beggar,"[82] is not called magnificent, but only someone who does so on big things. For a magnificent person is generous, but it does
30 not follow that a generous person is magnificent. The deficiency that pertains to this sort of active condition of the soul is called chintziness, and the excess is vulgarity or gaudiness or anything of that sort, that goes to excess not in the amount spent on what one ought to spend on, but in making a great display of oneself with things one ought not to spend on, or in a way in which one ought not. We will speak about these people later.

The magnificent person seems like someone with knowledge, for such a person is able to contemplate what is fitting and to spend great
1122b amounts in a harmonious way. For just as we said at the start,[83] an active condition is determined by ways of being at work, and by those things with which the activities are involved. Now the expenditures of a magnificent person are great and fitting, and so are his works, for in that way the great amount spent will also be appropriate to the work. And so the work must be worthy of the expense, and the expense must be worthy of the work, or even exceed it. And the magnificent person will spend on such things for the sake of the beautiful, since this is shared in common by the virtues, and also will spend with pleasure and lavishly, since keeping precise accounts is chintzy. And such a person will consider how the work will be most beautiful and most
10 splendid, rather than at how much cost and how to get it for the least. So necessarily the magnificent person is also generous, for the generous person too will spend what one ought and as one ought, since generosity is concerned with these things, but it is in these qualities that the greatness, as in greatness of scale, of the magnificent person shows itself, and makes the work more suitably grand from an equal expense. For the excellence of a work is not the same as that of a possession, since a possession that is worth the highest price, such as gold, is the most valued, but the work that is valued most is one that is great and beautiful (for the contemplation of such a thing is wondrous, and what is magnificent is wondrous), and the excellence of a work, its magnificence, is in its grandeur.

Among things that are spent on, there are some that we call honor-
20 able, such as those that concern the gods—offerings devoted to them, temple buildings, sacrifices—and similarly what concerns any deity, as well as everything related to a common love of honor, for instance where people believe that one ought to equip a dramatic chorus, or fit out a warship, or even give a civic feast, in a splendid way. But in all these things, as was said, one takes into account, in relation to the one

---

[82] *Odyssey*, XVII, 421.

[83] That is, at the start of the discussion of virtue of character, especially 1103b 21-31.

who performs the action, who it is and what family and property belong to him, since it ought to be worthy of these, and suit not only the work but also the person doing it. Hence, a poor person could not be magnificent, since there is no property out of which such a person could spend appropriately, and one who tries to do so is foolish, since it is beyond what he can afford and beyond what he needs to do, while what comes from virtue is done rightly. But magnificence is appropriate to those who 30 have such means, either on their own or from their ancestors or those with whom they are connected, as well as to those who are well born or well thought of or anything of that sort, since all these things include greatness and worth.

So it is especially a person of this sort who is magnificent, and in such expenditures that magnificence consists, as was said, for they are the greatest and most honored, but there are also all those private functions that happen only once, such as a wedding and anything that may be of 1123a that sort, or anything there may be which the whole city, or people of high position, take seriously, or receptions and send-offs for foreign visitors, with gifts bestowed and given in return; for a magnificent person is lavish not on himself but on things shared in common, and his gifts have some likeness to offerings devoted to the gods. And it is characteristic of a magnificent person to furnish a house in a manner suitable to his wealth (for even this is a kind of adornment), and in connection with this to spend more on those works that are long lasting (for these are the most beautiful), and to spend what is appropriate on each thing, since it is not the same things that befit gods and humans, or that are fitting in a temple 10 and in a tomb. And since, among expenditures, each is great in relation to its kind, and the most magnificent expense is great in a kind that is great, while the most magnificent expense in these circumstances is one that is great there, then what is great in a work is different from what is great in expense; for a very beautiful ball or bottle has the magnificence appropriate to a gift for a child, even though the value of it is small and requires no generosity. For this reason it belongs to the magnificent person to make the result magnificent in whatever kind he makes it (for such a thing is not easily surpassed), and in a condition in accord with the worth of the expenditure.

The magnificent person, then, is of this sort, but the person who goes to excess and is vulgar overdoes it by spending more than is needed, as 20 was said. For on small occasions for spending, such a person spends a lot and makes a big display that is out of tune, for example by bringing food fit for a wedding to a pot-luck dinner, or, when outfitting a chorus of comic actors, bringing them onstage in the opening scene in royal purple, [84]

---

[84] The opening scene of a comedy would establish that it is to be a comedy, depicting people worse off than the audience, and not setting a dignified tone suited to tragedy. Apparently the Athenians considered Megarian comedies especially crude and capable of anything.

as people might do at Megara. A vulgar person will do all these kinds of things not for the sake of the beautiful, but to make a show of wealth, and thinking that he will make himself wondrous by these means, and will spend little on things on which one ought to spend a lot, and a lot where one ought to spend little. A chintzy person will come up short in everything, and even when spending the greatest amounts, will spoil the beauty of the result over something small, hesitating over whatever he does and looking for a way to spend the least, complaining about even that, and believing that he is doing more in every case than he needs to. These active conditions of the soul, then, are vices, but they do not bring reproach since they are not harmful to one's neighbor nor especially disgraceful.

Chapter 3. Greatness of soul,[85] even from its name, seems to be concerned with great things, and let us first take up what sort of great things they are; it makes no difference whether one examines the active condition or the person answering to the active condition. Now the person who seems to be great-souled is one who considers himself worthy of great things, and is worthy of them, for one who does so not in accordance with his worth is foolish, and among those who answer to the description of virtue there is no one who is foolish or senseless. So the great-souled person is the one described, for someone who is worthy of little and considers himself worthy of that is sensible, but not great-souled, for greatness of soul is present in something great, just as beauty is present in a body of full size, while small people can be elegant and well-proportioned but not beautiful. But someone who considers himself worthy of great things, but is unworthy, is vain, though not everyone is vain who considers his worth to be greater than it is. But someone is small-souled who considers his worth to be less than it is, whether he is worthy of great or moderate things, or even if, being worthy of little, he considers himself worthy of still less. And

---

[85] *Megalopsuchia* is translated sometimes as "pride," sometimes as "high-mindedness," but either of these choices misses at least half its meaning, while "magnanimity" shifts the problem into Latin and carries the wrong connotation. In the *Posterior Analytics*, 97b 14-26, Aristotle raises the possibility that it might be a word used in two distinct ways, referring to people like Achilles who do not tolerate insults, but also to people like Socrates who do not care about either good fortune or bad fortune. Even if that is true, one use might be primary while the other is derivative from it. Friedrich Nietzsche, in *Beyond Good and Evil*, § 212, takes greatness of soul to be the aristocrat's attitude of contempt for anyone who is not himself, assumed with irony by the low-born Socrates as a piece of one-upsmanship. But the truly great soul might have a standard of worth that has nothing to do with personal superiority. In his treatment of magnificence, Aristotle accepts a popular standard of judgment and purifies it dialectically, shifting its focus from how much is spent to how it is spent, and from the self-display of the spender to the enhancement of common life. Something similar happens with greatness of soul.

most small-souled of all would seem to be the one who is worthy of great things, for what would he do if he were not worthy of that much? So while the great-souled person is an extreme by reason of magnitude, he is a mean by reason of doing things the way one ought, for he assesses himself in accord with his worth, while the others exceed or fall short of theirs.

Now if one who is great-souled considers himself worthy of great things and is worthy of them, and is especially one who considers himself worthy of the greatest things, there would be one thing that these involve most. But worth is spoken of in relation to external goods, and we would set down as greatest of these the one that we assign to the gods, and at which people of high standing aim most of all, and which is the prize given for the most beautiful deeds; and of this kind   20 is honor, for this is the greatest of external goods.[86] So the great-souled person is concerned with honors and acts of dishonor in the way one ought to be. But even without an argument it appears that great-souled people are concerned with honors, for it is honor most of all of which they consider themselves worthy, and honor that is in accord with their worth. But the small-souled person falls short in relation both to himself and to the honor claimed by the great-souled person, while the vain person is excessive in relation to himself, though not in relation to the great-souled man.

And the one who is great-souled, if in fact he is worthy of the greatest honors, must be the best human being; for the one who is better is always worthy of more, and the one who is best is worthy of what is greatest. Therefore it is necessary for one who is great-souled in the true sense to be good, and what is great in each virtue would   30 seem to belong to someone who is great-souled. And it would by no means be fitting for someone great-souled to run away with wildly swinging arms, or to be unjust. Why would someone to whom nothing is great do anything shameful? And for one who examines the virtues each by each, it would obviously be completely ridiculous for someone who is great-souled not to be good. Nor would he be worthy of honor if he were base, since honor is the prize for virtue,   1124a

---

[86] Although this clause is stated without qualification, it is a conclusion found by looking at the way people attempt to bestow or attain something that a being of the highest worth would be worthy of. Soon, at 1124a 19 below, a shred of doubt will be attached to this conclusion that no external good excels honor, and at 1159a 25-26 the reason for this will be found; at 1169b 8-10, that conclusion will be overturned. The dialectical examination of all goods began at 1104b 30-31 with a broadly comprehensive list, that was narrowed down at 1110b 9-11; the consideration of external goods begins with a plausible opinion about the greatest of them, that eventually breaks down under the weight of other evidence. These are two of the ways dialectic proceeds, and in these instances the two strands of inquiry come to be woven together.

and is allotted to those who are good. Greatness of soul, then, seems to be a certain kind of adornment of the virtues, since it makes them greater, and does not come about without them. For this reason it is difficult to be great-souled in truth, for it is not possible without the beauty that belongs to goodness.[87]

Someone who is great-souled, then, is especially concerned with honors and acts of dishonor; such a person will be moderately pleased at honors that are great and come from serious people, taking them as hitting the mark of what is due, or even less than is due, since there could be no honor worthy of complete virtue, though he will accept them nonetheless, since they have nothing greater to offer him. But he will have utter disdain for honor that comes from random people or is for minor matters, since it is not these of which he is worthy, and he will have a similar attitude toward acts of dishonor, since they will not justly apply to him. And while, as was said, someone who is great-souled is especially concerned with honors, he will surely also hold himself moderately toward wealth and power and every sort of good fortune and bad fortune, however it may come about, and will be neither overjoyed when in good fortune nor overly distressed when in bad fortune. For he is not even that way about honor, though he takes it to be the greatest thing, for power and wealth are chosen on account of honor—at any rate those who have them want to be honored for them—and to that person for whom even honor is a small thing, the other things are small as well. That is why great-souled people seem to be arrogant.[88]

But the things that come from good fortune also seem to contribute toward greatness of soul, for those who are well born consider themselves worthy of honor, and so do those who are powerful or rich,

---

[87] As at 1099a 5-7, Aristotle plays on the self-congratulatory name the Athenian aristocracy used for itself, but it has by this point in the inquiry acquired a serious meaning. So too, the "adornment" (*kosmos*), which for the magnificent person was his house (1123a 7), is now seen as the sense of worth that comes from virtue of character rather than from money or empty self-esteem. Greatness of soul is the first of four virtues that Aristotle will find to require the presence of all the virtues of character. (See also 1129b 25-27, 1144b 30-1145a 2, and 1157a 18-19, 29-31.) It is a persistent theme of the Platonic dialogues that any virtue presupposes all virtue.

[88] This paragraph is a masterpiece of Aristotle's dialectic. If greatness of soul centers around worth, its concern with honor cannot be simply for the sake of honor. If honor is desired on account of worth, honor itself is measured and limited. Honor was found to be the greatest of *external* goods (and even then only provisionally on the basis of a certain kind of evidence), and now it is seen to be a small thing when measured against the inner knowledge of worth that is unmoved by and contemptuous of inappropriate honor and undeserved dishonor. Those who look down on others are given the opportunity, by this argument, to look down on their own excesses.

since they are in a superior position, and everything that is superior in respect to something good is held in higher honor. This is why things of this sort make people more great-souled, since they are honored by some people, but in accordance with truth, only someone good is honorable, and someone to whom both belong is considered more worthy of honor. But those who, without virtue, have the sort of good things that come from fortune consider themselves worthy of great things unjustly, and are not rightly called great-souled, since there is no worth or greatness of soul without complete virtue. But those who have goods of that sort also become arrogant and insolent, for with-   **30** out virtue it is not easy to carry off one's good fortune harmoniously, but not being able to carry it off, and believing that they are superior   **1124b** to others, they look down on them, even while they themselves act in whatever way they happen to. For they mimic the great-souled person without being similar to him, and do this in the ways they can; so while they do not do the things that come from virtue, they look down on other people. For the great-souled person looks down on others justly (since he holds his opinion truly), but most people are disdainful at random.

A great-souled person, because he holds few things in high honor, is not someone who takes small risks or is passionately devoted to taking risks, but he is someone who takes great risks, and when he does take a risk he is without regard for his life, on the ground that it is not on just any terms that life is worth living. And he is the sort of person who does favors but is ashamed to have them done for him, since the   **10** former belongs to one who is superior, but the latter to one who has someone superior to him. And he is apt to do a favor of greater worth in return, since in that way the one who did the first favor will be left owing something to him, and will be the one who gained a benefit. And great-souled people seem to remember favors they have done, but not those which were done for them (since the one the favor is done for is lesser than the one who does it, and he wants to have the upper position), and they hear about the former with pleasure, but are displeased by hearing about the latter. And that is why Thetis does not tell Zeus about the favors she did for him, nor did the Spartans tell the Athenians, but spoke of the favors done them.[89]

And it is characteristic of a great-souled person to ask for help

---

[89]   In the *Iliad*, at I, 503-4, Thetis barely alludes to the time she saved Zeus, a story her son had heard from her in detail many times (I, 393-407). Thucydides, in *The Peloponnesian War*, IV, 17-20, reports a speech made in Athens by Spartan representatives after the stunning defeat they had suffered on Pylos; they make no mention of the fact that they had saved Athens from the tyrant Hippias ninety years earlier, but talk about the gratitude Athens will gain by sparing its enemies now. This speech, which Aristotle may have known in other versions, seems close to what he describes here.

from no one, or only reluctantly, but to assist others eagerly, and to be
20   highhanded toward those of high station or good fortune, but moderate
toward those of a middle station, since it is difficult and dignified to be
superior to the former, but easy with the latter, and to stand on one's
dignity with the former is not bad manners, but among lowly people
it is bad form, as it would be to act tough toward the weak. It is also
characteristic of such a person not to go after things held in popular
esteem, nor those in which other people are pre-eminent, and to be a
slow starter and full of delay, except where there is great honor or a
great deed, and to be inclined to do few things, but great and notable
ones. And he is necessarily open in hating and open in loving (for
concealing such things belongs to one who is fearful, as does having
less concern for truth than for people's opinion), and speaks and acts
openly (for he is freespoken on account of being contemptuous of
30   others' opinions, and truthful, except for those occasions when he is
not because he is being ironic[90] toward ordinary people), and is not
1125a capable of leading his life to suit anyone else, other than a friend, since
that is fit for a slave, which is why all flatterers are servile and lowly
people are flatterers.

Nor is a great-souled person much given to wonder, since nothing
is great to him. Nor is he apt to bear grudges, for it is not characteristic
of one who is great-souled to remember things against anyone, not of
any sort and especially not wrongs, but rather to overlook them. Nor
is he a gossip, for he will not talk either about himself or about anyone
else, since he is not concerned to be praised himself or for others to be
blamed, so again he is not apt to give praise, and by the same token he
does not bother to speak ill even of his enemies, except to insult them.
10   He least of all is apt to complain about necessities or small matters, or
to ask for help, since to be that way would imply that he took them
seriously. He is the sort of person who possesses beautiful and useless
things, rather than things that are productive and beneficial, since that
is more suited to one who is self-sufficient. And a great-souled person
seems to have a slow way of moving, a deep voice, and a steady way of
speaking, since a person who takes few things seriously is not anxious,
and one who thinks nothing is great is not intense, but shrillness and
haste are results of these qualities.[91]

---

90 This "gracious" vice belonged distinctively to Socrates. (See 1127b 22-31.) It
comes under the general heading of not acting tough toward the weak, but
it was not only people of humble station whom Socrates treated ironically. In
Plato's *Gorgias*, Socrates is more frank with Polus, who is young and foolish,
and still more so with Callicles, who is very young and insolent, than he is with
Gorgias, one of the most admired and smug men in Greece. As tends to be the
case with irony, one can never be sure where that of Socrates starts or stops.

91 This final touch seems to some readers to be made tongue-in-cheek, and the
picture above of someone who is annoyed to be reminded that he ever needed

Such is the great-souled person, while the one who comes up short is small-souled, and the one who goes to excess is vain. Now even these do not seem to be people with vices (since they do not do harm), but people who are in error. For the small-souled person, while being   20
worthy of good things, deprives himself of the things he deserves, and seems to have something bad about him from his not considering himself worthy of what is good, or to be ignorant of himself, since he would have reached out for the things he was worthy of if they were good. Such people, though, are not thought to be fools, but too hesitant, but such an opinion seems to make them even worse, for the various sorts of people aim at the things that are in accord with their worth, but these stand aside from beautiful actions and pursuits as though they were unworthy, and likewise go without external goods. But vain people are foolish and ignorant of themselves, and are that way openly, for they stake a claim to things that are held in honor when they are not worthy of them, and then they are refuted. And they adorn themselves with   30
clothes and fashion and things of that sort, and want it to be obvious that the trappings of good fortune belong to them, and talk about these things as though they were going to be honored on account of them. But smallness of soul is positioned more opposite to greatness of soul than vanity is, since it both occurs more and is worse.

So greatness of soul is concerned with great honor, as was said.

Chapter 4. But it appears that there is also a virtue concerned with   1125b
honor, as was mentioned in the first remarks,[92] which would seem to stand toward greatness of soul pretty much as generosity stands toward magnificence. For they both stand apart from what is great, but give us the disposition one ought to have toward what is moderate or small, and just as there is a mean condition in the getting and giving of money, and also an excess and a deficiency, so too in reaching out for honor there is what is greater and what is less than it ought to be, as well as that which comes from where it ought and in the way it ought. For we blame the one who has a passion for honor both for going after honor more than one ought and for aiming at getting it from where one ought not, and we   10
blame the one who lacks the passion for honor for not choosing to gain

help may seem a defect of character, but it should be remembered that virtues are mean conditions of feeling as well as of inclinations to action. On the whole, Aristotle seems to prefer a well-grounded sense of worth and dignity, even if it has a comic side, to a sense of modesty and shame, which he thinks adults ought to have outgrown (1128b 15-21). He definitely counts greatness of soul a virtue, though he seems to rank it lowest of those virtues around which various people organize their whole lives. And this last sentence gives the clearest mark of the person of serious moral stature (*ho spoudaios*), taking few things seriously, and shows how the word grows to have the opposite of its root meaning of one who is anxious, urgent, or full of haste.

92   In Bk. II, Chap. 7, the first sketch of the virtues of character, at 1107 24-31.

honor even for beautiful acts. But there are times when we praise the one who has the passion for honor as manly and passionately devoted to the beautiful, and the one who lacks the passion for honor as moderate and sensible, just as we said in the first remarks. For it is clear that, since being "passionately devoted to such-and-such" is spoken of in more than one sense, we do not always apply being passionately devoted to honor to the same thing, but use it either in praising what is more than most people have or in blaming what is more than it ought to be. And since the mean condition is without a name, the extremes seem to dispute as though over deserted territory. But in things in which there is excess and deficiency, there is also a mean, and people do reach out

20   for honor both more and less than one ought, so that it is also possible to do so as one ought; what is praised, then, is this active condition of the soul, which is the nameless mean concerning honor. In relation to the passion for honor it appears as a lack of the passion for honor, but in relation to the lack of the passion for honor it appears as a passion for honor, and in relation to them both it is in a certain way both. This seems to be so in connection with the other virtues also, but here it is the extremes that appear to be the opposites since the mean does not have a name.

Chapter 5. Gentleness is a mean condition concerning anger. While the mean is nameless, and the extremes are pretty much so too, we are applying the word gentleness to the mean, though its meaning inclines toward the deficiency, since that has no name. The excess might be called

30   a certain kind of irritability, since the feeling is anger, though the things that cause it to be present are many and varied. Now someone who is angered at things and at people one ought to be angered at, and also as and when and for as long as one ought to be, is praised, so this would be a gentle person, if in fact gentleness is praised. For a gentle person means someone who is undisturbed and not led by his passions, but who becomes severe in the way, and in those circumstances, and for as

1126a   long a time, as reason prescribes, but such a person seems to err more on the side of deficiency, since one who is gentle is not inclined to take revenge, but is more apt to forgive. But the deficiency, whether it is a certain slowness to anger, or whatsoever it may be, is blamed. For those who do not get angry at things one ought to get angry at seem to be foolish, as do those who do not get angry as one ought, or when or at whom one ought, for they seem not to perceive it and not to be pained, since they do not get angry and are not apt to defend themselves. For holding back when one is being foully insulted, and overlooking it when it happens to those close to one, is slavish.

The excess also occurs in all respects (namely, getting angry at

10   people one ought not to get angry at, and in circumstances in which one ought not, and more than one ought, and more quickly, and for a longer time), though surely not all of them are present in the same person.

For this would not be able to happen, since a bad thing destroys even itself, and if it were complete in all respects it would become unbearable. Irritable people, then, get angry quickly at people one ought not to get angry at, or in circumstances in which one ought not, and more than one ought, but they stop being angry quickly, which is the best quality they have. And this follows with them because they do not hold anger in, but insofar as their anger is open on account of its sharpness, they retaliate, then leave off. Hotheaded people are sharp-tempered to excess, and irritable toward everything and everyone; hence the name. Bitter people resist letting go, and are angry for a long time, for   20
they hold on to their rage; but an end comes when one retaliates, for revenge puts an end to anger, introducing a pleasure that replaces the pain. But when this does not happen, such people carry a burden, for since they are not open about it, no one else helps persuade them out of it, and the anger within oneself needs time to soften. People of this sort are the most troublesome to themselves and to those most dear to them. And we speak of as harsh those who treat people severely on grounds upon which one ought not, or more than one ought, or for a longer time, and do not reconcile without revenge or punishment. We place the excess more opposite to gentleness, since it also occurs more,   30
for it is more human to take revenge, and harsh people are worse for living with.

And what was said in the earlier remarks[93] is clear also from what is being said, for it is not easy to determine how and with whom and in what circumstances and for how much time one ought to be angry, and at what point one does so rightly or goes astray. But the person who deviates a little is not blamed, whether the deviation is toward the more or toward the less, for sometimes we praise those who underdo   1126b
it and call them gentle, while sometimes we call those who are harsh manly, as people capable of ruling. But for deviating how much and in what way one is to be blamed is not easy to give an account of by a formulation, for such things are in the particulars, and the judgment is in the perceiving. But this much is clear at any rate, that the mean active condition is praised, in accord with which we get angry with the people whom one ought to get angry with, on the grounds on which one ought, as one ought, and all such things, while the kinds of excess and deficiency are blamed, to a small extent when they occur slightly, to a greater extent when they occur more, and to a great extent when they occur to a considerable degree. It is clear, then, that one must hold to the mean active condition. So let the active conditions connected with   10
anger have been discussed.

Chapter 6. In social relations, in living with others, and in sharing

---

[93] See 1109b 14-26, where anger is the example used to show that, even if hitting the mean is difficult, turning back from the extremes is always right.

words and deeds, some people seem to be obsequious, who compliment everything in order to please, and object to nothing, but believe that they must not be responsible for any pain to those they happen to be around. Those who, from an attitude opposite to that of these people, object to everything, and do not consider at all the pain they cause, are called hard to get along with and contrary. So it is not unclear that the active conditions spoken of are blamed, nor that the mean in these things is praised, in accord with which one will be accepting of the things one ought to be accepting of, and as one ought to be, and likewise one will not take a hand in the things one ought not to take

20   a hand in. There has not been any name given to it, but it seems most like friendship.[94] For it is the sort of person who is in accord with this mean active condition that we have in mind in speaking of a kind friend, though that also includes feeling affection. But it is different from friendship because it is without feeling and without affection for one's associates, for without liking or disliking, but just by being this sort of person, one is accepting of each thing in the way one ought to be. Such a person will do things the same way toward those he knows and those he doesn't, those he is accustomed to be around and those he isn't, except for doing them in the way that is fitting in each case, since it is not appropriate to be considerate in the same way of both customary associates and strangers, nor to do what causes them pain in the same way.

In general, then, it was said that such a person will associate with people in the way one ought, and, having reference to what is beautiful

30   and what is advantageous, will aim either at not causing them pain or at joining in their pleasure. For such a person seems to be concerned with pleasures and pains that turn up in social relations; in those situations in which it is not a beautiful thing, or is a harmful thing, for him to join in pleasing others, he will not take a hand in it, and will choose to do what gives pain—also, if joining in would bring disgrace to the one doing so, and that not a small one, or bring harm, while his opposition to it would cause little pain, he will not be receptive to it but keep his hands off. But he will associate in different ways with people of

1127a   high position and those he just happens to be around, and with those who are more and less known to him, and similarly in accord with other differences, allotting what is fitting to each sort, choosing for its

---

[94] In the same way that justice is reserved for special discussion in Bk. V because it has two forms (1108b 7-9), friendship will turn out to have three forms and occupy Bks. VIII and IX. Friendship is a full-fledged virtue of character, and in its complete development it becomes the primary such virtue. It is distinct from friendliness as the natural predisposition of a person inclined to feel a liking for others (1157b 28-32). The minor social virtue described in this chapter differs from both; it is the active condition of someone who can judge when, and when not, to go along with the crowd.

own sake to join in giving pleasure, but being cautious about giving pain, and thinking out the likely consequences—with respect to what is beautiful or advantageous, I mean, in case these would be too great. And for the sake of great pleasure in the long run he will give a little pain. The person at the mean, then, is of this sort, and is not named; the sort of person who joins in pleasures from an aim of being pleasant, and for no other reason, is obsequious, while the sort who does so in order to get some benefit for himself in money or what money can buy is a flatterer, and it was said that someone who keeps his hands   10 off all common pleasures is hard to get along with or contrary. And the extremes themselves seem to be the things that stand opposed, since the mean is nameless.

Chapter 7. The mean condition related to bragging is concerned with pretty much the same situations, and it itself is also nameless. But it is not a bad idea to go on to such things too, for we might get a better knowledge of the things connected with character by going through them each by each, and we might be more persuaded that virtues are mean conditions by noticing that it is that way in all cases. Now those who associate with a view toward pleasure and pain in living with others have been discussed, so let us speak about those who are truthful and those who are deceitful in words and deeds alike,   20 and in the way they present themselves. Now the braggart seems to be someone who takes upon himself a reputation for things that do not belong to him, or exaggerated over those that belong to him, while the ironic person, on the contrary, seems to disown things that do belong to him or understate them, but the person at the mean, being someone who calls each thing by its right name, is apt to be truthful in his life as well as in speech, acknowledging the things that belong to him, and nothing greater or less, as his own. And it is possible to do each of these things for the sake of some particular end or for none, but each person says and does things that correspond to the sort of person he is, and lives in that way, when he is not acting for the sake of any particular end. By itself, what is false is base and blameable, and what is true is beautiful and to be praised. So too, the truthful person,   30 who is the mean, is praised, while both kinds of deceptive people are blamed, but more so the braggart. Let us speak about both sorts, but first about the truthful sort.

Now we are not talking about someone who is truthful in contractual agreements, nor about the things that are coextensive with injustice and justice (since these pertain to another virtue), but who is truthful   1127b in speech and in life on occasions when nothing of that sort is at stake, from being that way by an active condition of the soul. And someone of this sort seems to be a decent person; for one who is passionately devoted to the truth, even in situations in which telling the truth makes no difference, will be truthful still more in situations in which it does make a difference, since he will be on guard against falsehood when it is shameful, when it is something he was on guard against even by itself, and such a person is praised. He will lean more toward something that understates the truth, since this appears to be more in harmony with one for whom exaggerations are hard to bear.

10   The one who takes upon himself more credit than belongs to him for the sake of no end, while he seems like someone base (or else he would not take delight in a lie), appears to be empty-headed rather than bad, but if it is for the sake of some end, one who does so for the sake of reputation or honor is not blamed too much as a braggart, but someone who does so for money, or for things that can be turned into money, is more disgraceful. A braggart is not a braggart in his predisposition, but in his choice, for it is from an active condition of the soul and from being just that sort of person that one is a braggart. In the same way, a liar, too, is either someone who delights in the lie itself, or someone who is grasping at reputation or gain. So those who brag for the sake of reputation make a pretense of the sort of things for which there is praise or congratulation, while those who do so for 20 gain pretend to things that give enjoyment to their neighbors and that can escape discovery that they are not so, pretending, for instance, that they are prophetic or wise or skilled in medicine. Most people make a pretense of and brag about things of that sort, since they have in them the attributes mentioned.

    Ironic people, who speak in understatement, appear to be more gracious in their characters, for they do not seem to speak for the sake of gain, but as a way of avoiding pretentiousness. These people especially deny things that are in high repute, as Socrates used to do. But those who deny things that are minor and obvious are called hyperprecious[95] and are easier to look down on; and sometimes it seems to be a means of bragging, like Spartan clothes, for not only the excess but also too great 30 a deficiency are boastful. But those who use irony in a measured way in connection with things that are not too commonplace and obvious show themselves to be gracious by being ironic. And it is the braggart who seems opposite to the truthful person, since he is worse.

    Chapter 8. But since in life there is also relaxation, and in this there is a playful way of passing the time, here too there seems to be a 1128a harmonious way of associating with people—sorts of things that one ought to say, and a way of saying them, and likewise a way of taking what is said. And the sort of people among whom one is speaking or to

---

95   Many of the vivid alternative names for vices come from comic poets. At the risk of displaying the vice itself, I have to confess the inadequacy of my best efforts to translate this one. It has a first half that means prissily fastidious (*baukos*), jammed onto a word for shameless people who stop at nothing (*panourgoi*). The sort of person meant might claim, in a self-satisfied tone, to be too stupid to use a computer.

whom one is listening will also make a difference. And it is clear that in connection with these things too there is an excess and a deficiency with respect to a mean. Now those who go to excess in making people laugh seem to be crude buffoons, greedily eager to do anything for a laugh, and aiming at causing laughter rather than at speaking gracefully without causing pain to the one who is made fun of. But those who do not say anything funny themselves, and are disdainful toward people who do, seem to be boorish and rigid. Those who are playful in a harmonious way are called charming, as being readily flexible, 10 for such acts seem to be motions that come from one's character, and just as bodies are judged by their ways of moving, so too are people's characters.

But since something to laugh at is always at hand, and most people delight in playfulness and mockery more than one ought, buffoonish people are also called charming as if they were delightful, but that charming people are different, and in no small way, is clear from what has been said. And a property that belongs to the mean active condition is adroitness, and it is characteristic of one who is adroit to say and listen to things of a sort that are fitting for someone decent and and of a generous spirit. For there is something that is appropriate for such a person to say by way of playfulness, and also to listen 20 to, and the playfulness that belongs to a generous spirit differs from that of a slavish spirit, as does that of an educated person from that of someone uneducated. One may see this also in old-fashioned and modern comedies, since foul language was the source of laughter in the former, but subtlety instead in the latter, and these differ no small amount with respect to gracefulness. Might one then define the person good at joking as saying what is not inappropriate to a generous spirit, or as not causing pain to one who hears it or even causing merriment [in the one made fun of]? Or is this sort of thing not even definable? For different things are hateful and pleasant to different people. So also are the things someone will listen to, for what one puts up with hearing, it seems one also does. Now one will not do just anything, for 30 a joke is a certain kind of slander, and the lawmakers prohibit some things from being said in slander, so perhaps they also ought to have prohibited some things from being said in jest. But someone with a gracious and generous spirit will hold himself to such limits, being like a law to himself.

Of this sort, then, is the person at the mean, whether he is called adroit or charming. But the buffoon is too weak to resist a joke, sparing neither himself nor anyone else if he is going to cause a laugh, and saying things of a sort that a gracious person would by no means say, 1128b and some that he would not even listen to. But the boorish person is useless in this sort of social life, for while contributing nothing he is disdainful toward everything. But the relaxation and playfulness in life seem to be necessary. So there are three mean conditions in life that have been spoken of, and all are concerned with sharing in certain words and actions. They differ in that one is concerned with truth and the others with pleasure, and of those concerned with pleasure, one is present in playful situations and the other in social occasions throughout the rest of life.

10   **Chapter 9.** It is not appropriate to speak about a sense of shame[96] as if it were a virtue, for it seems more like a feeling than like an active condition. It is defined, at any rate, as a certain kind of fear of a bad reputation, and it ends up being pretty much the same as a fear concerned with terrifying things, for people who are ashamed blush, while those who are afraid of death turn pale. Both, then, appear to be bodily in some way, which seems to belong more to a feeling than to an active condition. The feeling is not fitting at every time of life, but only in the young. For we think it necessary for those at that time of life to have a sense of shame because, since they live by feeling, they err in many ways, but are held back by shame. And we praise those among the
20   young who display shame, but no one would praise an older person for being filled with shame, since we think he ought not to do anything to which shame applies.

For shame does not belong to decent people, if it comes about for base acts (since one ought not to do such things, and if some things are truly shameful, while others are so according to opinion, it makes no difference, since neither sort ought to be done, and so shame ought not to be felt); and it belongs to someone base to be the sort of person to do any of the things that are shameful. And to be such as to be ashamed if one does anything of that sort, and for that reason think that one is a decent person, is absurd, since shame is for willing acts, but a decent person would never willingly do things that are base. A sense of shame
30   could be something decent only hypothetically, since if one were to do those things, one would be ashamed, but this is not the way it works with virtues. And if shamelessness, or not being ashamed to do shame-

---

[96] A sense of shame (*aidôs*) is a respectful attitude that holds one back from something. In the *Odyssey* its meaning ranges from modesty about nakedness or grief (VI, 220; VIII, 86), to reverent fear of the gods (IX, 269), to loving respect for a king. In this work, Aristotle uses it for the sensitivity to praise and blame that sends Hector and Diomedes into battle (1116a 27-29), and for the innate love of the beautiful that is a precondition for virtue (1179b 7-13). It is not simply a feeling, since all shame involves thinking (see *Topics*, 126a 8), but neither is it as deliberately chosen or willingly acquiesced in as the active states of character by which we take responsibility for our responses to our feelings (1105b 25-26, 1114b 22-23). Aristotle does not regard as distinct in kind the intense shame (*aischunê*) that makes someone blush and the milder attitude that shows itself as a difficulty in raising one's eyes to meet those of another (see *Rhetoric*, 1384a 35-b 1), the up-from-under look that was always seen in pictures of Diana Spencer.

ful things, is base, that doesn't make it any more the case that someone who is ashamed of doing such things is decent. Self-restraint[97] is not a virtue either, but something mixed, but this will be shown about it in a later section. But now let us speak about justice.

BOOK V

Chapter 1. About justice and injustice, one must consider exactly   1129a what sort of actions they turn out to be concerned with, and what sort of mean condition justice is, and what something just is a mean between. And let our examination be along the same line of inquiry as the preceeding discussions. Now we see that everyone intends justice to mean the sort of active condition of the soul out of which people are inclined to perform just actions and out of which they act justly and want what is just, and in the same way everyone speaks of injus-   10 tice as the active condition out of which people act unjustly and want what is unjust. Hence, for us too, let these things be set down first as in an outline. For it is not the same way with active conditions as with kinds of knowledge and capacities,[98] since the same capacity or kind of knowledge seems to belong to opposite things, while one active condition does not belong to things that are opposite; for example, one does not do opposite things out of health, but only healthy things, for we speak of walking in a healthy way when one walks as a healthy person would.

Often, then, one opposite active condition is discerned from its opposite, while active conditions are often discerned from those in whom they are present, for if being in good shape is something evident, then also being in bad shape becomes evident, and being in good   20 shape is evident from those who are in good shape, and the things conducive to being in good shape are evident from that. For if being in good shape is having firm flesh, then necessarily being in bad shape is having flabby flesh, and what is conducive to being in good shape is what produces firmness in flesh. And it follows for the most part that if

[97]   Self-restraint (*en-krateia*), which will be discussed in Bk. VII, Chaps. 1-10, is the condition of someone for whom each temptation requires a new effort of resistance. In the virtue of temperance (*sôphrosunê*), a stable equilibrium of character has been formed, in which one is neither enslaved to desire nor constantly restraining it.

[98]   The word here translated as capacity (*dunamis*) is translated in Bk. II, Chap. 5, as predisposition. These are two main types of potencies, not mere potentialities but inner states that press toward outward manifestation. In Bk. IX (Θ), Chap. 2, of the *Metaphysics*, Aristotle explains the distinction as dependent on involving or not involving reason. A doctor has the capacity to cause disease or death as well as restore health and preserve life, because the knowledge of the latter includes a knowledge of their opposites. But a predisposition is an irrational potency, and an active condition is a cultivated and chosen state of the soul, that incline the one who has them in only one direction.

one side is meant in more than one sense, the other side is also meant in more than one sense, for instance, if this is the case with the just, then it is also the case with the unjust. And it does seem that justice and injustice are meant in more than one sense, but since their ambiguity is between meanings that are close together, it escapes notice, and is not, as in the case of things far apart, so obvious; for example (since a difference is great that is in the look of things), what is called a latch means, ambiguously, what is beneath the neck in animals and that by which people latch their doors.[99]

So let the topic be taken up, in how many senses someone is called unjust. Now the lawbreaker seems to be unjust, and so does someone who is greedy and inequitable, and so it is also clear that someone who is law-abiding and someone who is equitable will be just. Therefore, what is just is what is lawful and equitable, and what is unjust is what is unlawful and inequitable. And since the unjust person is greedy, he will be concerned with good things--not all of them, but as many as good and bad fortune have to do with, which are always good simply, but not always good for a particular person. Human beings pray for these and pursue them, but they ought not, but ought instead to pray that the things that are good simply be good also for them, and choose the things that are good for them.[100] And the unjust person does not always take the larger share, but also the smaller in the case of things that are simply bad, but because the lesser evil also seems to be a certain kind of good, and greed is for what is good, for this reason someone who is unjust seems to be greedy for more. But such a person is inequitable, for this is comprehensive and something common.

But since the law-breaker is unjust and the law-abiding person is just, it is clear that everything lawful is in some way just, for the things determined by the lawmaking art are lawful, and we speak of each of these as just. But the laws talk publicly about everything, and aim at either the common advantage of all, or the advantage of the best people or of those who are in charge, in a manner determined either by virtue or by something else of that sort. So in one sense, we speak of the things that produce and preserve happiness or its parts in the political community as just. But the law also orders one to do the deeds

---

[99] The word *kleis* was applied to the collarbone, which is a sort of latch between the neck and chest; this would be an instance of ambiguity by derivation (1096b 27).

[100] At 1094b 18-19, Aristotle pointed out that wealth can harm or even ruin the people who have it. In the *Metaphysics*, at 1029 b 3-12, he compares the job of ethics to dialectical learning in the sense that each aims at what is simply good or true, but begins with people as they are. Dialectical learning begins with one's present opinions, but examines them to penetrate to the truths they partly contain and partly obscure; ethics must also consider the conditions of the soul that make it possible to see what is good clearly and use it appropriately. Socrates's prayer at the end of Plato's *Phaedrus* strikes the note Aristotle recommends.

of a courageous person, such as not to leave one's assigned place or run away or throw down one's arms, and the deeds of a temperate person, such as not to commit adultery or be wildly extravagant, and those of a gentle person, such as not to hit people or slander them, and similarly with the things that are in accord with the other virtues and vices, commanding the one sort and forbidding the other, rightly when the law is laid down rightly, but in a worse way when it is tossed off carelessly.

This sort of justice, then, is complete virtue, though not simply but in relation to someone else. And for this reason, it often seems that justice is the greatest of the virtues, and "neither evening's nor dawn's light is so wondrous," and we say proverbially "in justice all virtue is together   30 in one."[101] And it especially is complete virtue because it is the putting to use of complete virtue, and is complete because the one who has it is also capable of putting it to use in relation to someone else, and not just by oneself, for many people are able to put virtue to use among those at home but unable to do so in situations that involve someone else. And for this reason the words of Bias seem to be well said, that ruling will   1130a reveal a man, since one who rules is involved with someone else and within a community from the start. But for this same reason, justice, alone among the virtues, seems to be someone else's good,[102] because it is in relation to someone else, for one does things that are advantageous to another person, either to one who rules or to one who partakes in the community. So the worst person is one who makes use of vice in relation to himself and toward his friends, while the best person is not the one who makes use of virtue in relation to himself, but the one who does so toward someone else, for this is a difficult task.

This sort of justice, then, is not a part of virtue but the whole of virtue, nor is the sort of injustice opposite to it a part of vice but the   10 whole of vice. In what respect virtue and this sort of justice differ, is clear from the things that have been said, since they are the same thing, but what it is to be each of them is not the same[103]; insofar as it is related to someone else, it is justice, but insofar as it is simply a certain kind of active condition of the soul, it is virtue.

Chapter 2. But we are inquiring about the sort of justice that is present in a part of virtue, for there is one, as we assert. And likewise

---

[101]   The first line quoted is from the *Melanippe*, a lost play of Euripides, and the proverb comes from the poet Theognis.

[102]   This opinion is voiced in Plato's *Republic* by Thrasymachus (343C), on his way to a definition of anything just as the advantage of the stronger (344C) and his characterization of justice as very well-bred simple-mindedness (348C).

[103]   In the same way that the phrases "morning star" and "evening star" have different meanings, but both refer to Venus, justice in this broad sense still does not mean the same thing as virtue, but it turns out to name it from a certain perspective.

we are inquiring about the injustice that is particular. Here is a sign that there is such a thing: with the other vices, the one who engages in them—someone who throws down his shield out of cowardice, or speaks ill of people out of harshness, or does not help people with money out of stinginess—is being unjust but is not taking more than his due of anything, but when someone does take more than his due, it is often not a result of any vice of that sort, and certainly not a result of all of them, but it is a result of some vice (since we blame it), namely of injustice. There is, therefore, another sort of injustice as a part of the complete sort, and something unjust present in a part of what is unjust in the comprehensive sense of violating the law. Also, if one person commits adultery for the sake of making a profit, gaining that in addition, while the other gives money and takes the loss on account of desire, the latter would seem to be dissipated rather than greedy, but the former would seem to be unjust and not dissipated; therefore it is clear that the injustice comes from making the profit. Also, in connection with all the other unjust acts, a reference is always made to some particular vice—for instance, if one commits adultery, to dissipation, if one leaves a fellow soldier in danger, to cowardice, if one hits someone, to anger—but if one makes a profit, it is referred to no vice other than injustice.

So it is evident that there is another sort of injustice besides the complete sort, which is present in a part of it, having the same name because its definition is in the same general class. For both have their power in relation to another person, but the one is concerned with honor or money or safety, or some one thing if we had a name that includes all these, and is for the pleasure that comes from gain, while the other is concerned with everything that a serious person is serious about.[104] That, then, there is more than one kind of justice, and that there is one that is distinct from the whole of virtue, is clear, but one must grasp what it is and of what sort. Now the unjust has been distinguished into the unlawful and the inequitable, and the just into the lawful and the equitable. Injustice in the sense of the unlawful is the sort that was spoken of above, but since the inequitable and the unlawful are not the same but differ as a part from a whole (for everything inequitable is unlawful,[105] but not everything unlawful is inequitable), the unjust and

---

[104] Particular injustice concerns the things that one can only have by depriving others of them. The complete sort of injustice is also detrimental to one's relations with other people, but not by taking a greater share of anything. Gentleness of temper, for example, costs nothing and benefits everyone, and showing respect does not lessen one's own honor; these are things one might be serious about but not greedy for.

[105] "Lawful" is being used in the sense specified at 1129b 19-25, meaning what is in accord with proper legislation. Laws may of course be made thoughtlessly or tyrannically. Inequities would then be legal without being lawful.

injustice are also not the same as but different from those that are meant in the sense of the unlawful, the ones as parts, the others as wholes; for this sort of injustice is a part of the complete sort of injustice, and likewise one sort of justice is a part of the other sort of justice. And so one must speak about the sort of justice that is in the part, and the sort of injustice that is in the part, and in the same way about what is just and unjust.

So let the justice and injustice that are lined up with the whole of virtue, the one being the usage of all virtue, the other of vice, in relation   20
to someone else, be set aside. And it is clear how one ought to define what is just and unjust in this sense, for pretty much the bulk of the things that are lawful are the things that are ordered from complete virtue, since the law orders one to live in accord with each virtue, and forbids one to live in accord with each vice. And the things that tend to produce complete virtue are those of the ordinances of law that are enacted concerning education for the public. As for the education for each person, as a result of which each is a good man simply, one ought to distinguish later whether it belongs to politics or some other discipline, for perhaps it is not the same thing to be a good man and a good citizen in every situation.[106]

One form of the justice that is a part of virtue, and of what is just   30
as a result of it, is that which is involved in distributions of honor or money, or as many other things as are divisible, among those who share in the political community (for in these it is possible both to have an unequal amount or one amount equal to another), while one form is   1131a
the justice that sets things straight[107] in transactions. Of this latter, there are two parts, for among transactions, some are willing and others unwilling, willing transactions being of such kinds as selling, buying, lending at interest, giving security for a loan, investing, entrusting to another's care, and renting to another (which are called willing because the source of these transactions is a willing person),[108] while among the unwilling ones, some are stealthy, such as stealing, adultery, poisoning, leading someone into prostitution, corruptly influencing slaves,

---

[106]   The last point is addressed in the *Politics*, Bk. III, Chap. 4. The connection between private education and politics comes back in the last chapter of the *Nicomachean Ethics*, X, 9.

[107]   This is usually called corrective justice, and it typically comes into play after an injustice has arisen, but it also gets things straight in advance, as in drawing up a contract.

[108]   The use of the singular seems to mean that, from the point of view of either party to the transaction, the other person is the source of it. One can be just or unjust in dealing with others who are willing or unwilling. After the fact, legal action may seek to correct injustice (with civil penalties for the abuse of a willing person, and criminal penalties for the abuse of someone who is unwilling), but the primary action of this sort of justice, in the law and in each person, is to get things straight in the first place.

assassination by treachery, and false witness, and others are violent, such as assault, imprisoning, murder, rape, mutilating, verbal abuse, and slanderous insult.

10   **Chapter 3.** But since the unjust person is inequitable and what is unjust is inequitable, it is clear that there is also some mean in relation to what is inequitable; but this is what is equitable, for in any sort of action in which there is a greater and a lesser amount of something, there is also an equal amount. So if what is unjust is inequitable, what is just is equitable, the very thing which seems so to everyone even without an argument. And since an equal amount is a mean, what is just would be a mean. And in least terms, what is equal is in two things; it is necessary, then, that what is just is both a mean and something equal, and is something relative to and for certain people, and insofar as it is a mean, it is between certain things (and these are the greater and the lesser amounts), while insofar as it is something equal, it is present in two things, but insofar as it is just, it relates to certain people. Therefore what is just, in least terms, has to be in four things, since there are two

20   people in relation to whom it happens to be just, and two things in which it is present. And the same relation between the things as between the people will be the equality,[109] for as the things in which it is present are to one another, so too are the people to one another. For if the people are not equal, they will not have equal things, but from that source come fights and complaints, whenever people who are equal have or are given things that are not equal, or people who are not equal have or are given things that are.

Also, this is clear from what is in accord with merit, for all people agree that what is just in distributions must be in accord with some sort of merit, although not all people mean the same thing by merit, but those who favor democracy mean freedom, those who favor oligarchy mean wealth, others mean being well born, and those who favor aristocracy mean virtue. Justice, therefore, is a certain kind of proportion,

30   for proportion is not merely something peculiar to the numbers of arithmetic, but belongs to number in general,[110] for proportionality is equality of ratios, and in four things in least terms. That the proportionality of distinct terms is in four things is obvious, but even a continuous proportion is in four things, since it uses one term as two and names it

1131b   twice, as in "as A is to B, so is B to C." The B, then, is mentioned twice, so that, if B set down twice, there will be four things in proportion. And what is just is also in four things in least terms, and the ratio is the same, for the things are distinguished in similarity to the people

---

[109] The same word (*isos*) has been carrying the two meanings "equal in amount" and "equitable in character." The underlying relation that makes people and transactions equitable now emerges as an equality not of amounts but of ratios.

[110] The Greek word for number (*arithmos*) meant primarily not the pure numbers of arithmetic but any multitudes of countable things.

for whom they are just. Therefore as the A term is to the B, so is the C to the D, and hence alternately, as A is to C, so is B to D, and so too is the whole to the whole,[111] which is exactly what the distribution links up, and if they are put together in this way they are linked up justly. Therefore, the linking together of the A term with the C, and of the B with the D, is what is just in a distribution, and what is just in this sense is a mean, while what is unjust is what is disproportionate, for what is proportional is a mean and what is just is proportional.

Mathematicians call this sort of proportionality geometrical, for in a geometrical proportion, it follows that the whole [formed by the antecedents] is to the whole [formed by the consequents] as either antecedent is to its consequent. But this is not continuous proportionality, since there cannot be a term that counts as one and is both a thing that is just and a person for whom it is just. So what is just in this sense is what is proportional, and what is unjust is what is disproportionate. Therefore there comes to be a greater amount and a lesser amount, which is exactly what turns out in actions, for an unjust person has more, while the one to whom injustice is done has less of something good. In the case of something bad it is opposite, for the lesser evil, in relation to the greater evil, comes within the meaning of good, since the lesser evil is more choiceworthy than is the greater, and what is chosen is good; the more choiceworthy a thing is, the greater the good. This, then, is one form of the just.

Chapter 4. The remaining one is the justice that gets things straight, which comes about in transactions of both the willing and the unwilling sort. And this sort of justice has a different form from the preceding one. For the justice that distributes common property is always in accord with the kind of proportionality described, for even if the distribution is made from public monies, it will be in the same ratio which the

10

20

30

---

[111]   To start with, A and B were people, while C and D were (say) sums of money. Alternating this proportion is illegitimate mathematically, since there is no ratio between a person and a dollar, but is perfectly intelligible in the situation to which the mathematical language is being applied. It says that person A is to (deserves) C dollars as (on the same grounds that) person B is to (deserves) D dollars. "So too is the whole to the whole" is an elliptical way of saying that composing the alternate ratios [(A+C):C::(B+D):D] and re-alternating [(A+C):(B+D)::C:D] brings back the original ratio of the two people A and B. That is, A with C dollars in his pocket and B with D dollars in his, maintain the same relation as do their relative merits, and neither has been unjustly enriched at the expense of the other. Proofs that these transformations of a proportion preserve proportionality in the results may be found in Euclid's *Elements*, Bk. V, Props. 16 and 18. But note that this whole mathematical treatment of distributive justice depends on a ratio of human beings with respect to what they deserve, a qualitative relation for which the quantitative value of the things distributed to them is at best a metaphor, a visible sign of the community's respect.

amounts paid in as taxes have to one another, and what is unjust in the sense opposite to this sort of justice is what violates the proportion. But what is just in transactions is something equitable, and what is unjust

1132a   is something inequitable, but not according to the former kind of proportionality, but according to an arithmetic proportion.[112] For it makes no difference whether a decent person cheated someone of a low sort, or a low sort of person cheated a decent one, or whether a decent or a low sort of person committed adultery; but the law looks only to the difference arising from the harm, and treats people as equals, if one of them does injustice and the other suffers it, and if one of them caused harm and the other has been harmed.

So the judge tries to equalize what is unjust in this sense, since it is an inequality; for whenever one person has been wounded and another has caused the wound, or one person has committed murder and another has been murdered, the suffering and the doing are divided

10   unequally, but the judge tries, by means of the penalty, to make things equal, taking away the gain. For "gain" is spoken of as a way of speaking simply in such cases, even if it would not be an appropriate word for some of them,[113] such as for someone who causes a wound, or loss for the one who suffers it, but whenever what is suffered is measured, the one thing is called loss and the other gain. So while what is equal is a mean between the greater and the less, gain and loss are greater and less in opposite ways, gain being a greater amount of something good and a lesser amount of something bad, and loss being the opposite; between them the mean is what is equal, which we say is just, so that the justice that sets things straight would be the mean between loss and gain. For this reason too, whenever people have a dispute, they

20   appeal to a judge, and going to a judge is going to justice, for the judge is meant to be a sort of ensouled justice, and people seek out a judge as a mean, and some people call them mediators, on the grounds that, if they hit the mean, they will hit upon what is just. Therefore what is just is a certain kind of mean, if the judge is.

---

[112]   The geometric proportion governs the similarity of figures. A two-inch by three-inch rectangle is similar to one that is four by six inches. The arithmetic proportion is governed by increments of addition and subtraction. Three exceeds two by the same amount that five exceeds four. So while 6:4 preserves the geometrical relation, or ratio, of three to two, it is five that has the same arithmetic relation to four that three has to two.

[113]   As in the case of distributive justice, where a qualitative relation of human worth is made manifest in a quantitative ratio, the justice that sets things straight assimilates all wrong done by one person to another to a quantitative gain and loss. The penalty that fits the crime has to measure the "degree" of guilt by taking into account such things as intent and any special obligation the criminal may have had to the victim. Premeditated matricide, for instance, produces a greater imbalance than accidental manslaughter, and the penalty in each case seeks to measure the "gain."

And the judge evens things up, just as, when a line has been cut into unequal parts, one takes away the part by which the greater segment exceeds the half, and adds this to the smaller segment. And when the whole has been divided in half, people say they have what belongs to them, when they get what is equal. And what is equal is a mean between the greater and the less by arithmetic proportionality. And this is the manner in which the just gets its name, because it adjusts things in halves, as if one were to call it "the adjusted" and the judge the adjuster.[114] For whenever something is subtracted from one of two equal things and something is added to the other, that other will be in excess by these two increments, since, if something were subtracted from the one but something was not added to the other, that other would have been in excess by the one increment only. Therefore it will exceed the mean by one increment, and the mean will exceed that from which it was subtracted by one increment. And therefore we recognize by this pattern what one needs to take away from the one who has more, and what to add to the one who has less, for one must add that by which the former exceeds the mean to the one who has less, and take away from the greatest amount that by which the mean is exceeded. The lines AA', BB', CC' being equal to one another, from AA', let AE be subtracted, and to CC', let C'D be added, so that the whole CC'D exceeds AE by GC' plus C'D, and therefore exceeds BB' by C'D.[115]

But these words "loss" and "gain" are taken from willing exchange, for having more than one had is called gaining, and having less than at first is called losing, as in buying and selling and all the other transactions to which the law gives a free hand. But whenever neither more nor less results, but the very amounts that came from them, people say they have what is theirs and neither lose nor gain. So too, what is just in transactions that are not willing is a mean between a certain kind of gain and loss, a having of something equal both before and after.

30

1132b

10

20

---

[114] Literally: "the just (*dikaion*) gets its name because it is in halves (*dicha*), as if one were to call it *dichaion* and the judge (*dikastês*) *dichastês*." This word for judge applied in Athens to each member of what we would call a jury.

[115]

A	E	A'	
B		B'	
C	G	C'	D

Note that C'D need not equal EA'. AE and CC'D come before the judges, who must adjust the arithmetic mean (CC'D-AE)/2 to determine the just result BB'. For example, a drunk driver, who has taken a small gain in convenience getting home, may have inflicted a much greater loss on his victims. The mathematical metaphor is a pattern that cannot be applied by calculation, but only by judgment. And the judgment of the mean in matters of justice, as with the mean in relation to anger (1126b 4) and in everything that has to do with virtue of character (1109b 23), is in the perceiving of it.

Chapter 5. To some people it seems that reciprocity is what is simply just, as the Pythagoreans used to say; for they defined what is simply just as what is undergone in reciprocity to another. But reciprocity does not fit either distributive justice or the justice that gets things straight—even though people want it to mean this, and want the justice of Rhadamanthus[116]:

> If one suffers what one did, that would be the straight upright way

—for it often sounds the wrong note. For instance, if one who has a position of authority hits someone, it is not right for him to be hit back, and if someone hits the one in authority over him, it is right not only for him to be hit but also for him to be punished. Also, willing and unwilling transactions differ greatly. But while in associations that involve exchange, what is just in this sense holds them together, it is something reciprocal by way of proportionality, and not by way of equality. For a city stays together by paying things back proportionately, since people seek either to pay back evil, and if they cannot, that seems to be slavery, or to pay back good, and if they cannot do that, exchange does not happen, and they stay together by means of exchange. This is also why people put a temple of the Graces by the roadway, in order that there should be reciprocal giving, for this is a special feature of graciousness, that one ought to do a kindness in return to the one who has been gracious, and ought oneself in one's turn to take the initiative in being gracious.

And linking things up along the diagonal[117] makes reciprocal exchange be proportionate. Take a housebuilder A, a leatherworker B, a house C, and a shoe D. What is needed, then, is for the housebuilder to get the leatherworker's product from him, and himself give him in exchange his own product. Now if a proportional equality is worked out first, and then a reciprocal exchange takes place, what was described will be the case; but if it is not worked out, the exchange is not equal, and the parties do not stay together. For nothing prevents the product of one person from being worth more than that of the other, and it is necessary then that these be equalized. And this is the case with the other arts as well, for they would have become extinct if one could not make, as a producer, a certain amount and a certain kind of thing and,

---

[116] A mythical judge from whom, in the afterlife, no crime is hidden and none goes unpunished. The reciprocity associated with him is strict retaliation, but a simple reversal of temporal order gives us the reciprocity sacred to the Graces, or the golden rule, converting paying back into giving what one hopes to get.

[117] An inverse proportion is involved, since each producer must be matched up with an appropriate amount of the other person's product, which must be increased or decreased in the inverse ratio. Worth of A's product : Worth of B's product :: Quantity of B's product : Quantity of A's product. See 1133a 22-23 below.

as a consumer, receive something as much as and of the same quality as this. For a community does not arise between two doctors, but between a doctor and a farmer, and in general between people who are different and not equal; but these need to be equalized.

Hence all things of which there is exchange need to be comparable in some way. For this purpose, the currency was brought in, and it becomes in a certain way a mean, since it measures all things, and so also their excess and deficiency, and thus however many shoes are equal to a house or to some food. It is necessary, then, that, exactly as a housebuilder is to a leatherworker,[118] there are just that many shoes to a house (or to the food), for if this is not so, there will be no exchange nor community, and this will not be possible unless they are equal in some way. Therefore it is necessary for all things to be measured by some one thing, as was said above, but in truth this is need, which holds everything together, for if people were in need of nothing, or did not have similar needs, then there would either be no exchange or not the same kind. But by conventional agreement, the currency has become a sort of interchangeable substitute for need, and for this reason it has the name currency,[119] because it is not natural but by current custom, and it is in our power to change it or make it worthless.

So there will be reciprocity when things are equalized, and thus, exactly as a farmer is to a leatherworker, [there is that much of] the product of the leatherworker to the product of the farmer. But it is necessary to put the products into this form of proportionality not when they have been exchanged (or else one extreme will have both excesses),[120] but when the people still have their own products. That way they will be equals and sharers, because this is the sort of equality that is capable of coming about in their case, namely, farmer A, food C, leatherworker

20

30

1133b

---

[118] The ratio that determines equivalent amounts of commodities is between the arts or skills. (The parenthetical reference to the food anticipates the version of the example below at 1133a 32-33.) If it were simply a matter of noticing that it takes (say) 100 times as long to build a house as it does to make a shoe, the equation would be easy to make, but there is also a difference in degree of skill, as well as in how scarce those who have the skill may be. Reciprocally equal exchange is thus a combination of the distributive principle of geometrical proportionality (the numbers of commodities received are in the ratio of the relative worth of their producers), with the corrective principle of restoring arithmetic equality (the value of each commodity received is in the inverse ratio of number of them).

[119] Currency (*nomisma*) is what is by custom or law (both of which are meant by *nomos*), and gives us the English derivative "numismatics" for coin collecting.

[120] This wording has caused much confusion and various conjectural interpretations, but it seems simply to mean that the inverse ratio is applied to what the two people produce, rather than to what they get. If A's work is twice as valuable as B's, then the inverse factor of ½ is applied to his own product before the exchange, not to the amount of B's product he is to receive.

B, and his product equalized as D, but if it were not possible for things to be reciprocated in this way, there could be no sharing. And that it is need that holds them together as some one thing, is clear, because they do not exchange when they are not both in need of one another, or when one of them is not in need of the other, as when someone needs something one has, such as wine, and gives in exchange his export

10   license for grain, and then this needs to be equalized.

But for the purpose of a future exchange that will take place when there is need, if nothing is needed now, currency is a sort of guarantor for us, since the bearer of this must be able to get what he needs. But then this currency too undergoes the same thing, since it does not always command an equal amount; nevertheless, it tends to stay more constant. Hence, all things ought to be valued in currency, for in this way there will always be exchange, and if this, then also a shared community. So the currency, like a unit of measure, equalizes things by making them commensurable, for there would be no community if there were not exchange, and no exchange if there were not equality, and no equality if there were not commensurability. Now while in truth it is

20   impossible for things that differ so much to become commensurable, it is sufficiently possible for what is needed. So there has to be some one unit of measure, and this by current acceptance, on account of which it is called currency, for this makes all things commensurable since they are all measured by the currency. A house is A, ten minae are B,[121] and a bed is C. If the house is worth five minae, or equivalent to it, A is one-half B, and the bed C is one-tenth part of B; so it is obvious how many beds are equivalent to a house, namely five. And that this is the way exchange was before there was currency is clear, for it makes no difference to speak of five beds for a house or of the amount the five beds are worth.

30   What, then, is unjust, and what is just, have been stated. And now that these things have been distinguished, it is clear that doing what is just is a mean between doing injustice and having injustice done to one, for the former is having a greater amount and the latter is having a lesser amount. And justice is a certain kind of mean condition, but not in the same way that the other virtues are, but because

1134a   it is concerned with a mean quantity,[122] while injustice is concerned

---

Otherwise A would get half the amount of a product half as valuable, and B would get both excesses, or four times what he is entitled to.

[121]   One mina was worth one hundred drachmae. Using the rate of one drachma a day as a good salary for a worker or soldier, which it had been in Athens at the time of the Peloponnesian War, would make the bed in this example cost several weeks' wages, and the house would take around a year and a half to earn.

[122]   The heavily mathematical treatment of justice up to this point omits any reference to the beautiful, which was said to be the end and aim of all virtue

with extreme quantities. And justice is that by which the just person is said to be inclined to do what is just by choice, and inclined to distribute things, both to himself in comparison with someone else, and to another person in comparison with someone else, not in such a way that more of what is choiceworthy goes to himself and less to his neighbor, nor the opposite way with what is harmful, but so that each gets what is proportionately equal, and similarly with another person in comparison with someone else. And injustice is the opposite in relation to what is unjust, and this is excess and deficiency of what is beneficial or harmful, contrary to proportion. Hence injustice is an excess and a deficiency, because it is concerned with an excess and   10 a deficiency, an excess for oneself of what is simply beneficial and a deficiency of what is harmful, or in the case of two other people, the whole distribution is made in a similar manner and contrary to proportion, in whichever direction it happens to be. And with an unjust transaction, having injustice done to one is less than the mean, and doing the injustice is in excess of it. So about justice and injustice, what the nature of each is, let it have been stated in this way, and similarly about what is just and unjust in general.

Chapter 6. But since it is possible for someone to do injustice without yet being unjust, what sort of unjust act is it, by doing which someone *is* unjust in each form of injustice, such as a thief or adulterer or robber? Or are they not distinguished in that manner? For someone might even   20 have intercourse with a married woman, knowing who she is, though not because the act has its source in choice but from passion. So while he does something unjust, he is not unjust; just as someone who is not a thief still stole something, one who is not an adulterer still committed adultery, and it is similar in other cases.

Now the way reciprocity is related to justice has been stated above,[123] and it must not be forgotten that what is being sought is not only what is just simply but what is just in political life. And this is found among those who share a life that aims at being self-sufficient, and among those who are free and are equal either proportionally or numerically; so with those for whom this is not the case, there is no justice toward

---

of character (1115b 12-13, 1122b 6-7). This suggests that justice is in some way an incomplete, or undeveloped, virtue, and this will be confirmed in the discussion of friendship in Bks. VIII and IX. The active condition of the soul that is necessary and sufficient to make shared life possible may not raise the life that is shared to the form that most fulfills human capacities. Justice may still be a necessary step toward that higher condition. And injustice is not merely a matter of the quantity of wrong in an act, but a condition of the soul that determines deliberate choice, as the beginning of the next chapter reminds us.

[123] In particular, at 1132b 33-1133a 2, it was said that it holds the city together.

30   one another in a political sense, but something that is just in a certain way and by means of a likeness.[124] For there is something just for those for whom there is also law pertaining to them, and among whom there is injustice, since the judgment of justice is a discrimination between what is just and unjust. And among those among whom there is injustice, there is also the doing of injustice (though among those who do injustice, there is not injustice in all of them), and this is distributing more to oneself of what is simply good, and less of what is simply bad.

1134b   And this is why we do not allow a human being to rule, but the law, because a human being does this for himself and becomes a tyrant. But the ruler is a guardian of what is just, and if of what is just, then also of what is equal. And since there seems to be nothing to gain for him if he is just (for he does not distribute more of what is simply good to himself unless this is in proportion to what he deserves, and hence he labors for someone else, which is the reason people say that justice is someone else's good, as was said before), some sort of compensation must therefore be given, and this is honor and reverence; but those for whom such things are not sufficient become tyrants.

10   What is just for a master of slaves or for a father is not the same as what is just in these senses, but it is similar to it, for there is no injustice in its simple sense toward things that are one's own, and a piece of property,[125] or a child, until it is of a certain age and independent, is just like a part of oneself, and no one chooses to harm himself; hence there is no injustice toward oneself, nor, therefore, anything just or unjust in the political sense. For these are in accordance with law, and among people for whom it is natural for there to be law, and these are people among whom there is an equality of ruling and being ruled. Hence there is something just in relation to a wife, more so than in relation to a child or to pieces of property, for this is the justice that belongs to household management; but this too is different from the political sort.

Chapter 7. Of the political sort of justice, one kind is natural and another is conventional. What is naturally just has the same power every-

20   where, and is not affected by whether it seems so to people or not, but what is conventionally just is something that at first makes no difference

---

[124] The end of the chapter shows that Aristotle is thinking of the various relations within a family or household, where the slaves are not free, the children are not equal, and the whole group is not self-sufficient but part of a larger community. Justice in the full sense comes into being with the distance and responsibility of fellow citizens.

[125] Aristotle's complex attitude toward slavery is presented in the *Politics*. He considers ownership of a human being to be beneficial, just, and in accord with nature (1255a 1-3) only when the slave is incapable of directing his own life, because he is incapable of forethought (1252a 31-34), of initiating any reasoning (1254b 20-23), and of deliberating (1260a 12). The enslaving of people captured in war rests on custom and force alone, and is disadvantageous to both master and slave (1255b 4-15).

to do this way or some other way, but when people have established it, does make a difference, such as being released for a ransom of one mina, or sacrificing a goat but not two sheep, and also those things that people set down by law for particular situations, such as sacrificing to Brasidas,[126] and things of the sort that are decided by a vote. And it seems to some people that all justice is of this sort, because what is by nature is unchangeable and has the same power everywhere, just as fire burns both here and among the Persians, while they see what is just being changed. But this is not the way it is, though it is so in a certain sense, and while among the gods, no doubt, nothing changes at all, among us there is something that is by nature even though everything is changeable; nevertheless, one kind of thing is by nature and another   30 kind is not by nature.

What sort of thing, among the things that are capable of happening in different ways, is by nature, and what sort is not but is conventional and by agreement, even if both are equally changeable, is clear.[127] And the same distinction will fit other things, for the right hand is stronger by nature, and yet it is possible for everyone to become ambidextrous. The things that are just by convention and expediency are like units   1135a of measure, for the measuring units for wine and grain are not equal everywhere, but where they are sold they are greater, and where they are bought they are less. Similarly, the things that are just not naturally but by human convention are not the same everywhere, since the

---

126 Not a god or legendary hero, but a Spartan general who set the city of Amphipolis, an Athenian colony in Thrace, free from Athenian control, and died defending it when Athens tried to take it back. The people of Amphipolis rewrote history by tearing down all remnants of their actual founder, and declaring that honor for Brasidas. See Thucydides, *The Peloponnesian War*, IV, 102-108 and V, 6-11.

127 There are three things at work here. First, all natural things admit of exceptions and of incidental variations, since natural patterns determine the way things are for the most part (*hôs epi to polu*; see especially *Physics* 198b 35-36). Second, where human beings are involved, choice can combine with nature to produce something nature alone would not provide; the ambidextrous person mentioned below is an example of this kind, and so are clothes and houses. But most important in this context is the sort of thing mentioned above, the particular expression of which at first makes no difference, but once established becomes the embodiment of its natural core. A simple example is the fact that human beings have the power of speech by nature and universally, but can only express it through the arbitrary and conventional medium of a particular language such as Greek or English. The superficial fact is that all language is relative to places and peoples, but the deeper truth is that language is natural to us simply as humans. Similarly, a student who claimed that there is no justice by nature because all values are relative might still complain that his bad grade in an ethics class was unfair. The distinction between natural and conventional justice is clearer in practice than in popular opinion.

kinds of constitution are not the same either, though the only one that is everywhere according to nature is the best kind. Each of the things that are just and lawful holds the position that universals do in relation to particulars, for the actions are many, but each thing that is just is one, since it is universal. And an act of injustice differs from what is

10   unjust, and an act of justice from what is just, since something is unjust by nature or by the ordering of a constitution, and this very thing, once it has been done, is an act of injustice, but until it is done it is not yet an act of injustice but something unjust, and similarly with an act of justice (or rather it is called in general a just deed, while an act of justice refers to what is done to correct an act of injustice). One must consider each of them later, what forms there are of them, and how many, and what exactly they turn out to be concerned with.

Chapter 8. But since the things that are just and unjust are as described, one does injustice or acts justly whenever one does them willingly, but whenever one does so unwillingly, one neither does injustice nor acts justly other than incidentally. For people do things which

20   happen to be just or unjust, but an act of injustice and a just deed are defined in terms of what is willing and unwilling, for it is only when an act is willing that it is blamed, and by the same token it is then an act of injustice, so that there will be something unjust that is not an act of injustice, if willingness is not attached to it. By a willing act I mean, as was said before,[128] what someone does from among things that are up to him, knowingly and not being ignorant of whom he does it to, what he does it with, or for what end he does it, for instance whom he hits, with what, and for the sake of what, doing each of those things neither incidentally nor being forced to. (For example, if someone were to take one's hand and hit someone else, one would not be willing, for the act is not up to oneself.) And it is possible for the person who is hit to be one's father, and for one to recognize that he is a human being and one

30   of those who are present, but be ignorant that he is one's father, and let such distinctions be made similarly with that for the sake of which one acts,[129] and for the circumstances of the whole action.

So that of which one is ignorant, or of which one is not ignorant but which is not up to oneself, or is done as a result of force, is an unwilling act. And there are also many among the things that belong to us

1135b   by nature that we do and undergo knowingly, none of which are either willing or unwilling, such as growing old and dying. Similarly, among what is just and unjust, there is also something done incidentally. For someone might give back something held in trust unwillingly and out of fear, whom one ought not to speak of as doing what is just or acting justly other than incidentally. Similarly, one ought to speak of someone

---

[128]   See 1111a 3-b 3.

[129]   The earlier example was of giving someone something to drink to save his life, which had the effect of killing him (1111a 13-14).

who is forced, and unwillingly does not give back something held in trust, as being unjust and doing unjust things incidentally. And among things done willingly, we do some from having chosen to, but others that we have not chosen, the ones that were chosen being those that were deliberated about in advance, and the unchosen willing acts being those that were not deliberated about in advance.[130]

Now since there are three kinds of harm done in communities,[131] those that involve ignornace are mistakes, whenever one did not act upon the person, or do the deed, or act with the instrument, or act for the sake of the end that one had assumed. For he believed either that he was not throwing anything, or not this thing, or not at this person, or not for the sake of the result, but it turned out not to be for the sake of the result he supposed, for example when he acted not in order to wound but to nudge, or not the person he did, or not with what he used. Whenever, then, the harm results contrary to what might reasonably be supposed, it is an accident, but when it is not contrary to what might reasonably be supposed, but is without malice, it is an act of negligence (for whenever the source of responsibilitiy is in oneself, one commits an act of negligence, but when it is external, one causes an accident.) But whenever one acts knowingly but not deliberatrely, it is a wrong, as are all those acts of injustice that are done out of spiritedness or all the other passions that are necessary or natural attributes of human beings, for in doing harm and being in the wrong in these ways people do injustice, and the deeds are acts of injustice, but they are not on that account unjust or vicious people, for the harm does not come from vice. But when it is from choice, the person is unjust and vicious.

Hence it is beautifully judged[132] that acts that arise out of spiritedness are not from forethought, for it is not the one who acts with spirit who is the source of it, but the one who made him angry. Moreover, what is in dispute does not concern what did or did not happen, but the justice of it, since the anger is occasioned by an apparent injustice. For it is not the case, as among people who have made contractual agreements, that they are disputing about what happened, and that one of them is necessarily a crook (unless they do it out of forgetfulness), but agreeing about the fact, they are disputing about which way is just, and the one who deliberately started it is not ignorant of what he was doing, so the one [who retaliated] believes injustice was done to him

---

130 At 1111b 6-10, animals, children, and all of us when we act on the spur of the moment were said to be acting willingly but not from choice.

131 This is a common legal distinction between mistakes (*hamartêmata*) and wrongs (*adikêmata*), and, within the former, between accidents (*atuchêmata*) and acts of negligence (*hamartêmata* in the narrower sense).

132 This is one of only two references to the beautiful in Bk. V (the other being at 1136b 22). It is applied not to an action embodying justice but to an act of judging. See the note to 1133b 33.

1136a   but the other does not. But if someone does harm by choice, he does injustice, and as a result of these sorts of acts of injustice the one who does them is an unjust person, whenever what is done is contrary to proportion or equity. Likewise, whenever someone acts justly, having chosen to do so, he is a just person, and someone acts justly even if he merely acts willingly. Of unwilling acts, some are the sort that admit of forgiveness, but others are not forgiveable. For those things that people do in error not only while being ignorant but also as a result of ignorance are forgiveable,[133] but those that are done not as a result of ignorance but while one is ignorant and as a result of a passion that is unnatural and inhuman are not forgiveable.

10   **Chapter 9.** One might raise as an impasse, to see if distinctions have been made adequately about doing injustice and having injustice done to one, first of all whether it is possible for things to be as Euripides has said,[134] when he wrote absurdly,

"I killed my mother, a brief tale."
"Willingly while she was willing, or unwillingly while she was not?"

For is it truly possible to have injustice done to one willingly or not, but is it always something unwilling, just as doing injustice is always willing? Or is suffering injustice always one way or the other, or is it sometimes willing and sometimes unwilling? And similarly with having justice done to one, since acting justly is always something willing, so 20   that it is reasonable that the ways of being acted upon would be opposed in a similar way to the corresponding actions, and both suffering injustice and having justice done to one would be willing or both unwilling. But it would seem absurd even in the case of having justice done to one, if it were always willing, for some people have justice done to them when they are not willing. And next, someone might raise this as an impasse, whether everyone on the receiving end of an unjust act has something unjust done to him, or whether it is the same way with being acted upon as with acting; for it is possible to take part in just things on either side incidentally, and it is clear that it is the same also with unjust things, for doing things that are unjust is not the same as doing injustice, nor is being on the receiving end of unjust things the same as having injustice done to one. And it is the same with acting justly and 30   having justice done to one, since it is impossible to have injustice done to one unless someone is doing injustice, or to have justice done to one

---

[133] The act results from ignorance if it produces remorse and regret, signs that one acted unwillingly, but things done while one is drunk or enraged may be nonwilling acts without being unwilling. See 1110b 18-27. The sick or animal-like state produced by unnatural and inhuman passions is discussed in Bk. VII, Chap. 5 and the end of Chap. 6.

[134] This is presumably a fragment of the lost play *Alcmaeon*, ridiculed for its weak motivation at 1110a 28-29.

unless someone is acting justly.

But if doing injustice is simply harming someone willingly, and someone who is willing is someone who knows upon whom and with what and in what way he is acting, and someone without self-restraint himself willingly harms himself, then such a person would suffer injustice willingly and it would be possible for someone himself to do injustice to himself. But this too is one of the impasses, whether it is   **1136b** possible for oneself to do injustice to oneself. Also, through lack of self-restraint a willing person could be harmed by another willing person, so that it would be possible to have injustice done to one willingly. Or is the definition not right, but to "doing harm knowing to whom and with what and how" there ought to be added "against that person's wishes"? Then, although someone is harmed and is on the receiving end of unjust things willingly, still no one willingly has injustice done to him, since no one, not even the person without self-restraint wishes this, but he acts contrary to his wishes. For no one wishes for something he believes not to be of serious worth, and the person without self-restraint does what he believes one ought not to do. One who gives away things that belong to him, as Homer says Glaucus gave Diomedes "gold for   10 bronze, worth a hundred cattle for what was worth nine,"[135] does not have injustice done to him, since giving it is up to him, while having injustice done to him is not up to him, but someone who does injustice needs to be present. As for having injustice done to one, then, it is clear that it is not something willing.

Of the things we brought up, there are still two to mention: whether it is ever someone who gives out more than is deserved who is unjust, or only the one who has more, and whether it is possible oneself to do injustice to oneself. For if the thing mentioned first is possible, and someone who gives out more, rather than the one who has more, is doing injustice, then if anyone knowingly and willingly distributes more to someone else than to himself, he himself is doing injustice to   20 himself. Moderate people seem to do this very thing, since a decent person is inclined to take less than others. Or is this not a simple matter? For if it happened this way, the giver might have gotten more of some other good thing, such as reputation, or simply the beauty of it.[136]

---

[135] One of the most memorable scenes in the *Iliad* is the encounter of Diomedes and Glaucus at VI, 119-236. Boasting turns into a rare moment of friendship in the midst of war, and the great comparison of human life to dead leaves buried under succeeding generations, imitated by every epic poet since, is proved false in the very speaking of it, since it is the memory of their dead grandfathers that surfaces to unite the two men. Homer closes the scene, which has pulled our attention away from the war, with an ironic line (234) that says in effect, "how stupid—he thought friendship was worth more than money."

[136] This is the most revealing remark Aristotle makes in this discussion about the relation of justice to the beautiful, since the beautiful act requires going

Further, the claim is refuted by the definition of being unjust, for the giver suffers nothing that is contrary to his own wishes, so that he does not suffer injustice on that account, but, if anything, suffers only harm. And it is clear that it is not always the one who has more who is doing injustice, but also the one giving out more, since it is not the one to whom an unjust thing belongs who is doing injustice, but the one to whom doing this unjust thing willingly belongs, and this is the one in whom the source of the action is, and this is in the one who gives and not in the one who gets the larger amount. Still, since

30   "doing" is meant in more than one way, and there is even a sense in which an inanimate weapon commits a murder, or a hand, or a house slave who was ordered to, one who is not doing injustice may yet do unjust things.

Again, if someone judges a case in ignorance, he is not doing injustice in relation to what is just as far as the law is concerned, nor is the judgment an unjust one, but there is a sense in which it is unjust, since legal justice is a different thing from justice in the primary sense. But

1137a   if someone judges a case unjustly knowingly, he himself is also taking more than his due, either in doing a favor or taking revenge. So just as if he were someone who had taken a portion of the unjust gain, the one who judges unjustly from these motives has more than his share, for even if he had decided on that basis about a piece of land, he would have gotten not land but money.

People believe that it is up to them to do injustice, and hence they believe that it is easy to be just, but it is not; for to have intercourse with one's neighbor's wife, or to hit one's neighbor, or to put money in one's hand is easy and up to them, but to do these things while being

10   in a certain condition is neither easy nor up to them. And similarly, people think there is nothing wise about recognizing what is just and unjust, because the things about which the laws speak are not difficult to understand (but these are not the things that are just, except incidentally). But to know how just things are done and distributed is a bigger job than to know what is healthy, although even there it is easy to know about honey and wine and hellebore, or about burning and cutting, but how one ought to dispense them for health, and to whom and when, is such a big job that it is the same as being a doctor. But for the same reason cited, people believe that doing injustice belongs to a just person no less than being just does, because the just person is not less but even more capable of performing each of these actions[137];

20   and he is able to get together with a married woman or to hit some-

beyond what justice calls for. See the note to 1133b 33.

[137]   See the note to 1129a 13. Popular opinion confuses the expertise that comes from knowledge with the competence that belongs to a cultivated and chosen active condition of character. Socrates, in the Platonic dialogues, is constantly pressing people to reflect on this assumption, asking why the just person, if

one, and a courageous person is able to throw away his shield and to run away in whichever direction he turns, but to be cowardly or to do injustice is not to do these things, except incidentally, but to do them while being in a certain condition, just as being a doctor and healing is not cutting or not cutting and giving or not giving drugs, but doing so in a certain way.

What is just is present among those who share in things that are simply good, and are capable of having an excess or deficiency in these things. For some, there is no such thing as an excess of them, for instance, perhaps, for the gods, while for others, those who are incurably corrupt, no portion of these things is of benefit, but all of them cause harm, but for the rest they are good up to a certain amount, and this is a human   30
amount.

Chapter 10. Concerning decency[138] and what is decent, how decency is related to justice and the decent to the just, is the next thing to state. For they appear to those who examine them neither to be simply the same nor to be different in kind. And sometimes we praise a decent act or man in such a way that we also transfer the word to other things, when we   1137b
are praising them, in place of "good," making it clear that what is more decent is better. But sometimes, to those who follow up the argument, it seems absurd if what is decent is praised despite being something aside from what is just. For either what is just is not of serious worth, or what is decent is not just, if they are different; or if they are both of serious worth, they are the same thing. The impasse concerning what is decent follows from roughly these reasons, but they are all correct in a certain way, and not at all mutually contradictory. For the decent thing, though it is better than a certain kind of just thing, is just, and is not better than what is just by being of some other kind. Therefore the same thing is just and decent, and while both are things of serious   10
worth, what is decent is superior.

It produces an impasse because, while what is decent is just, it is not so according to the law, but is a setting straight of what is legally just.

---

he is skilled at guarding property, would not also be the best thief (*Republic* 333C-334A), and why the students who learn how to argue about justice from *Gorgias* would not be a menace to society as legal advocates (456C-460A).

[138] Decency (*epieikeia*) is usually translated in this chapter as "equity" in its technical legal sense, but an equitable person (*ho isos*), as spoken of in the beginning of Bk. V, is someone who wants dealings and distributions to be equal, either numerically or proportionally. The condition meant here has to do with making exceptions to laws or rules or to strict equality. A simple example might arise if the social security law is changed to produce a more equitable distribution of burdens and benefits; one generation will have paid too much under the old scheme, and will then receive proportionally too little under the new one, and some special provision would have to be made to do what is decent in the circumstances.

The reason is that every law is universal, and there are some things about which it is not possible to speak rightly when speaking universally. In situations, then, in which it is necessary to speak universally, but not possible to speak rightly, the law takes in what applies to the greater number of cases, not failing to recognize the error, and it is nonetheless right, for the error is not in the law or in the lawmaker, but in the nature of a particular case. For the material of which actions consist is that way straight from the start. So whenever the law speaks universally, but what turns out in this case lies outside the thing said universally, then it is right, insofar as the lawmaker leaves something out and errs by speaking simply, to set straight the thing left out, which even the lawmaker himself would say if he were there, and which, if he had known, he would have put in the law. Hence what is decent is just, and is better than a certain kind of justice, not better than what is simply just, but better than the error that results from speaking simply. This is the nature of what is decent, a setting straight of a law, insofar as it leaves something out as a result of being universal. For this is also the reason why not all things are in accord with law, because it is impossible to set down a law about some things, so that there is need of a decree. For a rule for something indeterminate is also indeterminate, as is the lead straightedge used in housebuilding on Lesbos; for the ruler is altered to fit the shape of the stone and does not stay rigid, and the decree is altered to fit the circumstances.

What, then, is decent, and that it is just and better than a certain kind of justice, is clear. And it is also evident from this what a decent person is, for someone who is inclined to choose and to do things of that sort, and who is not rigidly precise about justice to a fault, but is inclined to take less, even when he has the support of the law, is decent, and this active condition of the soul is decency, being a certain kind of justice and not a different active condition.

Chapter 11. Whether it is possible to be unjust to oneself or not is evident from what has been said. Of the things that are just, some are things prescribed by law that go along with all virtue; for example, the law does not condone killing oneself, and what it does not condone it forbids. Also, whenever someone willingly does harm contrary to law, not paying back harm done to him, he is being unjust, and a willing person is one who knows to whom and with what he is doing something; and someone who cuts his own throat out of passion does this willingly, outside the law itself, which the law does not permit, and therefore he is being unjust. But to whom? Is it not to the city, rather than to himself? For he undergoes this willingly, but no one has injustice done to him willingly. Hence the city applies a penalty, and some sort of dishonor is attached to the one who destroys himself, as someone who does injustice to the city.

And also, by an act by which the one being unjust is merely unjust and not of low character in general, it is not possible to be unjust to oneself. (For this is different from the former case, since there is a way in which the unjust person is bad in that respect, just as a coward is bad in a certain respect, rather than as having vice as a whole, so not even in this respect is one being unjust.) For then at the same time, the same thing would be subtracted from and added to the same thing, but this is impossible, and so it is always necessary for what is just or unjust to   20 involve more than one person. Moreover, injustice is something willing and from choice and prior in time, since someone who, because something was done to him, does the same thing back in return, does not seem to be unjust; but when someone acts on himself, he suffers and does it at the same time. Also, he would be having injustice done to him willingly. And on top of these things, no one is unjust without some particular act of injustice, but no one commits adultery with his own wife, or breaks into his own house, or steals his own property. And in general, doing injustice to oneself is also refuted by the distinction made about having injustice done to one willingly.

And it is clear too that while both suffering and doing injustice are   30 bad (since one is having less, and the other is having more than the mean, which corresponds to health in the medical art and to being in good shape in the art of gymnastic training), nevertheless doing injustice is worse; for doing injustice involves vice and is blamed, and vice either complete and unqualified, or nearly so (since not every unjust thing done willingly involves injustice[139]), but being on the receiving end of injustice entails no vice or injustice. So suffering injustice is less bad in itself, though nothing prevents it from being a greater evil incidentally.   1138b But this is not a matter of concern to the art that studies these things; art declares pleurisy a more serious disorder than a sprained ankle, even though the latter might sometimes become so incidentally, if, when one has a sprain, it turns out that, as a result of falling, one is captured or killed by enemies.

But metaphorically and through an image there is such a thing, not as justice by oneself toward oneself, but among certain things within oneself, and not all justice but the sort practiced by a master of slaves or head of a household. For in arguments of that sort,[140] the part of the soul having reason is set over against the irrational part; so it is to those who   10 are looking at these parts that there seems to be injustice toward oneself,

---

[139]   See 1135b 8-11 and note.
[140]   The principal and most influential argument that treats justice within each human being by way of an image is in *Plato*'s *Republic*. The three-part soul is such a useful and revealing way of thinking about ourselves that it is easy to forget that it is a metaphor, and a double one at that. Things that are genuinely present in the soul are projected into an imaginary city, where they become stratified into distinct groups of citizens; then an inquiry into justice in that imaginary city is conducted for the sake of understanding the right ordering

because among these parts it is possible to suffer something contrary to one's desires. Just as between someone ruling and someone who is ruled, then, there would be a certain justice also among these.

So concerning justice and the other virtues of character, let distinctions be made in this way.

BOOK VI —Types of Human Knowledge

Chapter 1. Now since what we said earlier is that one ought to choose the mean, and not the excess or deficiency, and the mean is as right reason says, let us explicate this. For in all the active conditions of the soul described, as also with all others, there is some target to which the one who has a rational understanding looks off as he tightens or loosens his grip, and there is some boundary marking the mean conditions which we claim are between an excess and a deficiency, a boundary in accord with right reason. But while speaking this way is truthful, there is nothing clear in it, for in all other pursuits about which there is knowledge it is true to say this, that one ought not to bear down or let up too much or too little, but the mean amounts and according to right reason. But having this understanding alone, one would know nothing more, as if someone were to say that one ought to apply to the body whatever the medical art calls for and in the way the one who has it says. Hence it is necessary in connection with the active conditions of the soul as well, not only that this be said truly, but also that it be determined what the right understanding is and what defines this.

Now we claim that the virtues of the soul are distinguished into those that belong to character and those that belong to thinking. We have gone through what concerns the virtues of character, but in connection with the rest, let us discuss them after speaking first about the soul. Now it was said before that there are two parts of the soul,[141] the part that has reason and the irrational part, but now one must make a division in the same way concerning the part that has reason. Let two parts that have reason be assumed, one part by which we contemplate the sorts of beings of which the governing principles are incapable of being other than they are, and one part by which we contemplate things capable of being otherwise; for in relation to things different

---

of the human soul. The political metaphor divides things in the soul that might be as inseparable as the convex and concave sides of a breadthless curve (see 1102a 28-31 above), while the "psychological" metaphor distorts the city by implying that is capable of too much unity (see *Politics*, 1263b 29-37).

141   This was accepted at 1102a 26-28 as a popular way of speaking that does no harm. A more careful and complex consideration of the question may be found throughout *On the Soul*. At 411a 27-b 12 of that work, Aristotle suggests that all activities of the soul belong to it as a whole, at 429b 11-22, that recognizing something by perception and thinking what something is are two different applications of the same power, and at 432a 22-b 8, that desire is present in all thinking.

in kind, that which, among the parts of the soul, is by nature related
to each, is also different in kind, if recognition is present in the parts   10
of the soul by some sort of likeness and kinship. Let one of these be
called the knowing part and the other the calculating part,[142] since
deliberating and calculating are the same and no one deliberates about
things that are incapable of being otherwise, so that what calculates
is one particular part of that in the soul which has reason. Therefore,
one must grasp the best active condition of each of these parts, since
that is the virtue of each, and the virtue of a thing is related to its
particular work.

Chapter 2. Now there are three things in the soul that govern action
and truth: sense-perception, intellect, and desire. Of these, sense-perception is the source of no action; and this is clear since animals have
sense-perception but do not share in action.[143] But what affirming and   20
denying are in thinking, pursuing and avoiding are in desiring, so that,
since virtue of character is an active condition of the soul that determines
choice, while choice is deliberate desire, for these reasons the rational
understanding must be true and the desire right if the choice is of serious worth, and what the one affirms, the other pursues. Now this is
the sort of thinking and truth that pertains to action; in thinking that is
contemplative, and not pertaining to action or to making anything, truth
and falsity mark it as working well or badly, since this is the work of the
whole thinking activity, but of the activity of thinking that pertains to
action, what marks it as working well is truth that stands in agreement   30
with right desire.

The source of action, then, is choice—the origin of motion rather
than the cause for the sake of which it takes place—while the source of
choice is desire combined with a rational understanding which is for
the sake of something. Hence there is no choice without intellect and
thinking, or without an active condition of character, since in action
there is no such thing as doing well or the opposite without thinking
and character. Thinking itself moves nothing, but thinking that is for
the sake of something and pertains to action does cause motion, for   1139b
this is also what originates the capacity to make something, since one
who makes something always makes it for the sake of something and

---

142   This is a temporary name (*to logistikon*) for what Aristotle will call, at 1140b
      26-27, the part that forms opinions. It refers here to calculating in a broader
      sense than the mathematical one, or to reasoning in a narrower sense than
      the general one that would apply to all deductive thinking. The divisions of
      the thinking soul echo those on the "divided line" in *Plato's Republic* (509D-
      511E), but even there the names are somewhat fluid, and here the evidence
      for them is taken from our thinking about life and action.
143   An action (*praxis*) is chosen, and presupposes deliberation and forethought.
      Everything an animal does is guided by sensory imagination (*On the Soul*,
      434a 6-8).

the thing made is not simply an end (but it is relative to something and aims at something), though a thing done is. For good action is an end, and desire aims at this. For this reason choice is either intellect fused with desire or desire fused with thinking, and such a source is a human being.

And nothing that has happened is chosen; for instance no one chooses for Troy to have been sacked, since one deliberates not about what has been but about what is going to be and is possible, and what has happened is not capable of not having happened. So Agathon[144] rightly says

10   Of this power alone is even a god deprived,
        To make undone whatever has been done.

Truth, then, is the work of both of the thinking parts of the soul, so those active conditions by which each of them will most of all disclose truth are the virtues that belong to them jointly.

Chapter 3. So let us speak about them, starting anew from a higher standpoint. Let those powers with which the soul discloses truth by affirming and denying[145] be five in number, and these are art, knowledge, practical judgment, wisdom, and intellect. For in conceiving something or in an opinion it is possible to falsify things.

Now what knowledge is will be evident from the following, if one is to speak precisely and not to go by things that resemble it. We all assume that what we know is not capable of being otherwise. And with
20   things that are capable of being otherwise, whenever they occur outside our view, it escapes our notice whether they *are* or not. Therefore, a thing that is known *is* by necessity, and therefore it is everlasting, since all things that *are* simply by necessity are everlasting, and everlasting things are ungenerated and indestructible. Also, all knowledge seems to be teachable, and what is known is learnable. But all teaching comes from things that are already discerned, as we say also in the writings

---

144 Agathon was a prize-winning tragic poet, but none of his plays and few of his lines have survived. He is best known from *Plato's Symposium*, where he is presented as having a fluent style with pretty words and little thought (See 1140a 19-20). This odd little paragraph stands between and emphasizes two of the most important central claims of Aristotle's ethics: that a human being is an ultimate source of action, so much so that our choices could not be over-ruled even by a god, and that, since the choosing human being is a fusion of thinking and desire, the truth in which choice takes its stand involves what is variable and not yet existent as well as what is eternal and changeless.

145 Truth in affirming and denying belongs to discursive thinking. There is a deeper sense in which truth in contemplation means contact with what is simple and involves no predication, and a merging of the soul into the things it thinks. See the *Metaphysics*, 1051b 17-33, and *On the Soul*, 429b 3-6, 430a 5-6. The discussion here will go up to the threshold of that kind of thinking, which will be found to be at the root of both kinds of intellectual virtue, but not inquire into its nature or the conditions of its possibility.

on logic,[146] since teaching takes place either by means of examples or by deductive reasoning. An example[147] is in fact a source of something universal, while deductive reasoning is from things that are universal. Therefore there are sources from which deductive reasoning proceeds,   30 of which there is no deduction, and therefore what makes them known are examples.

Therefore,[148] knowledge is an active condition of the soul that governs demonstration, with as many other additional distinctions as we made in the logical writings,[149] for whenever someone is convinced of something in a certain way, and the sources of it are evident to one, one knows it. For if the sources of the conclusion are not more evident than it is, one will have knowledge only incidentally. So let what concerns knowledge be marked off in this way.

Chapter 4. Among things that are capable of being otherwise, there   1140a is something that is made and also something that is done, but making and action are different (and we are convinced of this about them even by popular writings), and so the active condition involving reason that governs action is also different from the active condition involving reason that governs making. Hence, too, neither of them is included by the other, since action is not a kind of making and making is not a kind of action. And since housebuilding is a particular art and as such is a particular active condition involving reason that governs making, and nothing is an art that is not an active condition involving reason that governs making, nor is there any such condition that is not an art, an art would be the same thing as an active condition involving a true   10 rational understanding that governs making. All art is concerned with the process of coming into being, and to practice an art is also to consider how something capable of being or not being, and of which the source is in the one who makes it and not in the thing that is made, may come into being; for art is not concerned with things that either are or come into being by necessity, or with things that are by nature, since those

---

146   This is said at the very beginning of the *Posterior Analytics*.

147   *Epagogê* is usually translated "induction," which suggests a generalization from many examples, but Aristotle makes clear in many places (for instance, *Posterior Analytics* 71a 7-9 and *Physics* 247b 5-7) that a single act of being brought face to face with the universal in a particular is sufficient. His meaning requires genuinely getting hold of something, not making a rough formulation that fits a lot of facts.

148   The word "therefore" (*ara*) is used four times in nine lines as the deductive character of knowledge (*epistêmê*) is deduced.

149   These qualifications, given in the *Posterior Analytics* (71b 20-23) explain the "in a certain way" of the next clause. The sources of conviction that produce knowledge must be true, primary, and indivisible, as well as better known than, prior to, and responsible for the conclusion. Deduction from hypothetical or arbitrary assumptions is not demonstration; even if the conclusion happens to be true, that sort of deduction does not give one knowledge, except incidentally.

things have their sources in themselves.

But since making and action are different, necessarily art has to do with making and not with action. And in a certain way chance and art are concerned with the same things,[150] as Agathon also says "art loves
20 chance and chance loves art." Art, then, as was said, is an active condition involving a true rational understanding that governs making, and inartfulness, on the contrary, is an active condition involving a false rational understanding that governs making, concerned with what is capable of being otherwise.[151]

Chapter 5. Concerning practical judgment, the way we might get hold of it is by considering whom we speak of as people with practical judgment. And it seems then to belong to someone with practical judgment to be able to deliberate beautifully about things that are good and advantageous for himself, not in part, such as the sort of things that are conducive to health or to strength, but the sort of things that are conducive to living well as a whole. A sign of this is that we also speak of people as having practical judgment concerning some particular
30 thing when they calculate well with a view to some particular serious end, among those about which there is no art. And so also generally, someone who is apt at deliberating would be possessed of practical judgment. But no one deliberates about things that are incapable of being otherwise, nor about things he himself is not able to do. So if knowledge involves a demonstration of things the sources of which are incapable of being otherwise, while there is no demonstration of these things we are speaking of (since all of them are capable of being
1140b otherwise), and there is no deliberating about things that are by necessity, then practical judgment would not be either knowledge or art, not knowledge because a thing done is capable of being otherwise, and not art because action and making are different in kind. It remains, therefore, that it is a truth-disclosing active condition involving reason that governs action, concerned with what is good and bad for a human being. For the end of making is different from itself, but the end of action could not be, since acting well is itself the end.

---

[150] Chance (*tuchê*) is the interference of two or more lines of causality which stem from natural or human agency. Art (*technê*), since it does not create out of nothing, is the blending of human with natural causality. Agathon likes the way their names sound together.

[151] The dialectical preliminaries of the argument of Bk. VI have now cleared the way for the intellectual virtues to begin to come to sight. The argument to this point may be sketched out thus: (Chap. 1) Virtue of character presupposes some sort of thinking. (Chap. 2) Since character governs choice, and choice is a fusion of thinking with desire, the thinking it rests on must itself combine a knowing of what is invariable with an understanding of what is variable. (Chap. 3) Knowledge of what is invariable is demonstrative, and must be governed by whatever in us knows its sources. (Chap. 4) Art is a skilled understanding of variable things, but only of how to make things, not of how to act.

It is for this reason that we believe that Pericles[152] and people of that sort are possessed of practical judgment, because they are able to see what is good for themselves and for human beings, and we regard those who manage households and handle political affairs as having such a capacity. For the same reason we give temperance[153] its name, as that which preserves practical judgment; and it does preserve this sort of judgment, since it is not every sort of judgment that pleasure and pain destroy and warp, such as that a triangle does or does not have a sum of two right angles, but the judgments that concern action. For the sources of actions are the ends for the sake of which the actions take place, but to someone disabled by pleasure or pain, the source immediately ceases to be apparent, and it does not seem to him that he needs to choose and to do everything for the sake of this end, since vice is destructive of the source.   20

So necessarily, practical judgment is a truth-disclosing active condition involving reason about human goods that governs action. But while there is a virtue that belongs to art, there is none that belongs to practical judgment, and in art, someone who makes an error willingly is preferable, while in connection with practical judgment this is worse, as it is in connection with the virtues. It is clear, then, that practical judgment is a virtue and that art is not. But since there are two parts of the soul that have reason, this would be the virtue of one of them, the part that forms opinions, since both opinion and practical judgment concern what is capable of being otherwise. But practical judgment is an active condition involving not just reason; a sign of this is that forgetfulness occurs in that sort of active condition, but there is no forgetting of practical judgment.[154]   30

Chapter 6. But since knowledge is a kind of judgment that concerns things that are universal and are by necessity, while things that are dem-

---

[152] During the period between the Persian and Peloponnesian Wars, Pericles emerged as the dominant figure in Athenian political life. Thucydides (*The Peloponnesian War*, II, 65) says that the Athenian democracy under Pericles was in fact an aristocracy of one, and describes the chaotic rivalries of lesser men after his death that led to Athens's ruin. But there are also suggestions in Thucydides's presentation of him (especially II, 38, 40, 43) that Pericles encouraged the greed for material things and lust for power that brought about that ruin. In the Platonic dialogues there is a similarly ambivalent presentation of Pericles, as a political man guided by a deeper philosophic education (*Phaedrus* 269E-270A), but also as one of those who led Athenians to think there was such a thing as greatness without virtue (*Gorgias* 519A).

[153] Temperance (*sôphrosunê*) is literally "sound-mindedness," or that which keeps thoughtfulness safe and sound.

[154] Practical judgment is the first of the active conditions of the thinking soul so far considered deemed worthy of being called a virtue. Art is rejected because it covers a range of skill rather than being good in itself, and because a deliberate use of it for a bad result is a possibility. Knowledge is rejected by the last criterion, since intellectual virtue must be integral to good character, which it makes no sense to speak of forgetting.

onstrated, and all knowledge, have sources (since knowledge involves reason), it could not be knowledge or art or practical judgment that gets hold of the source of what is known, since what is known is dem-
1141a   onstrated, while the latter two have to do with things that are capable of being otherwise. And so wisdom is not directed at these sources either, since it belongs to one who is wise to have a demonstration of some things. So if those conditions by which we disclose truth and are never in error, about things that either are not or are capable of being otherwise, are knowledge, practical judgment, wisdom, and intellect, and it cannot be any one of three of these (the three I mean being practical judgment, knowledge, and wisdom), it remains for intellect to be directed at the sources.[155]

Chapter 7. Wisdom in the arts we ascribe to those who are the most
10   precise at the arts, for instance to Phidias as a wise sculptor and to Polycleitus as a wise portrait sculptor, meaning by wisdom here nothing other than excellence at the art, but we believe that there are some people who are wise wholly and not in part—not wise in some other respect, as Homer says in the *Margites*[156]

The gods made him neither a ditchdigger nor a plowman,
Nor wise in any other respect.

So it is clear that wisdom would be the most precise kind of knowledge. Therefore, a wise person needs not only to know the things that follow from the sources but to discern truly what concerns the sources. So wisdom would consist of intellect and knowledge, a knowledge with
20   its head on, as it were, knowing what is most highly honored.

For it is absurd for anyone to believe that politics or practical judgment is the most serious kind of knowledge, if a human being is not the highest thing in the cosmos. So if what is healthful or good is something different for human beings and for fish, while what is white or straight is always the same thing, then also all would call the same thing wise, while what is in accord with practical judgment would differ; for in each kind, one says that what discerns well the things that concern itself is

---

[155]   It was deduced above, at 1139b 29-31, that it is by looking at examples (*epagogê*) that we are brought face to face with the universals from which reasoned demonstrations are made. It follows that intellect (*nous*) is that in us which grasps the universal, when a particular thing is perceived. This is not "abstraction," the mere ignoring of perceptible attributes that produces mathematical objects (see 1142a 18 below), but a contemplative act whereby the same activity that holds a perceptible thing together works directly on our souls. See *On the Soul*, Bk. III, Chap. 4.

[156]   The *Margites* was a comic epic poem, now lost, that was attributed to Homer. Aristotle considered it the first true comic writing, lifting the form above personal mockery to what is universally laughable, so that Homer was the originator of both tragic and comic poetry. (See *Poetics*, 1448b 28-1449a 2.)

possessed of practical judgment, and would turn those things over to that one. This is why people also speak of some animals as being possessed of practical judgment, the ones that manifestly have a capacity for foresight about their own lives. And it is also clear that wisdom and the political art could not be the same, for if people were to say that the art that has   30 to do with the things that are beneficial to themselves is wisdom, there would be many sorts of wisdom; for there is not one art concerned with the good of all living things, but a different one concerned with each kind, unless there is one medical art concerning all the things there are. And if it is the case that a human being is the best in comparison to the other animals, that makes no difference, for there are also other things that are much more divine in their nature than a human being, such as,   1141b most visibly the things out of which the cosmos is composed.

So from what has been said, it is clear that wisdom consists of both knowledge and intellect directed at the things that are most honorable in their nature. This is why people say of Anaxagoras and Thales, and others of their sort, that they are wise but not possessed of practical judgment, when they see them being ignorant of what is advantageous to themselves, and say that they know things that are exceptional and wondrous and difficult and miraculous, but useless, because they do not inquire about human goods. But practical judgment is concerned with human things and things about which it is possible to deliberate, for we say that this work belongs to the person of practical judgment most   10 of all, to deliberate well, but no one deliberates about things incapable of being otherwise, nor about variable things among which there is not some end, and that end a good achieved by action. And one who is a good deliberator simply is someone who, by his reasoning, is apt to hit upon what is best for a human being among actions.

And practical judgment is not only about what is universal, but needs to discern the particulars as well, since it has to do with action, and action is concerned with particulars. This is also why some people who do not have knowledge, and, among others, those who have experience, are more adept at action than others who do have knowledge; for if someone knows that light meats are easily digested and healthful, but is ignorant of which meats are light, he will not produce health, but someone who knows that poultry is light and healthful will produce   20 it more. Practical judgment is concerned with action, so that it needs to have both universals and particulars, or more so the latter. But even here there must be some overarching art.

Chapter 8. In fact, the political art is the same active condition as practical judgment, though what it is to be each of them is not the same.[157] As applied to the city, practical judgment in the overarching sense is the art of lawmaking, while in the sense having to do with particulars it has

---

157   See the notes to 1094a 27 and 1130a 12.

the common name, politics, and this governs action and deliberation, since a decree is an action to be performed as an ultimate particular thing. And this is why people speak of only those of the latter sort as being political, since they alone act, as if they were hands-on craftsmen.

30   Also, practical judgment seems to people to be especially concerned with oneself as one person, and this gets the common name of practical judgment, while other sorts are called household management, lawmaking, or politics, and within the latter, one sort deliberative and the other judicial. Now knowing what pertains to oneself is a species of knowing, but there is much difference within the genus; and someone

1142a   who knows and devotes his time to things that concern himself seems to be possessed of practical judgment, while political people seem to be busybodies. And so Euripides writes[158]

> How can I have good judgment, when I had the chance to be
> Numbered quietly among the many in the ranks,
>   Taking an equal part?
> For people who go beyond, doing something more...

For people seek their own good, and believe they ought to do this, and the idea that these are the ones who have practical judgment is taken from this opinion. And yet presumably it is impossible to seek one's

10   own wellbeing without household management or the political art. Also, how one ought to manage one's own concerns is unclear, and needs to be examined.

A sign of what is being said is why young people become skilled geometricians and mathematicians, and wise in respect to such things, but they do not seem to become possessed of practical judgment, and the reason is that practical judgment has to do with particulars, which become known by experience, but the young are not experienced, since it is length of time that produces experience. And then one might consider this, why it is that a child might become a mathematician, but not wise or knowledgeable about nature. Is it not because things of the one sort come from abstraction,[159] while the sources of things of the other sort

20   come from experience? The young are not convinced of the latter, but talk about them, but what the former things are is not unclear. Also, error in deliberating concerns either the universal or the particular; one may err either in thinking that all heavy water[160] is bad to drink, or that

---

[158]   The lines are from his lost play *Philoctetes*, spoken by Odysseus.

[159]   Aristotle's fullest description of abstraction is in the *Metaphysics*, 1061a 29-b 3. With mathematical things there is less to them than meets the eye; hence they are clear and distinct. Knowledge of nature is understood as requiring the sort of patient observation of living things that we now call ethology, or the patient beholding of the night sky that discloses the motion within it.

[160]   Not deuterium hydroxide, but muddy water. In mathematics, there is no

this water is heavy.

And it is clear that practical judgment is not knowledge, for it is directed at an ultimate particular, as was said, since the action to be performed is a thing of that sort. So it is at the opposite extreme from the intellect, for intellect is directed at ultimate terms of which there is no articulation, while practical judgment is directed at the ultimate particular, of which there is no knowledge but only perception—not the perception of the separate senses, but the sort by which we perceive that the ultimate figure in mathematics is a triangle, since there too there will be a stop. But this is perceiving more than practical judgment is; a   **30** different form of it belongs to the latter.[161]

Chapter 9. Inquiring and deliberating are different, since deliberating is a certain kind of inquiring. Now one ought to get an understanding about skilled deliberation, of what it is, whether it is a kind of knowledge or opinion or skill in guessing, or something of another kind. But it is not knowledge, since people do not inquire after things they   **1142b** know, but skilled deliberation is a kind of deliberation, and someone who deliberates inquires and calculates. And it is not skill in guessing either, since this is without a reasoned account and is something quick, while people deliberate for a long time, and say that one ought to be quick to do what has been deliberated, but to deliberate slowly. So too, intellectual imagination[162] and skilled deliberation are different, since intellectual imagination is a kind of skill in guessing. But neither is skilled deliberation any sort of opinion.

But since the one who deliberates badly errs, while the one who deliberates well does so rightly, it is clear that skilled deliberation is

particular to which to apply the universal (though in the productive arts one might apply them), but since deliberation must lead to choice, it involves the whole human being. See 1139a 29-b 5 above.

[161] At 1112b 16-24, Aristotle compared deliberation to analysis of a mathematical figure, each coming to a stop where a subsequent act begins. The example here seems richer, though. Not only is there some triangle from which a proof or construction might start, but we recognize by sheer seeing that there is no figure contained by fewer sides than a triangle in general. This is intelligent and imaginative seeing, that holds something constant in imagination while varying other things, and understands an example as standing for the whole of an infinite class. Deliberating is like that, though not so fully realized in imagination, which is perhaps the meaning of the last sentence. That deliberation rests on imagination is explicitly stated in *On the Soul*, 431a 14-18, b 3-10. That the things the virtues lead one to choose must be recognized by perceiving (and not deduced from rules) has been stated above, at 1109b 23 and 1126b 4.

[162] Intellectual imagination (*agchinoia*) is explained in the *Posterior Analytics*, I, 34, as a quickness at making connections through intermediate links. It seems to be an intellectual counterpart to the poet's gift for finding metaphors by an immediate recognition of similarities (*Poetics* 1459a 6-9).

10 some sort of rightness, though belonging to neither knowledge nor opinion. For there is no rightness of knowledge (since there is no error in it either), while rightness of opinion is truth; at the same time, everything about which there is an opinion has already been determined. But surely skilled deliberation is not without a reasoned account. Therefore what remains is that it belongs to thinking things through, for this is not yet an assertion, since opinion is not a process of inquiring but already a certain kind of assertion, while the one who deliberates, whether he deliberates well or badly, inquires after and calculates about something. But skilled deliberation is a certain kind of rightness of deliberation, so the first things to be sought are what deliberation is and what it is about.[163]

But since rightness has more than one meaning, it is clear that skilled deliberation is not rightness in every sense. For someone who lacks self-restraint or someone of bad character will, as a result of reasoning, hit upon what he proposes that he ought to do, so that he 20 will have deliberated rightly, despite the fact that he gets something extremely bad. But deliberating well seems to be something good, for skilled deliberation is the sort of rightness of deliberation that governs attaining something good. But it is possible to hit upon even this by false reasoning, and to hit upon what one ought to do, but not by the means one ought, because the middle term is wrong.[164] So not even this process by which one hits upon the thing one ought to do, though not by the means one ought to have used, is skilled deliberation yet. Also, it is possible by deliberating for a long time to hit upon what someone else arrives at quickly. Accordingly, the former is still not skilled deliberation, which is a rightness that results from what is beneficial in the end for which, the means by which, and the time in which it ought to occur.

Also, it is possible for something to be deliberated well either 30 simply or in relation to some end. But skilled deliberation in the simple sense is what gets things right in relation to what is the end simply, while a certain variety of it does so in relation to some particular end. So if deliberating well belongs to people with practical judgment, skilled deliberation would be rightness in accord with what is advantageous[165] in relation to the end, and practical judgment is a

---

[163] This was worked out in Bk. III, Chap. 3 above. The conclusion there is that it is step-by-step inquiry about means that lie in one's power to achieve some end, and Chap. 4 of Bk. III adds that the end wished for is discerned clearly as a result of virtue of character. Both of these earlier conclusions go into the following argument.

[164] A simple example of this, from 1116a 20-23 above, is Hector's reasoning that he ought to defend his city because people would subject him to public shame if he did not.

[165] The advantageous (*to sumpheron*) was included at 1104b 30-31 as one of

true conception of this.

Chapter 10. There is also astuteness or quick comprehension, in accordance with which we call people astute or quick-witted, which is not in general the same thing as knowledge, or as opinion (for then everyone would be astute), nor is it any of the partial kinds of knowledge, such as medicine, concerning what is healthy, or geometry, concerning magnitudes. For astuteness is not concerned with the things that always are and are unchanging, nor with any and every thing that comes into being, but concerns the things about which one might be at an impasse and might deliberate. Hence it is concerned with the same things as practical judgment, but astuteness is not the same thing as practical judgment. For practical judgment is something that imposes obligations, since the end that belongs to it is what one ought or ought not to do, while astuteness is only something that makes distinctions. For astuteness is the same thing as quick comprehension, and astute people are the same as those who are quick-witted.

And astuteness is neither the having nor the acquiring of practical judgment; but just as the act of learning is called understanding when one is using [rather than acquiring] knowledge, in this way, astuteness consists in using opinion for distinguishing those things that practical judgment concerns, when someone else speaks about them, and distinguishing them beautifully, since the "quickly" [of quick comprehension] is the same as "beautifully." And the word for comprehension, as in naming people of quick comprehension, comes from the comprehending involved in learning, for we often speak of learning when we mean comprehending.[166]

Chapter 11. What is called thoughtfulness, in accordance with which we speak of people as compassionate[167] and as being thoughtful, is a right discrimination of what is decent. A sign of this is that we say that a decent person is especially apt to be compassionate, and

1143a

10

20

---

the three forms of the good, along with the beautiful and the pleasant. The beautiful was singled out as the end governing virtue of character (1115b 12-13), and what is advantageous as a means to that end is now assigned to the intellectual virtue of practical judgment, as what governs its rightness.

[166] The precise linguistic distinctions of this chapter are hard to preserve in English. The word for astuteness (*sunesis*) is literally a "putting together," as we might speak of "putting two and two together." It is interpreted by Aristotle as a sort of second-hand practical judgment, that quickly sees the point when someone else displays practical judgment.

[167] Compassion in this chapter is *sun-gnômê*, which was translated as "forgiveness" in Bk. III, Chap. 1 (see 1110a 23-26), where the topic was responsibility. Here it is part of a cluster with *eugnômôn* (a considerate person) and *gnômê* (thoughtfulness). The root meaning of judgment or intention is tilted in the compounds, in their ordinary use, toward meaning a sympathetic or benevolent kind of thinking.

that having compassion about some matters is a decent thing. And compassion is a kind of thoughtfulness that governs a right discrimination of what is decent, "right" meaning that it is of what is truly decent. And it is reasonable that all these active conditions of the soul converge to the same meaning, for in applying thoughtfulness and astuteness and practical judgment and intellect to the same people, we are saying that they already have thoughtfulness and intellect and are possessed of practical judgment and astute. For all these capacities

30   are directed at things that are ultimate and particular, and someone is astute and considerate or compassionate in being able to discern those things a person of practical judgment is concerned with, since what is decent belongs in common to all good people in the way they act toward another person, while all actions are among things that are particular and ultimate; for the person of practical judgment needs to discern these, and astuteness and thoughtfulness have to do with actions, which are ultimate.

And intellect is directed at what is ultimate on both sides,[168] since

1143b   it is intellect and not reason that is directed at both the first terms and the ultimate particulars, on the one side at the changeless first terms in demonstrations, and on the other side, in thinking about action, at the other sort of premise, the variable ultimate particular; for these particulars are the sources from which one discerns that for the sake of which an action is, since the universals are derived from the particulars. Hence intellect is both a beginning and an end, since the demonstrations that are derived from these particulars are also about these.[169] And of these, one must have a perception, and this perception is intellect. This is why these capacities seem to be natural, and while no one is wise by nature, it seems that one has thoughtfulness and astuteness and intellect by nature. And a sign of this is that we believe that they come along with certain times of life, and this particular time of life includes

10   intellect and thoughtfulness, as though nature was the cause. So one

---

[168]   It was said above, at 1142a 23-27, that intellect and practical judgment stand at opposite extremes, directed at the unarticulated and indivisible terms of thought and the ultimate particulars of perception. The two extremes are now said to be united in the one faculty of intellect, that contemplates the universals contained in the ultimate particulars, which can be the only terms for a knowledge of truth. The same activity that holds a particular thing together is at work on the soul even in perception. Thus the claim that a single power stands at the root of theoretical and practical knowing rests on ultimate conclusions of the highest kind of philosophy, which are arrived at in Bk. III of *On the Soul* and Bk. XII of the *Metaphysics*. Here that claim asserts the unity of the human being.

[169]   This sentence is misplaced in the manuscripts, four lines below. An example of the sort of demonstration referred to is the one about "heavy" (muddy) water at 1142a 22-23. There is a major premise that makes a claim about a universal, and a minor premise that brings some perceived thing under that universal.

ought to pay attention to the undemonstrated statements and opinions of people who are experienced or old, or of people with practical judgment, no less than to the things they demonstrate, for by having an eye sharpened by experience, they see rightly.

What, then, practical judgment and wisdom are, and exactly what each is concerned with, and that each is the virtue of a different part of the soul, have been said.

Chapter 12. But one might raise an impasse about how these virtues are useful, for wisdom contemplates nothing by which a human being will be happy (since it is not directed at any form of coming into 20 being); and while practical judgment is that way, for the sake of what does one need it? Even if practical judgment is concerned with things that are just and beautiful and good for a human being, these are the things that it belongs to a good man to do, and we are no more able to perform these actions by knowing about them, if indeed the virtues are active conditions of the soul; it is just as it is with things that are said to belong to health and to being in good shape, not in the sense of producing those states, but the things that result from one's active condition, for we are no more able to do those things by having the arts of medicine and gymnastic training. And if what is to be said is that one has practical judgment not for the sake of these acts that result from one's active condition, but for the sake of the coming into being of that active condition, it would be of no use to people who are of serious moral stature; but it also would be of no use to people who are 30 not that way, since it makes no difference whether they have practical judgment themselves or heed the advice of others who have it. It would be sufficient for us to do as we also do concerning health, for we want to be healthy, but we still do not learn the medical art. What's more, it would seem to be absurd if something that is inferior to wisdom were to be in control over it, since whatever produces each thing governs it and gives orders about it.

So one must speak about these things, since at this point the only thing that has been done about them is to make an impasse out of them. First, then, let us assert that it is necessary for them to be choiceworthy 1144a in themselves, since each of them is the virtue of its respective part of the soul, even if neither of them produces anything at all. And in the next place, they do produce something, not in the way that the medical art produces health, but in the way that health produces health[170]; that is the way wisdom produces happiness, since by being part of complete virtue, it makes someone happy by being possessed and being at work. And the work of a human being is accomplished as a result

---

[170] This striking formulation is explained by 1143b 25-26 above. The primary cause of healthy life is the healthy active condition constantly at work in the body. The medical art can at best remove obstacles to it, or get it back on track.

of practical judgment and of virtue of character, since virtue makes
the end on which one sets one's sights right and practical judgment
makes the things related to it right. (Of the fourth part of the soul, the

10   nutritive part,[171] there is no virtue of such a kind, since acting or not
acting is not up to it.)

As for one's not being any more able to do what is beautiful and
just by means of practical judgment, one must begin from a standpoint
a little higher, taking the following as a start. Just as we speak of some
of those who do just things as still not being just people, such as those
who do the things that are prescribed by the laws either unwillingly, or
through ignorance, or for some other reason and not for their own sake
(even though they do what one ought and everything a person of serious moral stature would be moved to do), in this sense, as it seems, it is
possible to perform each action in such a way as to be good--and the sort

20   of way I mean is by choice and for the sake of the actions themselves.
Now virtue makes the choice right, but the being done of everything
that is naturally for the sake of that choice results not from virtue [of
character] but from some other capacity.

But it is necessary to say something for those who want to get a
clearer understanding of these things. Now there is a capacity which
people call cleverness, and this is such as to enable one to do the things
that are conducive to the object one has set down, and to achieve it. So
if one's object is something beautiful, this capacity is to be praised, but
if it is base, it is shamelessness. Hence we even call people with practical judgment clever and shameless. But practical judgment is not this
capacity, though it is not present without this capacity. But that "eye"

30   of the soul does not develop its active condition without virtue, as was
said[172] and as is clear. For demonstrative reasoning about things to be
done has as a starting point, "since such-and-such is the end and the
best thing," whatsoever it may be (for let it be some chance thing for
the sake of argument), and this does not show itself except to a good
person; for vice warps someone and makes one be wrong about the

---

[171]   At 1102b 30, this was called the vegetative part, having no share in reason,
while the desiring or appetitive part, though irrational, can listen to and
obey reason. That willing acceptance of rational assistance by the irrational
soul is virtue of character, while the power in the rational soul to render
such assistance is practical judgment. What contribution wisdom, directed
at unchanging truth, makes to human life is only suggested by tantalizing
analogies above (1144a 3-5) and below (1145a 6-11) here in Bk. VI. That question is returned to in Bk. X, after a deeper investigation of pleasure helps to
clarify it.

[172]   The eye for particulars that belongs to practical judgment and requires experience was mentioned at 1143b 13-14. That one's sight of the beautiful and
pleasant is made clear by virtue, and clouded by its absence, was said first
at 1113a 29-b 1.

sources that govern action. So it is clear that it is impossible to be possessed of practical judgment without being good.[173]

Chapter 13. And one must also examine again what has to do with virtue, since virtue too is in much the same situation that practical judgment is in as compared to cleverness—not the same as it, but similar to it—and that is the way natural virtue is related to virtue in the governing sense. For it seems to everyone that each of the types of character is present in some way by nature, since we are just or inclined to be temperate or brave, and have the other kinds of character straight from birth; however, we still look for something different that is good in the governing sense, and for such conditions to be present in another way. For the natural sorts of active conditions belong even to children and animals, but without intelligence these conditions are obviously capable of doing harm. This much anyway is likely to be observed, that just as it 10 goes along with a strong body without sight to fall forcibly because of not having sight, so too is it here; but if one gains intelligence, it carries over into action, and the active condition that resembles a virtue will then be a virtue in the governing sense.

So just as there are two forms present in the part of the soul that forms opinions, cleverness and practical judgment, so too are there two forms in the part that has to do with character, one of them natural virtue and the other virtue in the governing sense, and of these, the governing sort does not come about without practical judgment. It is for this reason that some people say that all virtues are forms of wise judgment, and the way Socrates used to look for virtue was in one sense right, though in another sense he was in error, for he erred in thinking that all virtues are forms of wise judgment, but he asserted beautifully 20 that there is no virtue without wise judgment.[174] A sign of this is that even now all people, when they define virtue, after stating the sort of active condition it is and what things it is related to, add "in accordance with right reason," and what is right is what is in accord with practical judgment. So it seems that everyone divines that virtue is this sort of active condition, one that is in accord with practical judgment. But this needs to be changed a little, for virtue is not just an active condition in accord with right reason, but one that *involves* right reason, and practical judgment is right reason concerning such matters. So Socrates

---

[173] Since being good requires action, and right action depends on practical judgment, good character and good judgment are mutually dependent (a conclusion drawn below at 1144b 30-32) and must develop together. This reflects the fact that neither desire nor thinking has the upper hand in determining choice (see 1139b 4-5).

[174] A characteristic Socratic argument may be found in Plato's *Meno*, 87C-89A, where the sameness of virtue and *phronêsis* is the explicit conclusion but goes beyond what is proven. In claiming starkly that "virtue is knowledge," Socrates's intention was not to state a doctrine but to shock people into thinking.

30   believed that the virtues are reasoned accounts (for he believed them
all to be kinds of knowledge), but we believe they involve reason. It is
clear from what has been said, then, that it is not possible to be good in
the governing sense without practical judgment, nor to have practical
judgment without virtue of character.

This might also refute the argument by which someone could make
the case that the virtues are separated from one another. For the same
person is not the most well favored by nature for all things, so that he
will have acquired one virtue already when he has not yet acquired
1145a another. For this is possible with natural virtues, but with those by
which one is called good simply, it is not possible, since all virtues will
be present together when the one virtue, practical judgment, is present. And it is clear that, even if it did not govern action, there would
be need of practical judgment because it is the virtue of a part of the
soul, but also that choice will not be right without practical judgment or
without virtue, since the latter makes one bring the end into action, and
the former makes one enact the things related to the end. But even so,
it is not the case that practical judgment is in authority over wisdom or
over the better part of the soul, just as the medical art is not in authority
over health; for medicine does not make use of health, but sees how it
may come about, and then it gives orders for the sake of health, not to
10   health. It would be similar if someone were to say that politics rules the
gods, because it gives orders about everything in the city.

BOOK VII

Chapter 1. After these things, one ought to state, making another
start, that there are three kinds of things to be avoided that have to
do with one's character: vice, lack of self-restraint, and an animal-like
state. The opposites of two of them are obvious, since we call the one
virtue and the other self-restraint, but in relation to the animal-like
20   state, it would be most fitting to speak of a virtue that transcends us,
something heroic and godlike, as Homer made Priam say about Hector
that he was exceedingly good, "and even seemed to be not the child of
a mortal man but of a god."[175] So if, as is said, people are turned from
humans into gods by a surpassing degree of virtue, it is clear that it
would be some such active condition that would be placed opposite to
one that is animal-like; for just as there is no vice or virtue belonging
to an animal, so too neither state belongs to a god, but the one side is
something more honorable than virtue, and the other is something of
a different kind from vice.[176] But since it is also a rare thing for there to

---

[175] See *Iliad* XXIV, 258-9.
[176] In Bk. I, Chap. 12 above, Aristotle argued that it would be ridiculous to praise
the gods, as though judging that they meet some standard of ours. Likewise,
it seems, it would be inappropriate to blame animals for falling short of such
a standard. This would imply that an animal-like human being had somehow
sunk beneath blame.

be a godlike man (as the Spartans are accustomed to speak of someone, when they admire him greatly, calling him a "gawdlike" man), so too an animal-like person is rare among human beings, and is found most   30 of all among the barbarians, though some instances occur on account of diseases or defects. But we also disparage people who surpass the rest of human beings in vice by calling them animal-like. But about this sort of disposition, one must make some mention later, and about vice there has been a discussion above.[177] But it is necessary to speak about lack of self-restraint and softness and luxuriousness, as well as about self-restraint and endurance, for one must not assume that either of   1145b them has to do with the same active conditions as virtue and vice, nor that they are different in kind.

One ought, as with other things, when one has set forth the appearances, and has gone through the impasses a first time, to bring to light in that way especially all the received opinions about these experiences, or if not that, then most and the most authoritative of these opinions. For if the difficulties are resolved, and something is left of the received opinions, it would have been made evident in an adequate way. Now it seems that self-restraint and endurance belong among things that are of serious stature and are praised, while lack of self-restraint and softness belong among things that are of a low kind and are blamed,   10 and that the self-restrained person is the same as one who stands by his reasoning, while the unrestrained person is one who stands aside from his reasoning. And the unrestrained person does things on account of passion while knowing that they are base, while the self-restrained person, when he knows that his desires are base, does not follow them, on account of reason. And while some people say that a temperate person is self-restrained and enduring, and that the latter sort of person is wholly temperate, others deny it; and some say that a dissipated person is unrestrained and an unrestrained person is dissipated, lumping them together, while others say that they are different. Sometimes

---

[177] The discussion of vice runs through the whole of Bks. II-V, but its crucial characteristics are identical to those of virtue of character, as given at 1105a 30-33: vice is knowingly and deliberately chosen for its own sake, and out of a stable active condition of the soul. In this sentence, the animal-like state is called a disposition (*diathesis*), a word used rarely in the *Nicomachean Ethics* to refer to all states of the soul in general (especially at 1108b 11), but vice, like virtue, is emphatically an active condition (*hexis*), one of the most frequently used, and most important, words in the whole work. Failure to translate it distinctively blurs the distinctions about to be made between virtue and self-restraint, and between vice and lack of self-restraint. Virtue and vice belong to the constancy of character, while the states about to be explored are rudderless. Two sentences below, restraint and unrestraint are called *pathê*, in its general sense of experiences, perhaps to anticipate that unrestraint is a *pathos* in its particular sense of a merely passive condition.

people deny that a person with practical judgment is capable of being unrestrained, but sometimes they say that some of those who have practical judgment and are clever are unrestrained. Moreover, people are spoken of as lacking self-restraint for spiritedness or for honor or for gain. These, then, are the things that are said.

Chapter 2. But one might raise an impasse about how anyone who conceives things correctly behaves without restraint. So some people deny that this is possible for one who knows, since it would be a terrible thing if, when knowledge is present, something else were to master it and drag it around like a slave, as Socrates believed; for Socrates used to fight against that proposition altogether, on the ground that there is no such thing as unrestraint, since no one acts contrary to what is best while believing that to be the case, but only from ignorance that it is.[178] Now this argument disputes things that are plainly apparent, and there is need to inquire, in connection with the experience, if it is from ignorance, what manner of ignorance it comes from. For it is clear that the person who behaves without restraint at least believes that to be contrary to what is best before he comes to be in a state of passion. But there are some who go along with the argument in some respects, but not in others, since they agree that nothing is more powerful than knowledge, but do not agree that no one acts contrary to what had seemed better, and for this reason they say that the unrestrained person is overpowered by pleasures when he has not knowledge but opinion.

But surely if it is opinion and not knowledge, and it is not a strong conception that does the resisting but a mild one, as in people who have doubts, there would be forgiveness for someone who does not stand firm in his own conceptions in the face of strong desires. But there is no forgiveness for vice, nor for anything else that is blamed. So is it when practical judgment resists that unrestraint occurs? For this is extremely strong. But that would be absurd, since at the same time the same person would be possessed of practical judgment and unrestrained, but no one would claim that it could belong to a person with practical judgment to do the most base things willingly. What's more, it has been shown above that the one who is suited for action is the person with practical judgment, since it is something directed at ultimate particulars and he is someone who has the other virtues.[179]

Also, if it is in having strong and base desires that someone is a self-restrained person, a temperate person will not be self-restrained

---

[178] The image of the slave is in Plato's *Protagoras,* 352 A-C. One place Socrates's argument appears is in the *Meno,* 77C-78B.

[179] These points repeatedly turn up as the results of arguments in Bk. VI, at or near the conclusions of Chaps. 7, 8, 9, 11, 12, and 13. The present paragraph shows that practical judgment is too strong a thing to fail in action, while mere opinion is too weak a thing to be blamed for failing.

nor a self-restrained person temperate, since it does not belong to a temperate person to desire too much or to have base desires. But he would certainly need to have them to be self-restrained, for if desires are good, an active condition preventing one from following them would be base, so that self-restraint would not in every case be of serious worth, while if they are weak and not base, it would be nothing grand, and if they are base and weak, it would be nothing big. Also, if self-restraint makes one stand firm in every opinion, it could be something base, for instance if it made one abide by a false opinion, and if unrestraint makes one stand aside from every opinion, being unrestrained could be something of serious worth, as in the case of Neoptolemus in Sophocles's *Philoctetes*; for he is praised for not abid-   20
ing by the things he was persuaded of by Odysseus, on account of being pained at lying.[180]

Another impasse comes from an argument that is a sophistry, for those who make it want to cross-examine someone into a paradox, so that they will be impressively clever when they reach it, and on account of the paradox, the inference that results turns into an impasse; for one's thinking is tied in a knot whenever one does not want to remain in place, on account of not being satisfied with the conclusion, but is not able to move forward, on account of not being able to refute the argument.[181]
Now it follows from one particular argument that senselessness combined with unrestraint is virtue, since, on account of the unrestraint, one does the opposite of what one believes, while one believes that good things are bad and that one ought not to do them, and thus will do what   30
is good and not what is bad. Also, someone who acts from conviction and by choice and pursues pleasures would seem to be better off than someone who does so not through reasoning but through unrestraint, since he could be more easily cured by being persuaded otherwise, while the unrestrained person is subject to the proverb by which we say "when water chokes someone, what should he drink?" For if he had been convinced of what he was doing, when he was persuaded   1146b
otherwise he would stop, but as it is, even when he is persuaded, he

---

[180] The point is not that lying is always wrong, but that Neoptolemus, after being rightly persuaded that lying is sometimes the better course, discovers by his experience with Philoctetes that the lie he told was wrong in those circumstances, and chooses to accept all the consequences of abandoning his opinion and trying to undo the damage it caused. Neoptolemus's character is such that this moral choice of the beautiful converges with following his own pleasure; see 1151b 17-21.

[181] The second clause describes the state produced by any impasse (*aporia*), a state which Aristotle considers a necessary precondition for any serious inquiry. His explanation is given in the *Metaphysics*, at 995a 24-b 4, and makes explicit what is meant by the image of the torpedo fish, or stingray, in Plato's *Meno* (79E-80D). But Aristotle also points out in the *Metaphysics* that sophists mimic philosophic inquiry outwardly, but differ from philosophers in their intentions (1004b 17-26).

nevertheless does something else.

Also, if there is unrestraint as well as self-restraint in connection with everything, what is unrestraint simply? For no one has every kind of unrestraint, but we speak of some people as unrestrained simply. Some such impasses as these, then, result, and of them, one must clear away some parts and leave others intact, for the resolution of an impasse is a discovery.[182]

Chapter 3. First, then, one must examine whether people are unrestrained knowingly, or not, and knowingly in what respect. Next, one must establish what the unrestrained and the self-restrained person are concerned with—I mean, whether they have to do with every sort of pleasure and pain or with certain definite kinds—and whether a self-restrained person is the same as or different from an enduring person, and similarly with as many other things as are alike in kind with this study. A starting point for the examination is whether the self-restrained and the unrestrained person have their distinctiveness by way of the things they are involved with or by the manner of it—I mean, whether the unrestrained person is unrestrained just by being involved with such-and-such, or not, but by being concerned with it in a certain manner, or not that either, but from both—and following upon that, whether unrestraint and self-restraint have to do with all things or not. For the person who is unrestrained in the simple sense is not concerned with everything, but with those things a dissipated person is concerned with, nor is he unrestrained simply by having a relation to them (since then unrestraint would be the same thing as dissipation), but by having a relation to them in a particular manner. For the dissipated person is led to them by his own choice,[183] believing that he always ought to pursue a pleasant thing that is at hand, while the unrestrained person does not believe that, but still pursues it.

Now as for its being true opinion but not knowledge contrary to which people behave without restraint, this makes no difference to the

---

[182]   This is what distinguishes genuine inquiry from sophistry. If one is stuck at an impasse, a new perspective or deeper formulation is the only way out, and this is both a discovery and something to which one is now committed.

[183]   This blending of the active and the passive characterizes vice, as it does virtue. It is the active condition or state of character for which Aristotle says we are jointly responsible (1114b 21-22), no matter what desirable things attract us and what sort of upbringing or training we have had. The language applied in this passage to unrestraint (*pros ta pathê echein pôs*) would ordinarily lead to calling it an active condition, but Aristotle, when he speaks directly about unrestraint, always calls it not a *hexis* but a *pathos* (1145b 5, 29, 1147b 8, 16, 1148b 6), a response to one's feelings and desires so feeble that it neither chooses nor rejects them, and remains as passive as they are. It is only in summary statements, when it is included with other states under one name, at 1151a 27, 1151b 29, and 1152a 35, that unrestraint is called a *hexis*.

argument, since some people who hold opinions are in no doubt, but think they know with precision. So if it is on account of having only slight belief that people with opinions will act contrary to their conceptions more than will people who know, knowledge will be no different from opinion, since some people believe in their opinions no less strongly   30
than others believe in the things they know, as Heracleitus shows.[184]
And since we speak of knowing in two senses (for both someone who has knowledge but is not using it, and someone who is using it, are said to know), it will make a difference whether one has knowledge but is not attentively considering, or is attentively considering, the things one ought not to do; for this [i.e., acting contrary to knowledge] seems terrible, but is not if one is not attentively considering it.

Also, since there are two ways of having premises, nothing prevents   1147a
someone who has both kinds from acting contrary to his knowledge when he is using the universal premise but not the particular, for actions are particulars. And there is also a difference with respect to the universal term, since it may be attributed to oneself or to the thing one is concerned with; for example, one may have the premises that dry food is beneficial to every human being and that oneself is a human being, or that such-and-such a food is dry, but whether this particular food in front of one is of that kind is a premise one either does not have or is not actively considering.[185] So as a result of these ways of having premises, there will be such an inconceivable amount of difference that for the unrestrained person to have knowledge in the one way would seem nothing strange, but for him to have knowledge in the other way would be astounding.

Also, a way of having knowledge different from those just men-   10
tioned belongs to human beings, for in having knowledge but not using it we see a different kind of having, such that one both has it in a certain way and does not have it, for instance when someone is asleep or insane or drunk. But surely people who are in states of passion are disposed in that same way, since rages and sexual desires and some other such states obviously also derange the body, and even make some people insane. It is clear, then, that one ought to speak of unrestrained people as being in a condition similar to these. And speaking the words that come from knowledge signifies nothing, since people who are in these states of passion recite demonstrations, or verses of Empedocles; those   20

---

184 This is usually taken as referring to Heracleitus's own style of making pro-
nouncements without argument, but it is also a constant theme of his that
human knowledge is all illusory. See, for example, in the Diels numbering,
fragments 1, 2, 5, 17, 26, 28, 40, 56, 78, 102, 104, and 108.
185 A similar example was used at 1141b 16-21 to show that an eye sharpened by
experience is more important to action than a knowledge of universals. Knowledge that merely links universal terms to one another and to oneself lacks the
kind of particular judgment that ends deliberation and dictates action.

who are first learning something also string words together, but do not yet know anything. For one must grow into knowing, and this requires time; and so one ought to assume that people who behave without restraint speak in the same way as actors playing a part.

Further, one might also look into the cause from the standpoint of nature[186] in the following way. For a universal premise is an opinion, but the other sort of premise is concerned with particulars, which are governed from the start by sense-perception, and when one conclusion comes from them, it is necessary then for the soul to affirm it, and in reasoning about doing something, for one to perform the action at once. For example, if one ought to taste everything that is sweet, and this thing here, as a certain one of the particulars, is sweet, it is necessary for someone who is able to and is not prevented, to do this at that same time he recognizes it. But when a universal premise is present in someone that prevents tasting it, and another that every sweet thing is pleasant, and this thing here is sweet (and this is at work on him), and a desire happens to be present, then while the one premise says to avoid this, the desire takes the lead, since it is able to set in motion each part of the body. And so, behaving without restraint results in a certain way from a proposition or opinion, which, while not in itself opposed to right reason, is opposed to it incidentally, since the desire, though not the opinion, is opposed.[187] And so for this reason animals are not unrestrained, because they do not have a universal conception, but imagination and memory of particulars.

As for how the ignorance is undone, and the unrestrained person comes to be someone who knows again, the explanation, which one needs to hear from people who study nature, is the same as in the case of someone who is drunk or asleep, and is not peculiar to this experience. But since the premise that comes last and governs actions is an opinion about something perceived, someone who is in a state of passion either does not have this, or has it in such a way that having it is not knowing it, but only saying it in the way someone who is drunk recites verses of Empedocles. And since the ultimate term is not a universal and does not

---

[186] "From the standpoint of nature" translates the adverb *phusikôs*. Aristotle generally contrasts arguments of this kind with those that are *logikôs*, or from the standpoint of logic, as for example at 204b 4-11 of the *Physics*.

[187] The opinion is "every sweet thing is pleasant." It is not in itself opposed to right thinking, and by itself it does no harm, leading only to the conclusion that this thing in front of me would be pleasant; the act of tasting it is still prevented by another opinion, such as that health, or having something to offer a friend, is better than indulging every momentary pleasure. It is the desire that substitutes, in an unrestrained person, for the missing premise "every sweet thing ought to be tasted," from which someone with the vice of dissipation deliberately acts. Hence, while vice is a misuse of choice, unrestrained behavior is a failure of choice (see 1148a 6, 9), in which the human fusion of desire and thinking (see 1139b 4-5) has been unbalanced with desire taking the lead.

seem to pertain to knowledge in the same way as something universal does, it also appears that what Socrates was looking for turns out to be the case.[188] For it is not when knowledge in the governing sense seems to be present that the experience of unrestraint occurs, nor is it this that is dragged around by passion, but a knowledge involving sense-perception. So about its being someone who knows or not, and how, while knowing, it is possible to behave without restraint, let it have been discussed to this extent.

Chapter 4. But one must discuss next whether anyone is unre- 20
strained simply, or every unrestrained person is so in some partial sense, and if it is the latter, what sorts of things an unrestrained person has to do with. Now it is clear that self-restrained and enduring people, and unrestrained and soft people, have to do with pleasures and pains. But since some of the things that produce pleasure are necessary, while some others are chosen for their own sake but admit of excess, the bodily sort being necessary (and I mean such things as have to do with nourishment and the need for sex, namely the sort of bodily pleasures we established that dissipation and temperance are concerned with[189]), the other sort not being necessary but being chosen for their own sake (and I mean such things as victory, honor, wealth, and that sort of good and pleasant 30
things), it is those who go to excess in relation to these latter pleasures, violating the correct rational understanding they have in themselves, whom we call unrestrained not simply, but adding something to it, saying that they lack restraint for money or for gain or for honor or for spiritedness but do not lack it simply, as though they are different and are called that by a likeness, as in the case of Human who won at the Olympic games; for in his case his generic name was only slightly dif- 1148a
ferent from his proper name, but nevertheless was different.[190]

A sign of this is that unrestraint is blamed not merely as a mistake but also as though it were a kind of vice, either simply or in some

---

[188] See 1145b 23-27. On Aristotle's account, Socrates is right in a sense, but genuine knowledge remains intact and uncompromised only because it is insufficient in the first place to determine action (see 1139a 34-36). It is a lack of character that makes unrestraint possible (compare 1148a 2-4). There is never a struggle between knowledge and desire, but where character has not been formed, knowledge and desire have not come into accord. It is in the early stages of the formation of character that something of the same kind and strength as desire can come to counterbalance it, and this is habit (see 1103a 23-26, b 23-25, 1104b 11-13).

[189] See Bk. III, Chap. 10.

[190] The Olympic champion boxer in 456 BC was named Anthropos. The "slight" difference attaching to his proper name is the phrase added to identify him as the Olympic champion, but it makes a big difference in the meaning of the name. Aristotle's point is merely that "unrestrained for..." does not necessarily name a subclass within unrestraint, but can be something essentially different that merely resembles unrestraint in the proper sense. See 1148b 4-14 and note.

partial sense, while none of these people [who lack restraint for some particular thing is blamed in that way]. And among those who are involved with the kinds of bodily enjoyment that we say a temperate or dissipated person is concerned with, someone who pursues excesses of pleasure, or avoids excesses of the pains of hunger, thirst, heat, cold, and of all things that involve touch and taste, not from choice but con-
10   trary to his choice and his thinking, is said to lack restraint not with an added qualification, that it has to do with these particular things, as with someone who lacks restraint for anger, but merely to lack it simply. Another sign is that people are called soft in relation to these pleasures, but not in relation to those others. And for this reason we put the unrestrained person in the same class as the dissipated person (and the self-restrained person in the same class as the temperate person), but none of those other people, since unrestrained and dissipated people are involved in certain ways with the same pleasures and pains. But while they are involved with the same things, they are not involved with them in the same way, but the latter choose them and the former do not choose them. For this reason we would speak of anyone who pursues excesses of pleasure without desiring them, or desiring them slightly, and who avoids moderate pains, as more dissipated than
20   that person who does so on account of having strong desire. For what would he do if youthful desire were to arise in him, and strong pain from necessary needs?

But since, among desires and pleasures, some are in the class of things that are beautiful and of serious stature (since some pleasant things are choiceworthy by nature), others are contrary to these, and yet others are in between, exactly the ones we singled out before,[191] such as money and gain and victory and honor, with regard to all those of this in-between sort, people are blamed not for feeling or desiring or loving them, but for the manner of it and for going to excess. This is why those who, contrary to reason, either are overpowered by or
30   pursue any of the things that are naturally beautiful and good, such as those who are more zealous about honor than one ought to be, or about their children and their parents—for these too are among good things, and people who are zealous about them are praised—though still there is some excess even in these cases, if someone, like Niobe,
1148b   were to fight even against the gods, or were to be the way Satyrus, who bore the epithet Devoted to his Father, was about his father, since he

---

[191]   At 1147b 29-35, these pleasures were singled out as belonging not to simple unrestraint (which involved only the necessary bodily pleasures), but to particular ways of appearing to lack restraint. The purpose there was a two-fold distinction of kinds of unrestraint. The threefold array in which these pleasures now occupy a middle place makes room for the discussion in the next chapter of animal-like behavior.

seemed to be too foolish—[192] So there is no vice involved in these things for the reason mentioned, that each of them is among things that are naturally choiceworthy in themselves, but even in them excesses are bad and are to be avoided. But in a similar way, there is no unrestraint about them either, since unrestraint is not only something to be avoided but is among things that are blamed, though on account of a likeness to that experience, people call it unrestraint while adding something about each sort, as one might speak of a bad doctor or a bad actor, whom one would not simply call bad.

So just as in those cases, since each of the instances is not badness but   10
is like it by analogy,[193] so too it is clear that in these cases one ought to conceive of unrestraint and self-restraint as being whatever is concerned with the same things as temperance and dissipation, while we speak of it as concerned with spiritedness by a likeness, for which reason we call someone unrestrained by adding "in relation to spiritedness" just as "in relation to honor" or "in relation to gain."

Chapter 5. But since some things are pleasant by nature, and of these some simply and others going along with kinds of animals and human beings, while others are not, but become pleasant in some cases because of defects, in others by habits, and in yet others by corrupted natures, it is possible to observe active conditions connected with each of these pleasures and closely resembling them. I am speaking of animal-like conditions, such as that of the human female who people say rips open   20
pregnant women to eat the babies, or the sorts of things people say some of the savages around the Black Sea enjoy, raw meat with some of them, human flesh with others, and others giving their children to one another to feast on, or what is reported about Phalaris.[194] These are animal-like conditions, but others come from diseases (and in some people from insanity, as with the person who sacrificed and ate his mother, or the one who ate the liver of his fellow slave), and still others resemble dis-

---

[192] This labyrinthine sentence simply ends without a predicate, the point of it being made more simply in the next sentence. Niobe was punished by the gods for excessive pride in the number of her children, and became a mountain peak that weeps all through every summer. Satyrus Philopator may have been someone who killed himself out of grief after his father's death.

[193] The word analogy is used here in a precise way: a bad doctor is to a skilled one as a bad character is to a virtuous one. The word "bad" has no content in common in the two uses, but only a formal sameness of relation. See 1096b 26-29 and note. Hence it can now be concluded that the qualifications having to do with spiritedness or honor, and so on, do not subdivide the general class of unrestraint, or add things to a common core of meaning, but set up analogies to a state of the soul essentially different from them.

[194] Phalaris was a tyrant, notorious for imaginative cruelty, of a city on Sicily. Since his best-known instrument of torture roasted people alive, it is not hard in the present context to guess what else was reported. See also 1149a 13-14 below.

eases or come from habits, such as plucking out one's hair or gnawing on one's nails, or even on charcoal or dirt, or sex acts between males,
30   for these result in some cases from nature, but in others from habit, as with people who have been abused since childhood. Now with those for whom nature is responsible for this, no one would say that they are unrestrained, just as one would not say that about women because they are not active but passive in sex, and it is the same with those who are in a disease-like condition as a result of habit.

Having either of these sorts of condition, then, is outside the
1149a   boundaries of vice, just as the animal-like condition is, and for a person who has such a condition to master it or be mastered by it is not a matter of simple unrestraint but of unrestraint by likeness, just as one ought not to speak of as unrestrained the person who has this kind of experience in connection with surges of spiritedness. For every sort of senselessness or cowardice or dissipation or harshness that goes to excess is either animal-like or disease-like, since someone who is by nature of such a kind as to be afraid of everything, even if a mouse squeaks, is cowardly with an animal-like cowardice, and the person who was afraid of a weasel was so as a result of a disease; and
10   among senseless people, some, who lack reason by nature and live by sense-perception alone, as with some remote races of barbarians, are animal-like, while others, who lack reason on account of diseases, such as people subject to epileptic seizures or the insane, are disease-like. And among these, it is possible for someone sometimes merely to have the condition and not be mastered by it—I mean, for instance, if Phalaris held back his desire to eat a child, or for some exotic sexual pleasure—but it is also possible to be mastered by it and not just to have it.

So just as, with vice, the sort that is human is simply called vice, while the other sort is spoken of with an added qualification, that it is animal-like or disease-like, but not simply vice, it is clear that in the same way one sort of unrestraint is animal-like, and another is disease-like,
20   while it is only the sort that corresponds to human dissipation that is unrestraint simply. So it is clear that unrestraint and self-restraint are concerned only with those things with which dissipation and temperance are,[195] and that concerning other things there is a different form of unrestraint, called that by a metaphor and not simply.

---

195   Temperance and dissipation are active conditions involving choice, concerned with the necessary pleasures of food and sex. Unrestraint, in its simple and proper sense, is a passive condition involving a failure of choice, concerning those same objects. When disease, bad habits, or natural defects push the objects of these necessary pleasures outside those that are natural to humans, a condition distinct from unrestraint, but resembling it, arises, just as, if those same unnatural objects were deliberately and regularly chosen, the result would be a distinct and inhuman kind of vice. The metaphor and

Chapter 6. But let us observe that a lack of restraint for spiritedness is less shameful than a lack of restraint for desires. For spiritedness seems to listen to reason to some extent, but to mis-hear it, just as servants in a hurry, who rush off before hearing everything that is said, get the instructions wrong, or dogs, before looking to see if it is a friend, bark if there is merely a noise. In such a manner, spiritedness, on account of   30
the heat and haste of its nature, when it has heard something but has not heard an order, rushes toward revenge. For reason or imagination revealed that there was an insult or a belittling, and spiritedness, as though reasoning that it is necessary to go to war against any such thing, immediately gets violently angry; while desire, if reason or sense-perception merely says that something is pleasant, rushes toward enjoyment. So while spiritedness follows reason in a certain way, desire does not,[196]   1149b
and so is more shameful. For while someone who lacks restraint for spritedness is in a certain sense giving way to reason, the other sort of person is giving way to desire and not to reason.

Also, there is more forgiveness for following natural tendencies, since even among desires, there is more forgiveness for those that are of a sort that is common to all people, and to the extent that they are common. But spiritedness and aggressiveness are more natural than desires that are for excess or desires that are not for necessary things, as with the man who defended himself on the charge that he beat his father, saying "he also beat his, and that one beat the one before him,"   10
and pointing to his son, "and he will beat me when he becomes a man; it's inborn in us." And the one who was dragged by his son used to order him to stop at the doorway, since he himself used to drag his father that far. Also, people who plot and scheme are more unjust. Now a spirited person is not a schemer, nor is spiritedness itself, but they are open, while desire is as people say of Aphrodite, "a weaver of

---

resemblance to unrestraint in these cases has to do with not restraining the objects of necessary desires within human bounds; the other sort of resemblance, that involves losing control of desires for things that are beautiful and good in themselves, is returned to in the next chapter.

[196] It may appear that the two cases are the same, but careful comparison to 1147a 31-b 3 shows that in unrestraint in its simple and proper sense, a desire is taking the place of a missing premise, while in the present case, spiritedness acts on a premise that seems to be implied. In the blended state of being active and passive at once, a simply unrestrained person is controlled by desire, while an overly spirited person is taking charge of things, but impatiently and on insufficient grounds. Aristotle's refusal to treat spiritedness as simply another desire, directed at revenge, is not a trivial distinction, though he does not press that distinction as far as others might. In Plato's *Republic*, spiritedness is treated as a third part of the soul that mediates between the rational and irrational sides of us and allows us to become whole. Aristotle prefers to think of human desire as infused with thought and human thinking as infused with desire. (See the notes to 1105a 8, 1113a 12, and 1139a 4.)

snares of the Cyprian race," and as Homer says in connection with her embroidered shawl, "speaking soft words, that steal the wits even from one with sturdy wisdom."[197] So if that sort of unrestraint is more unjust and more shameful than is the sort that has to do with spiritedness,
20   then unrestraint in the simple sense is also vice in a certain sense.

Also, no one commits a gratuitous insult from a feeling of pain, but everyone who acts in anger acts from being pained, while the one who gratuitously insults someone does so with pleasure. So if it is the case that those things are more unjust, at which it is especially just to be angry, then so is unrestraint that comes from desire, for there is nothing gratuitously insulting in spiritedness.[198] Accordingly, it is clear that unrestraint that has to do with desires is more shameful than the sort that has to do with spiritedness, and that what self-restraint and unrestraint *are*[199] connected with are bodily desires and pleasures.

But one must take up the differences among these bodily desires and pleasures themselves, for as was said at first, some of these are human and natural in both kind and amount, while others are animal-
30   like, and still others come from defects and diseases. Of these, it is only with the first sort that temperance and dissipation are concerned. That is why we do not speak of animals as either temperate or dissipated except by a metaphor, and if some particular kind of animals as a whole is exceptional in relation to another kind in insolence, destructiveness, or in being inclined to eat everything, since they do not have choice or
1150a   reasoning but stand out from nature as the insane do from human beings. But an animal-like state is less bad than vice, though more frightening, since the better part of the soul is not corrupted, as it would be in a human being, but the animal does not possess it. So it is like comparing something inanimate to something with a soul, as to which is worse,

---

[197] The first phrase quoted may be from Sappho. The second is line XIV, 217 of the *Iliad*, a partial description of the designs stitched on a garment Aphrodite gives Hera to help her ensnare Zeus.

[198] Gratuitous insult here translates *hubris*, which Aristotle describes in Bk. II, Chap. 2, of the *Rhetoric* as a belittling of someone for the mere pleasure of it. In that same place, he treats anger as the feeling arising from the opinion that one has been belittled gratuitously. Since the insolent person desires the warped pleasure that comes from feeling the power to hurt someone's feelings, he is classed with those who are unrestrained in their desires. Spiritedness in general may be roused in many ways, but Aristotle considers the sort of spiritedness that gets out of restraint as arising not from any desire but only to reduce the pain of feeling (correctly or incorrectly) unjustly insulted.

[199] By the emphatic placement and accent of the verb, Aristotle in effect says that the primary and governing meanings of self-restraint and unrestraint imply a connection with bodily desires and pleasures, setting up a variety of derivative senses in which the words may be used, with unrestraint for nonbodily pleasures, like that of insulting people, closer to the central meaning, and unrestraint for spirited responses farther away.

since the badness of something that has no source, as intelligence is a source, is always more innocent. It is much like comparing justice to a just human being, since there is a sense in which either one is worse; for a vicious human being can do ten thousand times as much evil as an animal.[200]

Chapter 7. But concerning the pleasures and pains and desires and aversions arising from touch and taste, which were distinguished above   **10** as those that dissipation and temperance have to do with, it is possible to be such as to give way even to those in relation to which most people are stronger, and it is possible to master even those in relation to which most people are weaker. Among these cases, people are unrestrained and self-restrained in connection with pleasures, and are soft and enduring in relation to pains. The active condition belonging to most people is in-between, even though people are more heavily weighted toward the worse side.[201]

And since some pleasures are necessary and others are not, and the former up to a certain amount and not as excesses nor as deficiencies, and it is the same way with desires and pains, someone who pursues pleasures beyond these, or these to excess and by choice, for themselves   **20** and for nothing else resulting from them, is a dissipated person; for necessarily this person is without regret, and is therefore incurable, since a person without regret is incurable.[202] Someone who falls short is the opposite, and someone at the mean is temperate. And similarly, someone who avoids bodily pains not from being overpowered by them but by choice is a dissipated person. But among those not acting by choice, some are led by pleasure, others by escaping the pain that comes from desire, so that they differ from one another. For it would seem to anyone to be worse if one who had no desire or a slight one were to do something shameful, than if someone did so from desiring it strongly, or if someone who was not angry were to hit someone, than if someone

---

[200]   These last three sentences are written in a sketchy way and leave room for a variety of interpretations. There are two points of comparison. The most frighteningly destructive animal is innocent in comparison to the slightest deliberate malice of a corrupt intelligence. But in the same way that justice itself is perfectly good, while a just human being, though fallible, can produce some good practical effects, animals and humans can be compared with respect to either inherent badness or incidental harm.

[201]   Since Aristotle repeatedly refuses to call unrestraint anything but a passive experience (see note to 1146b 22), it is notable that he here credits most of the human race with an active condition that holds out against our worst tendencies.

[202]   The necessary sequence is: choice implies lack of regret, which makes it impossible to change. In Greek the very name for the dissipated person (*a-kolastos*) suggests one who cannot be corrected, though at 1119a 33-b 7, Aristotle took it to mean one whose desires were not cut back or pruned in childhood.

30   did so in anger. For what would he do if he were in a passion? Hence a dissipated person is worse than an unrestrained person. But one of the things described is more a form of softness, while the dissipated person is of the other sort.[203]

The self-restrained person is the opposite of someone who is unrestrained, but the enduring person is the opposite of someone who is soft, for enduring consists in holding out against something, but self-restraint consists in overpowering it, and holding out and overpowering are different, just as not giving way is different from being victorious. Hence

1150b   self-restraint is preferable to endurance. And that person who falls short in relation to things most people resist and are strong enough for is soft and luxurious, for luxury is also a certain kind of softness. One who lets his cloak drag, so as not to be burdened by the pain of holding it, or who acts like someone who is sick, does not realize that he is miserable when he is like someone who is miserable. And it is similar with self-restraint and unrestraint, for it is not to be wondered at if someone gives way to pleasures or pains that are strong and excessive, but it is forgivable if he does so with resistance, like the Philoctetes of Thodectes

10   when he is struck by the viper, or the Cercyon in Carcinus's *Alope*, or like those who, having tried to hold back laughter, burst out laughing all at once, as happened to Xenophantus.[204] But it is to be wondered at if someone gives way to and is unable to resist those things that most people are able to hold out against, and it is not due to the nature of his race or to disease, like the softness in the race of the kings of Scythia, or as the female differs in strength from the male. And a childish person seems to be unrestrained, but is soft. For playfulness is relaxation, if it is a way of resting, and a childish person is among those who go too far in that direction.

Of unrestraint, one sort is impetuousness and another sort is weak-

20   ness. For people of the latter sort have deliberated, but, on account of passion, do not stick to the things they decided by deliberating, while those of the former sort are led by passion because of not having deliberated. For just as those who are on guard against being tickled do not respond to tickling, so too some people, having become aware beforehand and having foreseen what is coming and having awakened themselves and their reasoning in advance, do not give way to passion, whether it is pleasant or painful. People who are impatient and excitable[205] are

---

203   The sort of person who avoids pain by choice is a cross between the passive weakness of a soft character and the deliberate overindulgence of dissipation.

204   The two tragedies referred to are lost. The Philoctetes of Sophocles collapses on stage after a courageous struggle. Cercyon, a legendary king, is said to have been unable to endure the adultery of his daughter Alope. Xenophantus was the court musician of Alexander the Great.

205   The excitable are literally "melancholic." The theory of the four humors came from the Hippocratic tradition, but only centuries later, at the time of Galen,

especially unrestrained with the impetuous sort of unrestraint, since the former from hastiness and the latter from strength of feeling do not wait for reason, on account of being inclined to follow imagination.

Chapter 8. The dissipated person, as was said, does not have regrets, **30** since he stands by his choice, but every unrestrained person is capable of regret. Hence things are not as we made out in the impasse,[206] but the former is incurable and the latter is curable. For vice seems like such diseases as dropsy and consumption, and unrestraint like epileptic seizures, since the former is a continuous bad condition while the latter is not continuous. And the kinds to which unrestraint and vice belong are completely different, since vice is something one is not aware of having, while unrestraint is something one is aware of. And among **1151a** these unrestrained people themselves, the impulsive sort are better off than those who have reason but do not stick with it, since the latter give way to weaker passions, and are not lacking in prior deliberation as the others are. For a person who is unrestrained in this sense is like people who get drunk quickly and on a little wine, and on less than with most people. It is clear then that unrestraint is not vice (except, perhaps, in a certain respect), since the one is by choice and the other is contrary to choice; however, they are alike as far as actions are concerned, as with the words of Demodocus to the Milesians, "It's not that Milesians are stupid, just that they will do the sort of things that stupid people do"; **10** and while unrestrained people are not unjust, they will do injustice.

But since one sort of person is such as to pursue bodily pleasures to excess and contrary to a right understanding without being convinced, while the other is convinced to do so because of being the sort of person who is such as to pursue them, it is then the former who is easily persuaded otherwise and the latter who is not. For virtue keeps the source safe, while vice destroys it, and in actions the source is that for the sake of which one acts, just as in mathematics the sources are the hypotheses[207]; so neither there nor here is reason able to teach anyone the sources, but here it is virtue, either natural or habituated, that directs one to right opinion about the source. So a temperate person **20** is such as to have the source, while a dissipated person is the opposite, and there is someone who, on account of passion, stands aside from a

---

did they become associated with the four kinds of temperament, among which melancholy got a meaning closer to the one we give it.

[206] This was the second and less superficial sophistical argument given at 1146a 31-b 2.

[207] Aristotle ordinarily uses the word "hypothesis," as at 1128b 30, only for a conditional assumption, whereas the sources of mathematical reasoning are not assumptions but things known immediately, as is said at 1142a 25-29. His use of it here recalls the way Socrates speaks in Plato's *Republic* (510B-511D), understanding the sources of mathematics as provisional and hypothetical just because they are not the sources simply.

right understanding, whom passion masters so much so that he does not act in accord with the right understanding, but does not master so much so that he is the sort of person who is convinced that one ought to pursue such pleasures without restriction. This is the unrestrained person, who is better off than a dissipated person and is not simply base, since the best thing in him, the source, is preserved. And there is another sort of person opposite to this one, who is such as to stand firm and not to stand aside on account of passion. So it is clear from these things that the one is an active condition of serious worth, while the other is base.[208]

Chapter 9. Is a self-restrained person someone who stands firm in any and every sort of rational understanding and choice, or in one that is right, and is an unrestrained person anyone who fails to stand firm in any and every sort of choice and rational understanding, or in an understanding that is not false and a choice that is right? This was raised as an impasse above.[209] Or is it incidentally in any sort whatever, but in themselves a true understanding and a right choice that the former stands firm in and the latter fails to stand firm in? For if someone chooses or pursues one particular thing on account of another, he chooses and pursues the second in itself and the former incidentally. By "in itself" we mean simply. And so there is a sense in which it is any sort of opinion whatever that the one stands firm in and the other stands away from, but simply it is a true one.

But there are some people of a sort that stand firm in an opinion who are called stubborn, who are hard to convince and not easily persuaded out of anything. These people have some similarity to the self-restrained person, just as a wasteful person does to a generous one, or a rash person to a confident one, but they are different in many respects. For it is because of passion and desire that one of them does not change, since when it so happens, the self-restrained person will be readily convinced, but the others will not be convinced by reason, since they hold on to desire, and many of them are led by pleasures. People fond of their own opinions are stubborn, as are stupid and boorish people; those who are fond of their own opinions are so on account of pleasure and pain, for they enjoy being victorious when they are not persuaded out of them, and they are pained when their own opinions are deprived of authority like decrees. So they are more like an unrestrained person than a self-restrained one.

---

[208] Self-restraint, in comparison with virtue, is an immature state, in which character has not been formed. It is an active condition in an inefficient way, that has not become naturally infused into one's life. Unrestraint is here, as at 1151b 29 and 1152a 35 below, included among active conditions (see note to 1146b 22), either because of its resemblance to vice, or because it is thought of as a condition of exerting restraint that exists but repeatedly fails.

[209] See 1146a 16-21.

And there are some people who do not stand firm in their opinions, but not on account of unrestraint, such as Neoptolemus in Sophocles's *Philoctetes*; it is, however, on account of pleasure that he does not stand firm, but a beautiful pleasure,[210] since being truthful was a beautiful **20** thing to him, and he had been persuaded by Odysseus to lie. For not everyone who acts on account of pleasure in any respect is dissipated or base or unrestrained, but only someone who acts on account of a shameful pleasure.

But since it is also possible for there to be someone of a sort that enjoys bodily pleasures less than one ought, and who does not stand firm in a rational understanding, a self-restrained person is a mean between this sort of person and one who is unrestrained.[211] For the unrestrained person fails to stand firm in his understanding for something more, but this person does so for something less, while the self-restrained person stands firm and does not change for either reason. And if self-restraint is something of serious worth, both of the opposite active conditions must be bad, as they obviously are. But since one of **30** the two is evident in few people and on few occasions, then just as temperance seems to be opposite only to dissipation, so too self-restraint seems to be opposite only to unrestraint.

And since many things are spoken of in accordance with a likeness, the self-restraint attributed to a temperate person has also followed from a likeness. For the self-restrained person is of such a kind as to do nothing contrary to a rational understanding on account of bodily pleasures, and so is the temperate person, but the former has base desires **1152a** while the latter does not, and the latter is the sort of person who does not feel pleasure contrary to reason, while the former is the sort who feels it but is not led by it. The unrestrained person and the dissipated person are also similar, although they are different; both pursue bodily pleasures, the latter while believing that one ought to, but the former not believing that.

Chapter 10. Nor is it possible for the same person to be possessed of practical judgment and at the same time be unrestrained. For the person with practical judgment was demonstrated to be at the same

---

[210] In the overall dialectical motion of the inquiry, the meaning of the good, taken as threefold at 1104b 30-31, was reduced to two governing senses at 1110b 9-11, with the third meaning finding its subordinate place at 1142b 31-33. In this example, the two remaining senses of the good, the beautiful and the pleasant, merge. This merging was sketched out as a criterion of happiness at 1099a 24-31, but an understanding of its possibility requires an adequate account of pleasure, which will be sought just ahead in Chaps. 11-14.

[211] One might have expected the array to be completed by someone of excessive self-restraint, whom we might call inhibited, but Aristotle focuses on the failure of choice as what determines unrestraint and its extreme opposite. A way of feeling toward bodily pleasures overpowers thinking on both sides, producing opposite kinds of self-indulgence.

time someone of serious stature in character.[212] Also, it is not by knowing alone that someone is possessed of practical judgment, but also by
being able to act, but the unrestrained person is not able to act. But
nothing prevents a clever person from being unrestrained, which is why
some people sometimes seem to be possessed of practical judgment
but unrestrained, since cleverness differs from practical judgment in
the way explained in the first discussion of them, and though, in the
description of them, they are close, they differ with respect to choice. So
the unrestrained person is not even like someone who has knowledge
and is actively paying attention to it, but like someone who is asleep
or drunk. And though he acts willingly (since he acts while knowing
in some manner what he is doing and for what end), he is not vicious,
for his choice is that of a decent person, so that he is halfway to being
vicious.[213]

And an unrestrained person is not unjust, since he is not a schemer,
for one sort of them is not able to stand firm in the things he has deliberated, while the other, excitable sort doesn't even deliberate at all.
And so the unrestrained person is like a city that decrees everything it
needs to and has laws of serious worth, but makes no use of them, as
Anaxandrides joked:

> The city wanted to, inasmuch as it cares nothing about its laws.

But a vicious person is like a city that does make use of its laws, while
the laws it makes use of are vicious. Unrestraint and self-restraint have
to do with what goes beyond the active condition of most people, since
one stands firm more, the other less, than what most people are capable
of. And among unrestrained people, the excitable sort behave with an
unrestraint which is more easily cured than that of the sort who deliberate but do not stand by it, and those who are unrestrained by habit are
more easily cured than those who are so naturally. For habit is easier
to change than nature, and this is why even habit is hard to change,
because it seems to be like nature,[214] as Evenus says,

> I tell you, friend, it is exercise continued for a long time, and so
> This, for human beings, ends up being their nature.

What, then, self-restraint, unrestraint, endurance, and softness are,
and how these active conditions are related to one another, have been
said.

---

[212] See 1144a 22-1144b 1. That same passage is also the first discussion of cleverness, referred to five lines below.

[213] Literally "half-vicious," from which some readers have wrongly concluded
that vice is subject to gradations. The unrestrained person was described first
at 1095 4-11 as being like a young student who has all the theory of ethics
but unruly desires.

[214] This is the closest Aristotle comes to the formulation of later writers that
habit is a second nature.

Chapter 11. It belongs to one who engages in philosophic inquiry about politics to examine what concerns pleasure and pain, for he is   1152b the master craftsman of the end to which we look when we speak of each thing as bad or good simply. To investigate what concerns them is also something necessary, because we established that virtue and vice of character have to do with pains and pleasures, and most people say that happiness involves pleasure; this is also why people take the name blessedness from blissful enjoyment.[215] Now to some people it seems that no sort of pleasure is good, either in itself or incidentally, since the good and pleasure are not the same thing; to others it seems that,   10 though some pleasures are good, most of them are bad. And among these opinions there is yet at third, that even if all pleasures are good, it is still not possible for pleasure to be what is best.[216]

It is thought that it is not good at all because every pleasure is a perceptible process of coming-into-being into a natural state, while no sort of coming-into-being is of the same order as ends, as housebuilding is not of the same order as a house; and because a temperate person avoids pleasures; and because a person with practical judgment pursues the absence of pain, not what is pleasant; and because pleasures are an impediment to exercising judgment, and more so the more one enjoys them, as with the pleasure of sex, since no one could think about anything while engaged in it; and because there is no art of producing pleasure, even though every good thing is a product of an art; and because children and animals pursue pleasures. Of their not all being   20 of serious worth, the reason is that there are also pleasures that are shameful and are reproached, and that there are harmful ones, since some pleasant things are disease-like. And that pleasure is not the best thing, is because it is not an end but a process of coming-into-being. These are pretty much the things that are said.

Chapter 12. But that it does not follow from these things that pleasure is not good, nor even that it is not the best thing, is clear from these considerations: First, since the good has two senses (for there

---

[215] Aristotle suggests that *makarios* is derived from *(mala) chairein*. In Bk. I, Chap. 10, he associated blessedness with the external good fortune that does not produce happiness, but completes it.

[216] The popular attitude that confuses happiness with pleasure was set aside in Bk. I, at 1095b 14-22, as settling for a life fit for cattle. The prevailing fact that dominated the exploration of virtue of character was that pleasure is a powerful force that needs to be opposed (1104b 33-1105a 9, 1109b 1-12). But the discussion in this book of people who are unrestrained in a secondary and derivative sense has brought out the possibility of pleasures that are good in themselves and even beautiful (1147b 29-31, 1148a 22-b 14, 1151b 19). The current examination of pleasure, then, need not go back to the beginning of the question, but focuses on philosophic opinions. The first of the three is that of Speusippus (see 1153b 4-7 below), Plato's successor as head of the Academy, while the second and third are possibilities discussed in Plato's *Philebus*.

is what is good simply and what is good for something or someone in particular), natures and active conditions will follow the good in this respect, and so, consequently, will motions and processes of coming-into-being; and the bad ones seem to be the ones that, while

30   bad simply, are not bad for someone but preferable for that particular person, and some things that are not even preferable for that person are still preferable for him sometimes, for a short time, though not simply. And some of these are not even pleasures, but seem to be, as many processes as take place with pain and for the sake of healing, as do those applied to the sick.

Moreover, since one sort of good thing is a being-at-work, while another is an active condition, the processes that settle us into an active condition that is natural are pleasant incidentally, but there is in our desires a being-at-work of an active condition and nature that remains

1153a   constant,[217] since there are also pleasures that are without pain or desire, such as those of contemplating, that belong to a nature which is not deficient. A sign of this is that people do not enjoy the same thing as pleasant while the nature is being restored and when it has been settled into, but when it has been settled into they enjoy things that are pleasant simply, and while it is being restored they enjoy even things that are contrary to these, since people enjoy things that are sour and bitter, none of which is pleasant either by nature or simply. Neither, then, are the pleasures, for as the pleasant things differ from one another, so too do the pleasures that come from them.

Also, it is not necessary, as some people say, for there to be some other thing that is better than pleasure, as the end of a process of coming-into-being, since pleasures are not, nor do all of them even

10   involve, processes of coming-into-being; instead, pleasures are ways of being-at-work and are ends, and they do not result from states that are coming into being but from capacities that are being exercised. And not all pleasures have some other thing as an end, but only the ones that belong to those who are being brought into the completion of their nature. And therefore it is not right to claim that pleasure is a perceptible process of coming-into-being; rather, one ought to say that it is a being-at-work of an active condition in accord with nature, and instead of "perceptible," unimpeded.[218] The reason it seems to some people to be a process of coming-into-being is that it is good in the governing sense,

---

[217]   In Plato's *Gorgias*, Callicles describes the best life as the one with the maximum influx of pleasure, and the temperate life as the life of a stone (494A-B). Aristotle's claim is that the natural state is not inert but constant through being at work. This is the central postulate of all his thinking. Here it explains why there can be such a thing as "right desire" (1139a 24), or anything inherently and naturally pleasant.

[218]   It is not that being perceptible and being unimpeded have any relation to one another, but when pleasure was assigned to the class of processes of

since they believe that being-at-work *is* a process of coming-into-being, but it is something different.

The argument that pleasures are bad because some pleasant things are disease-like is the same as saying health is bad because some health-ful things are bad from the standpoint of making money. Both are bad in this particular sense, but are not for that reason bad, since even   20
contemplating is sometimes harmful to one's health. And there is no impediment either to wise judgment or to any other active condition in the pleasure that comes from each, but only in pleasures of different kinds, since the pleasures that come from contemplating and learning make one contemplate and learn more. And it turns out reasonably that no pleasure is the product of art, since there is no art of producing any other way of being-at-work either, but only of producing a capacity, even though the arts of perfumery and cookery seem to be productive of pleasure.[219]

And the arguments that a temperate person avoids pleasure, and a person of practical judgment pursues a life free of pain, and that children and animals pursue pleasure, are all resolved by the same thing. For since it was explained that in a certain way pleasures are good simply   30
and in a certain way not all of them are good, the sort of pleasures that animals and children pursue, and those in relation to which a person of practical judgment pursues freedom from pain, are those that involve desire and pain, namely the bodily pleasures (since these are of that sort), or the excesses of these, as a result of which a dissipated person is dissipated. Hence it is these that a temperate person avoids, since even a temperate person has pleasures.

Chapter 13. It is agreed, however, that pain is something bad,   1153b
and is to be avoided, since it is either simply bad, or bad by being an impediment. But what is opposite to something that is to be avoided, insofar as it is something to be avoided and something bad, is good. It is necessary, then, for pleasure to be something good. For from the way Speusippus used to refute this, by arguing that pleasure is like the greater, which is opposite to both the lesser and the equal, no refuta-

---

coming-into-being, its appropriate specific difference was perceptibility, since many digestive and metabolic processes that restore natural states are imperceptible. On that view, pleasure is the feeling we have when a natural state is disturbed but being restored. But if the class pleasure belongs to is that of being-at-work, its appropriate specific difference is lack of disturbance of the exercise of our natural powers, and pleasure is the active enjoyment of being what we are.

[219] In Plato's *Gorgias*, cookery is an example of a knack that comes from experi-ence for producing pleasure by flattery or pandering rather than by art. (See 462C-465E.) Socrates's point there is that what pleases anyone's senses is an irrational matter of taste, of which no general account can be given. Aristotle's point here is that even genuine arts like medicine and lawmaking do not pro-duce the pleasures of health or happiness, but only the conditions for them.

tion follows, since he would not say that pleasure is something bad in its very being.[220] And nothing prevents pleasure from being the best thing, even if some pleasures are bad, just as a certain kind of knowledge might be the best thing, even if some kinds of knowledge were
10   bad. And perhaps it is even necessary, if there is an unimpeded way of being-at-work belonging to each active condition, and happiness is the being-at-work either of all of these or of some one of them, for the one that is most unimpeded to be the state that is most worthy of choice; but this is a pleasure. Therefore some pleasure would be the best thing, even though many pleasures were bad, and if it so happens, simply bad.

And this is why everyone believes that the happy life is pleasant, and interweaves pleasure into happiness, with good reason, for no way of being-at-work that is complete is impeded, and happiness is among things that are complete. Hence, someone who is happy has need in addition of the goods of the body, and of goods that are external and from fortune, in order that he not be impeded on account of them. And those who claim that someone who is being tortured, or someone who
20   falls into great misfortunes, is happy if he is a good person are either intentionally or unintentionally talking nonsense. But because of the additional need of fortune, it seems to some people that good fortune is the same thing as happiness, which it is not, since even good fortune, when it is excessive, is an impediment, and perhaps it is no longer a just thing to call it good fortune, since the limit that determines it is related to happiness.

And the fact that all animals and human beings pursue pleasure is something of a sign of its being in some way the best thing:

> Nothing that's said amounts to nothing at all if many peoples say it.[221]

But since they do not all have the same nature or the same best active
30   condition, nor even seem to, they do not all pursue the same pleasure either, though they all pursue pleasure. But perhaps it is even the case that people pursue not what they think they do or would say they do, but the same pleasure, since all things have in their nature something

---

[220] Both Speusippus's argument and Aristotle's counterargument are more amply stated at 1173a 5-13, but are still not fully explicit. The greater and the lesser are two species of the unequal, which is what is opposite to the equal, just as cowardice and rashness are two species of vice in relation to fear and confidence. For Speusippus's analogy to hold, pleasure would have to be something inherently bad in the same way pain is, so that the two could constitute a single class of things opposed to the good neutral state; this would mean that any pleasure would always destroy or impede natural activity.

[221] Line 763 from Hesiod's *Works and Days*.

divine.[222] But the bodily pleasures have taken over the hereditary name because we most often steer toward them and everyone has a share in them, so since these are the only pleasures they know, people believe   1154a they are the only ones there are.

And it is also clear that, if pleasure and being-at-work are not good, it will not be possible for a happy person to live pleasantly; to what end would he have need of pleasure, if it is not good? It would even be possible for him to live in pain, since pain would be neither bad nor good if pleasure is neither. So why would he avoid pain? So the life of a person of serious moral stature would not be any more pleasant unless the ways of being-at-work that constitute it are as well.

Chapter 14. Concerning the bodily pleasures, one must examine the arguments to the effect that some pleasures, such as the beautiful ones, are most certainly worthy of choice, but not the bodily pleasures   10 with which a dissipated person is concerned. But then why are the pains opposite to those pleasures bad? For the opposite of a bad thing is a good thing. Are they good in the sense that they are necessary, because what is not bad is good? Or are they good up to a certain amount? For of those active conditions and motions of which there is no excess over what is for the better, there is no excess of pleasure either, but of those of which there is an excess, there is also an excess of pleasure. But there is an excess of things that are good for the body, and someone is base by pursuing that excess, and not the necessary pleasures, since every-one in some way enjoys pleasing food[223] and wine and sex, though not all people do so as one ought. But in the case of pain the situation is opposite, since it is not the excess of pain one avoids but all of it; for there is no pain opposed to an excessive pleasure except for a person   20 who pursues that excess.[224]

However, one ought to state not only what is true but also the reason behind what is false, since this contributes toward confidence in what one is saying; for when one gives a reasonable explanation of why what is not true appears to be true, it makes people be more confident of what is true, and so one ought to say why the bodily pleasures seem more to be preferred. First, then, it is because they drive out pain, and

---

[222]   This passage parallels Diotima's account of love in Plato's *Symposium*. See especially 205B and 207A-208B. That theme begins in Aristophanes's speech, at 192C-D, with the observation that sexual desire obviously has some deeper longing for fulfillment within it.

[223]   The word translated "pleasing food" (*opson*) refers to any food other than bread. In Plato's *Republic* (372D), Glaucon's spirited rejection of Socrates's healthy city is provoked by the lack of this sort of food, not for the sake of pleasure or taste, but because it marks out human meals as having a dignity beyond the feeding of animals.

[224]   This thought is expanded below at 1154b 2-6. Where character has not been developed, and more satisfying pleasures have not been found, people have nothing to turn to but the childish sources of pleasure they are acquainted with, and the absence of these comes to be felt as pain.

as a result of excesses of pain, people pursue pleasure that is excessive, and bodily pleasure in general, as though it were a cure. But the cura-
30   tive pleasures become violent, and hence people pursue them, because of the way they appear over against their opposite. And so pleasure seems not to be a thing of serious worth for two reasons, as was said,[225] since some pleasures are acts of a base nature (either from birth, as with an animal, or from habit, such as those of a base human being) while others are curative of something defective, and having something is
1154b   better than coming into having it; though the latter sort result in states of completion and thus are of serious worth incidentally.

Also, bodily pleasures are pursued on account of being violent, by people who are not capable of enjoying other pleasures; they even provide themselves with thirst in certain ways. When this is harmless it is not blameworthy, but when it is harmful it is something base.[226] But they do not have any other sort of things from which to get enjoyment, and by their nature a neutral state is painful to many people. For an animal is always exerting effort, as those who study nature bear witness, claiming that seeing and hearing are painful, but we are used
10   to them by now—so they claim. Similarly, in youth, because they are growing, people are in the same condition as those who are inebriated, and youth is pleasant; but people who are excitable by nature need perpetual curing since their bodies are continually being stung on account of the way they are blended, and they are always in a state of violent desire, but pleasure drives out pain, not only the pleasure opposite to the pain but any random pleasure, if it is strong. Through these means people become dissipated and base.

But pleasures that do not involve pains do not have an excess. These come from things that are pleasant by nature and not incidentally. By things pleasant incidentally, I mean those that cure pain, for because curing results from some action of the part that remains healthy, they
20   seem for that reason to be pleasant. But what is pleasant by nature is what causes the action of such a nature.[227] But nothing that is the same is always pleasant because our nature is not simple, but there is also something else present in it, as a result of which we are perishable; so

---

[225] See 1152b 20-23.
[226] An ancient commentator suggests that one may induce thirst by more exercise as well as by eating salty snacks.
[227] At 1152b 33-1153a 4, Aristotle distinguished pleasure in its true sense as the awareness of our own being-at-work. While the return to such a condition from a disturbance of it is pleasant, it is only so because of our awareness of what remains undisturbed throughout. Genuine bodily pleasure, then, comes from maintaining good bodily condition, and the strong sensation that accompanies large swings out of and back into it is an illusion if it is interpreted as strong pleasure. Intense pleasure would then seem to come from settling into a constant state of engagement with the proper objects of our nature.

if something of one sort acts, this is contrary to nature with respect to the other nature, though when they are equalized, what is done seems neither painful nor pleasant. Otherwise, if the nature of anything were simple, the same action would always be most pleasant. Hence, a god always enjoys a pleasure that is one and simple, for there is a being-at-work not only of motion but also of motionlessness, and there is a greater pleasure in rest than in motion. But change of everything is sweet, according to the poet,[228] on account of some badness, for just as   30 it is a bad human being who is easily changeable, it is also a bad nature that needs change; it is not simple and not suitable.[229]

So what concerns self-restraint and unrestraint, and what concerns pleasure and pain, have been discussed, and what each is and in what way some of them are good and the others bad. And what remains is that we speak about friendship.

BOOK VIII

Chapter 1. It would follow, after these things, to go through what   1155a concerns friendship, since it is a certain kind of virtue,[230] or goes with virtue, and is also most necessary for life. For no one would choose to live without friends, despite having all the rest of the good things, since

---

[228] Euripides, line 234 of *Orestes*.

[229] Human nature, or any compound nature, is not perfectly suited to its own ends. If the greatest pleasures of a human being as such are found in sustained activity, this is still wearisome to the bodily materials of which we are made, which is why we eventually die. (See also *Metaphysics*, 1050b 22-28.) It is not the compounding of bodily life with thinking that is at issue, since animals too have compound natures. Even the pleasure the whole body feels in vigorous exercise of its powers is eventually overtaken by the need of its material to lie down, as mere earth on the earth. The "equalization" referred to here is not that of a well-balanced life, but a keeping of activity to a minimal level that sacrifices its own proper pleasure to minimize the pain of weariness. Hence, freedom from pain means avoidance of life, while any sort of fulfill-ment means accepting some changeability. The whole topic of pleasure is reviewed in Bk. X, together with a return to the topic of happiness.

[230] At 1108a 26-28, Aristotle gave the name friendship, or friendliness, to a minor virtue related to deciding when to go along with the crowd for pleasant social occasions. In his fuller discussion of this virtue in Bk. IV, Chap. 6, he says it really has no special name and merely resembles friendship. Here he means not that it is one particular virtue but that it is a state of character involving choice that must have some relation to virtue as a whole. The phenomena of friendship are so varied and extensive that this requires pro-longed examination. Friendship bears to virtue a relation somewhat similar to that of unrestraint to vice. Unrestraint differs in kind from vice (1150b 35-36), but is similar enough to be blamed as "a certain kind of vice" (1148a 2-3). The discussion of unrestraint in Bk. VII served as a review of the topic of vice, and brought it to greater clarity. The discussion of friendship in Bks. VIII and IX serves a similar purpose for virtue of character.

for rich people and those who rule and have power, there seems to be the greatest need for friends. For what benefit would there be from such abundance if one were deprived of the opportunity to do favors, which arises most of all and in the most praiseworthy way toward friends?
10   And how could it be watched over and kept safe without friends? For the greater it is, the shakier its foundation is. And in both poverty and other misfortunes people believe that friends are the only refuge. And they believe that friends are helps to the young for avoiding error and to the old for caring for them and for action in which they fall short on account of weakness, and to those at their peak for beautiful actions "when two go together,"[231] since they are more capable of thinking and acting.

And friendship seems to be present by nature in a parent for a child and in a child for a parent, not only in human beings but also in birds and most animals, and for animals alike in kind toward one another, and
20   especially among human beings, which is why we praise those who are friends of humanity. And one might see among those who travel that every human being is akin and a friend to a human being. And friendship seems to hold cities together, and lawmakers seem to take it more seriously than justice, for like-mindedness seems to be something similar to friendship, and they aim at this most of all and banish faction most of all for being hostile to it. And when people are friends there is no need of justice, but when they are just there is still need of friendship, and among things that are just, what inclines toward friendship seems to be most just of all.[232] And friendship is not only necessary but also beautiful,
30   for we praise those who love their friends, and an abundance of friends seems to be one of the beautiful things. Moreover, people believe that it is the same people who are good men and friends.

But there is dispute about it on no small matters. For some people set it down that it is a certain kind of likeness and that those who are alike are friends. Hence people say "like to like" and "birds of a feather"
1155b   and that sort of thing.[233] Others, on the contrary, say that all such people

---

[231]   The quotation is from X, 224 of the *Iliad*, where it precedes one of the ugliest actions in the poem, but it had apparently become a proverb independent of its original context. See, for example, Plato's *Symposium*, 174D.

[232]   This is perhaps related to what Aristotle says in Bk. V, Chap. 10 about decency. There the emphasis is on the fact that justice must be universal, and decency ought to govern its application to particular situations. This whole paragraph serves to show that friendship is the fully developed virtue of character which supersedes justice. Friendship is more natural than justice, holds together the complete life of cities and not merely communities of commercial exchange (compare 1132b 31-1133a 5), is sufficient by itself to ends to which justice is necessary but not sufficient, and, like virtue of character in general, but unlike justice, achieves something beautiful. See the note to 1133b 33.

[233]   The first quotation is from XVII, 218 of the *Odyssey*. The second (literally "jackdaw to jackdaw") may possibly be from Epicharmus.

are "potters" in relation to each other. And they look for a higher and more natural reason for these same things, Euripides saying "earth is in love with rain" when it is dried out, and "solemn heaven filled with rain loves to fall to earth," and Heracleitus that "what is opposed holds together, and the most beautiful harmony comes from things that pull apart" and "all things come about by strife," while others, including Empedocles, are on the opposite side, for he says that like seeks its like.[234] But let those things in the impasses that have to do with nature be set aside (since they are not at home in the present inquiry), and let us examine all those that have to do with human things and pertain   10 to character and feelings, such as whether friendship comes about in all people, or whether it is impossible for people who are vicious to be friends, and whether there is one or more than one species of friendship. For those who believe that it is one, because it admits of more and less, are convinced by an indication that is not sufficient, since even things that differ in species are capable of being related as more and less; but this has been discussed before.[235]

Chapter 2. Perhaps the things that have to do with this might become clear if what is loveable is discerned, for it seems that not everything is loved, but only what is loveable, and that this is what is good or pleasant or useful; and what is useful would seem to be that   20 by means of which something good or a pleasure comes about, so that the good and the pleasant would be the things loved as ends.[236]

---

[234] The potters are from Hesiod's *Works and Days* (25-6: "potter has a grudge against potter, carpenter against carpenter, beggar against beggar, and singer against singer") and the lines of Euripides are from an unknown play. In the Diels numbering, the Heracleitus fragments are 8 and 80, and the reference to Empedocles is related to 22 and 109.

[235] The use of the word "species" makes clear what answer is implied, since those species themselves may be distinguished by being more and less of something within a genus. Burnet points to the discussion, in Chap. 6 of *On Sense Perception and Perceptible Things*, of sounds and colors that differ by imperceptible degrees but are grouped into species by our perception. There is no explicit discussion of this in the *Nicomachean Ethics*, but Aristotle may be referring to the numerous instances in which feelings or actions that are excessive or deficient determine states of character that differ in kind. It will turn out, in Chap. 4 below, that the species of friendship are even more distantly related.

[236] This passage parallels the distinction of the objects of choice as threefold (1104b 30-31), with one of the three subordinate to the other two (1110b 9-11); the remaining two, the beautiful and the pleasant, would need to merge to fulfill one of the criteria for happiness (1099a 24-31). Here the things distinguished are generalized objects of the sort of love that accompanies friendship. What appeared in the earlier distinction as the beautiful thing one might choose apart from considerations of pleasure, is replaced here by the thing that is loved as good apart from considerations of pleasure. Since love of the good is a thoughtful state of feeling, and choice of the beautiful is a deliberate thinking infused with desire, another kind of merging becomes possible.

But do people love the good, or what is good for themselves? For sometimes these are discordant; and it is similar with what is pleasant. And it seems that each person loves what is good for himself, and that, while the good is loveable simply, the good for each is loveable to each. And each person loves not what is good for himself, but what appears to be, but this will make no difference, since it will be what appears loveable.

But while there are three things on account of which people love, it is not friendship that is meant in the case of loving inanimate things, since there is no loving in return, or wishing for the good of that thing. (For it would no doubt be ridiculous to wish for good things for wine, but if one wishes anything, it is that it be preserved in order that one may have it.) But people say that one ought to wish for good things for a friend for his own sake. However, they call people goodwilled who wish for good things in that way when the same thing does not come from the other person, since they speak of goodwill in people who reciprocate it as being friendship. Or must one add, when they are not unaware of it? For many people are goodwilled toward those they have not seen, but believe to be decent or useful, and one of the latter might feel this same way toward the former. These people, then, are obviously goodwilled to one another, but how could one say they were friends when they are unaware of how they stand toward each other? Therefore it is necessary to have goodwill and wish for good things for one another, not being unaware of it, on account of some one of the reasons mentioned.

Chapter 3. But these reasons differ from one another in species, and therefore the kinds of loving and the kinds of friendship do too. So there are three species of friendship, equal in number to the kinds of things that are loved; for in accordance with each, there is a reciprocal loving which one is not unaware of, and those who love one another wish for good things for one another in the same sense in which they love. So those who love one another for what is useful do not love one another for themselves, but insofar as something good comes to them from one another. And it is similar with those who love on account of pleasure, since they are fond of charming people not for being people of a certain sort, but because they are pleasing to themselves. So those who love for what is useful have a liking based on what is good for themselves, and those who love for pleasure have a liking based on what is pleasant to themselves, and the other person is loved not for what he is, but insofar as he is useful or pleasant. Therefore, these are friendships of an incidental kind, since it is not insofar as the one loved is the very person he is that he is loved, but insofar as he provides, in the one case, something good, or in the other case, pleasure. Hence, such friendships are easily dissolved, when the people themselves do not stay the way they were, for when the others are no longer pleasant or useful they stop loving them. And what is useful does not stay the same, but becomes something different at a different time. So when that through which they were friends has departed, the friendship is dissolved, since the friendship was a consequence of that.

The sort of friendship that is for the useful seems to come about especially in the old (for those who are at such a time of life pursue not what is pleasant but what is beneficial), and in as many of those at their peak and of the young as pursue what is advantageous. Such people are not very likely to live together with one another, for sometimes they are not even pleasant to one another; so they have no additional need of such an association when the other person is not beneficial, since the other person is pleasant just so far as they have hopes of something   30 good from him. And it is among these friendships that people place those with foreign guests. But the friendship of the young seems to be based on pleasure, since they live in accord with feeling, and pursue especially what is pleasant to themselves and present at hand; but when the time of life falls differently, the pleasures too become different. Hence they quickly become friends and quickly stop, since the friend-ship changes at the same time as what is pleasant, and the turnover   1156b of this sort of pleasure is rapid. The young are also lustful, since the greater part of sexual love results from passion and is based on pleasure; this is why they love and stop loving quickly, often changing within the same day. And the young do wish to pass the time together and to live with one another, since what they get out of friendship comes about in that way.

But the complete sort of friendship is that between people who are good and are alike in virtue, since they wish for good things for one another in the same way insofar as they are good, and they are good in themselves. And those who wish for good things for their friends   10 for their own sake are friends most of all, since they are that way for themselves and not incidentally; so the friendship of these people lasts as long as they are good, and virtue is enduring. And each of them is good simply and good for his friend, since good people are both good simply and beneficial to one another. And they are similarly pleasant, since the good are pleasant both simply and to one another, for to each person, actions that are his own and such as his own are according to his pleasure, while the actions of the good are the same or similar. And it is reasonable that such friendship is lasting, for all those things that ought to belong to friends are joined together in it. For every friend-ship is for something good or for pleasure, either simply or for the   20 one who loves, and is from some sort of similarity, and in this sort all the things mentioned are present on account of themselves, since in this sort the people are alike, and all the rest of it; and what is good simply is also pleasant simply, and these things most of all are loved, and so the loving and the friendship among these people is the most intense and best.

But such friendships are likely to be rare, for such people are few.[237] Also, there is an additional need of time and intimate acquaintance, for according to the common saying, it is not possible for people to know one another until they use up the proverbial amount of salt together, and so it is not possible for them to accept one another before that, or to be friends until each shows himself to each as loveable and is trusted. Those who quickly make gestures of friendship toward one another want to be friends, but are not unless they are also loveable and know this, since wishing for friendship comes about as something quick, but friendship does not.

Chapter 4. This sort of friendship, then, is complete both in time and in the other respects, and in all of them, the same or similar things come to each person from the other, which is just what ought to belong to friends. And friendship on account of what is pleasant has a resemblance to this sort, since the good are also pleasant to one another. And it is similar with friendship on account of what is useful, since the good are that way to one another also. And the friendships between those [who seek pleasure or use] are most enduring when the same thing comes to them from one another, such as pleasure, and not only that but also from the same thing, such as between charming people, and not as with a lover and a beloved. For the latter do not take pleasure in the same things, but the lover in looking at the beloved, and the beloved in being paid attention to by the lover. And sometimes, when the bloom of youth fades, the friendship cools (since to the one the sight is not pleasing, and to the other the attentiveness is not forthcoming). On the other hand, many lovers remain friends, if, as a result of their intimacy, they become fond of each other's characters, when these are alike. But people who are involved in sexual relations not in exchange for something pleasant but for something useful are friends less fully and remain so less.

Those who are friends on account of something useful break up at the same time the advantage comes to an end, since they were friends not of one another but of what they got out of one another. So it is possible even for base sorts of people to be friends to one another for pleasure or for use, and for decent people to be friends to base ones, and for people who are neither one nor the other to be friends to any

---

[237]   At 1050a 15, Aristotle said that most people fall in between self-restraint and unrestraint, which implies all the more that most of us have neither virtue nor vice. But since this fullest kind of friendship is said to be present between people "insofar as they are good" (1156b 8-9), the capacity for genuine friendship becomes a measure of one's closeness to good character in general. Hence friendship turns out to reveal human goodness from a different aspect than virtue does, and in a certain way more fully.

sort whatever, but it is clear that only the good can be friends for themselves, since the bad do not enjoy their own kind unless some benefit   20
comes from them. And only the friendship of the good is resistant to slander, since it is not easy to be persuaded by anyone about someone whose character has been proved by oneself over a long time; between these people there is a trusting, and a never doing each other wrong, and everything else people consider worthy of friendship in its true sense. But in the other friendships, nothing prevents such trouble from being stirred up.

Since people use the word "friends" for those who are allied on account of what is useful, just as with cities (for alliances between cities seem to come about for the sake of advantage), and for those who are fond of one another on account of pleasure, just as with children, perhaps it is necessary that we too call such people friends, but say   30
there is more than one species of friendship, and that, while friendship in the primary and governing sense is between the good insofar as they are good, the remaining kinds are friendships only by a likeness, since the people are friends only in that respect in which there is something good and some likeness in them; for even the pleasant is good for people devoted to pleasure. But these other kinds are not very apt to be joined together, and the same people do not become friends on account of use as on account of pleasure, since, on the whole, incidental things are not linked up. And since friendship is divided into   1157b
these species, people of a low sort will be friends for pleasure or use, since they are alike in that respect, while the good will be friends for themselves, since they are friends insofar as they are good. The latter, then, are friends simply, but the former are friends incidentally and by resembling the latter.

Chapter 5. And just as in the case of the virtues, people are called good either with respect to an active condition or with respect to being at work, so too is it with friendship. For those who live together take pleasure in one another and provide good things for one another, while others, when sleeping or when in separate places, are not at work at it but still are in such a condition as to be at work in the manner of   10
friends. For places do not dissolve friendship as such, but only the being-at-work of it; but if the absence becomes long-lasting, it seems to cause forgetfulness of the friendship, which is why it is said that "lack of communication breaks up many friendships." And neither old people nor those with sour dispositions appear to be friendly, since the extent of pleasure is small in them, and no one is able to spend much time with what is painful or not pleasing; for nature appears to avoid what is painful most of all, and to aim at what is pleasant. But those who approve of one another but do not live together seem to be goodwilled rather than friends, since nothing is so characteristic of friends as living together; for those in need crave benefits, while those who are blessed   20

crave daily companionship, since it belongs to them least of all to be solitary. But it is impossible for people to spend time together who are not pleasing to one another, or who do not enjoy the same things, which is what a fraternal association[238] seems to involve. Friendship, then, belongs most of all to good people, as has been said repeatedly; for it seems that what is loveable and preferable is what is simply good or pleasant, while what is loved and preferred by each person is what is good or pleasing to that person, and to a good person, a good person is that way on both counts.

30   Affection seems like a feeling, but friendship seems like an active condition, for affection is no less present for inanimate things, but loving in return involves choice, and choice comes from an active condition. And people wish for good things for those they love for those others' own sake, not as a result of feeling but as a result of an active condition. And by loving the friend, they love what is good for themselves, for when a good person becomes a friend, he becomes good for the one to whom he is a friend. So each of them loves what is good for himself, and also gives back an equal amount in return in wishing as well as in what is pleasant; for it is said that "friendship

1158a   is equal relationship," and this belongs most of all to the friendship of the good.

Chapter 6. Friendship arises less among people of sour disposition and among those who are older, to the extent that they are harder to get along with and take less pleasure in company, since these things seem to pertain most to friends and to be most conducive to friendship. Hence, while the young become friends quickly, the old do not, since people do not become friends with those whom they do not enjoy, and it is similar with those of a sour disposition. Such people are still goodwilled to one another, since they wish for good things and present themselves on occasions of need, but they are not quite friends on account of not

10   spending their days together or enjoying one another, which seem to be the things most characteristic of friends.

To be a friend to many people in the complete kind of friendship is not possible, just as it is impossible to be in love with many people at the same time (for this seems like an extreme condition, of such a nature as to come about toward one person); and for the same person to find many people greatly pleasing at the same time is not easy, and it is perhaps not easy even for there to be many good people to

---

238   In Athens, at the time of the Peloponnesian War, these groups of rich young "comrades" were political parties. They participated in the oligarchic governments called the Four Hundred and the Thirty Tyrants, and one of the parties was suspected of an act of sacrilegious vandalism at the beginning of the Sicilian expedition. In Aristotle's time they were banned from political activity, but continued to exist as social clubs or fraternities.

be pleased by. And it is necessary to get experience and to come into intimate acquaintance with each other, which is of the utmost difficulty. But it is possible to be pleased by many people for usefulness and pleasure, since there are many people of those sorts, and their services are provided in a short time. Of these sorts, the one that is for pleasure seems more like friendship, whenever the same things come from both people, and they enjoy one another or enjoy the same things,   20
which is the sort of friendship that belongs to the young, since there is more generosity in these, while friendship for use is characteristic of vulgarly commercial people. And while those who are blessed have no need of useful people, they do need pleasant ones, since they want to live together with some people, and while people put up with what is painful for a short time, no one would continually endure it, not even the good itself if it were painful to him; that is why they look for pleasant friends.

Perhaps they ought to look for such people as are also good, and furthermore good for themselves, since in that way they would have all the things that are required in friends. But those who are in positions of power seem to make use of friends whom they keep divided, since some people are useful to them and others are pleasant, but not very often are the same people both. For they are not looking for people who   30
are pleasant because of virtue, or for people who are useful for beautiful deeds, but for charming people when they are aiming at pleasure, and for clever people to do what they order, and these attributes do not very often occur in the same people. It has been said that a person of serious stature is pleasing and useful at the same time, but such a person does not become a friend to a superior unless he is also superior in virtue; otherwise he cannot make things equal by being proportionally excelled.[239] But it is hardly customary for such people to turn up [in positions of power].

Now the friendships that have been discussed consist in an equal-   1158b
ity, since the same things come from both people and they wish for the same things for one another, or they exchange one thing for another, such as pleasure for benefit, and it was said that the latter sort are friendships to a lesser degree and are less enduring. They even seem, on account of likeness and unlikeness to the same thing, both to be and not to be friendships, for they appear to be friendships by likeness

---

[239]   In the context of distributive justice, in Bk. V, Chap. 3, proportionate equality simply meant that each was given what each deserved. How this translates into a friendship is not made clear until the following chapter. At first glance it might appear that opposite kinds of superiority would restore equality, and that two kinds of superiority on the same side would make the inequality worse. But the question is whether one can be friends with someone to whom one owes gratitude, but for whom one can have no respect.

to that which comes from virtue (since the one involves something pleasant and the other involves something useful, and these belong to that also), but in that friendship that comes from virtue is resistant to slander and lasting, while these quickly change, and differ in many other ways, they seem not to be friendships, by their unlikeness to that.

Chapter 7. But there is a different form of friendship that goes along with superiority, as of a father for a son, or generally of an older person for a younger, as well as of a husband for a wife or of any ruler for one who is ruled. And these also differ one from another, since the friendship of parents for children is not the same as that of rulers for those who are ruled, nor that of a father for a son as that of a son for a father, nor that of a husband for a wife as that of a wife for a husband. For a different virtue and a different work belongs to each of these, and the things on account of which they love are also different; so their affections and friendships are different too. And so, the same things do not come to each person from the other, nor should they look for the same things; but whenever children give parents what one ought to give those who have brought one into being, and parents give children what one ought to give one's offspring, the friendship of that sort of people will be lasting and decent. And in all the friendships that go along with superiority, the affection also ought to become proportional, that is, the better one, or the one conferring a greater benefit, ought to be loved more than he loves, and similarly in each of the other cases. For whenever the affection comes to be in accord with what is deserved, there comes to be a certain kind of equality, which seems to belong to friendship.

But what is equal in matters of justice does not seem to work the same way as what is equal in friendship, for in matters of justice, the equal is primarily what is in accord with what is deserved, and secondarily what is equal in amount, but in friendship it is primarily in accord with amount, and secondarily in accord with what is deserved. And this is clear if the divergence becomes great in virtue or in vice or in affluence or in anything else; for no longer are they friends, nor do they think they deserve to be. This is most manifest in the case of the gods, since they have the greatest superiority in all good things, but it is evident also in the case of kings, since those who are far inferior do not even think they deserve to be friends with them, nor do those who are worth nothing think they deserve to be friends with those who are best or wisest. In such cases there is no precise boundary up to which they are friends, for when many things have been taken away the friendship still remains, but when they are separated greatly, as from a god, it no longer does.

From this an impasse is raised, that perhaps friends do not wish for the greatest of goods for their friends, such as that they be gods; for then they would no longer have friends, and so there would be good things they do not have, since friends are good things. So if it was beautifully said that a friend wishes for good things for a friend for that friend's 10 own sake, that friend would need to remain whatever he is; thus one would wish for the greatest goods for someone who is still a human being. And perhaps not for all of these, since each person wishes for good things most of all for himself.

Chapter 8. Most people seem, on account of a passion for honor, to want to be loved more than to love. Hence most people are fond of flatterers, since a flatterer is a friend who is in an inferior position, or pretends to be that way, and to love more than he is loved; but being loved seems close to being honored, which most people aim at. But they do not appear to prefer honor for its own sake, but as something incidental, since most people delight in being honored by those in positions of power, on account of hope (for they believe they will get 20 something from these people if they lack anything, and delight in their honor as a sign that they will be well off). But those who crave honor from decent people who know them aim to confirm their own opinion about themselves; so they delight in honor, trusting in the judgment of those who say that they are good. Being loved, however, people enjoy for its own sake, and for this reason it would seem that it is something better than being honored, and that friendship is choiceworthy for its own sake.[240]

But friendship seems to be present in loving more than in being loved. A sign of this is that mothers delight in loving, for some of them give up their own children to be brought up, and feel love just in knowing them, not seeking to be loved in return if both are not pos- 30 sible; it seems to be sufficient for them if they see their children doing well, and they love them even if the children, in their ignorance, give back nothing of what is due to a mother. And since friendship is present more in loving, and those who love their friends are praised, the virtue belonging to friends seems to be loving,[241] so that those between whom this takes place in accord with worth are lasting friends, and 1159b their friendship is lasting.

---

[240] This result is a dialectical step beyond the conclusion at 1123b 20-21 that honor is the greatest of external goods. There, the evidence came from asking what we think is the greatest thing we have to give; here, what is asked, in effect, is what we treat as the greatest thing we can receive. The paragraph ascends from love as a reflection of honor that promises benefits, to honor proper, that confirms self-esteem, to being loved as an end in itself.

[241] It is not surprising that virtue is found on the active side of friendship, rather than the passive, but this result seems to be in conflict with the last observation in the preceding chapter. The sustained exploration of friendship leads eventually to the whole question of selfishness and selflessness in Bk. IX, Chap. 8.

And it is especially in this way that those who are unequal might be friends, since it could equalize them. Equality or similarity is friendship, and especially the similarity that comes from virtue, since such people are constant in themselves and stay constant toward one another; they have no use for anything base, and do not lend assistance to such things, and they even, in a manner of speaking, prevent them, since it does not belong to the good either to go astray themselves or to permit their friends to do so. But vice-ridden people have nothing stable about them, since they do not even remain similar to themselves, though they
10 become friends for a short time, while they take pleasure in one another's vices. Useful or pleasant people stay friends longer, for as long as they provide pleasures or benefits to one another.

And friendship for use seems to come about most of all between opposites, such as in someone poor for someone rich, or in someone ignorant for someone with knowledge, since the one will give something else in return, aiming at that which he happens to lack. One might pull a lover and beloved, or a beautiful and an ugly person, over into this group. And this is why lovers sometimes appear ridiculous, believing themselves worthy of being loved in the way they love; those who are similarly loveable ought perhaps to believe that, but those who have nothing of the sort about them are comical. But perhaps one opposite
20 does not desire the other for its own sake, but only incidentally, and the appetite is for the mean; this is what is good—for instance, for something dry not to become wet but to reach the mean, and similarly with something hot and with other things. But let these things be set aside, since they are too far outside the subject.

Chapter 9. Now it seems, as was said at the beginning,[242] that friendship and justice concern the same things and are present in the same things; for in every sort of community there seems to be something just, and also friendship. At any rate, people address their shipmates and fellow soldiers as friends, and it is similar with those
30 in other sorts of communities. To whatever extent that they share something in common, to that extent is there a friendship, since that too is the extent to which there is something just. And the proverb "the things of friends are common" is right, since friendship consists in community. All things are common to brothers and comrades, but certain definite things to other friends, more to some and less to others, since among the friendships too, some are friendships to a greater degree and others to a lesser. And the things that are just also vary,
1160a for they are not the same for parents toward children as for brothers toward one another, nor are they the same for comrades as for fellow citizens, and similarly in other sorts of friendship. So the things that are unjust are also different for each of these, and get increased by being

---

[242] At the beginning of Bk. VIII, at 1155a 22-28.

related to those who are more fully friends; for example, it is more terrible to cheat a comrade out of money than a fellow citizen, or to refrain from helping a brother rather than a stranger, or to hit a father rather than anyone else. And it is natural for what is just to increase along with friendship, since they are present in the same things and have an equal extent.

But all communities are like parts of the political community, for people come together for some advantage, and to provide for something   10
that contributes to life, and the political community seems to gather together from the beginning, and to remain together, for the sake of what is advantageous. The lawmakers aim at this, and people call the common advantage just. So the other communities aim at what is advantageous in a partial way; for example, sailors aim at what results from a voyage for making money, or something of that sort, and fellow soldiers aim at what results from warfare, grasping at money or victory or a city, and similarly with those who belong to a tribe or a district. But some communities, of people who celebrate festivals or subscribe to dining clubs, seem to come about for pleasure, since they are for   20
the sake of sacrifices or parties. But all of these appear to be under the political community, since the political community aims not at a present advantage but one that extends to all of life. But those who make sacrifices and congregations for these do so both to pay honor to the gods and to provide themselves with relaxations that involve pleasure. For the ancient sacrifices and congregations seem to have come about after the gathering of crops, as for the first fruits, since it was especially on these occasions that they had leisure. So all communities seem to be parts of the political community, and friendships of such kinds will go along with communities of such kinds.   30

Chapter 10. And there are three forms of constitutions, and also an equal number of deviations, as corruptions of these. The constitutions are kingship and aristocracy, and a third kind based on property assessments, which it seems appropriate to call timocratic, though most people are accustomed to call it constitutional rule.[243] Kingship is the

---

[243] A constitution is "the ordering of a city, of its other ruling offices and especially of the one that is in authority over them all." (*Politics* 1278b 8-10) An example of the third sort is Solon's constitution of Athens, in which the qualifications for various offices were determined by ownership of cultivated land, of a team of working animals, or of a horse; the fourth, propertyless class held no offices but served as the juries which constituted the whole of the judiciary (1273b 35-1274a 21). Since the exact apportioning of responsibilities in such a government had to be spelled out in an explicit constitution, it got the name of constitutional rule. Aristotle suggests the word "timocratic" because *timê* can mean both office and monetary value, but its root meaning is honor; in Plato's *Republic* timocracy is the name used for a regime governed entirely by considerations of honor (545B).

1160b best of these, and timocracy the worst. The deviation from kingship is tyranny, since both are monarchies, but they differ to the greatest extent, since a tyrant looks to his own advantage, while a king looks to that of those who are ruled. For someone who is not self-sufficient and superior in all goods is not a king, and such a person has no need of anything in addition, so he would look to things beneficial not to himself but to those who are ruled; one who is not of this sort would be a sort of king chosen by lot.[244] Tyranny is opposite to this, since the tyrant pursues what is good for himself. And it is more apparent in this case that it is the worst; the opposite of the best is the worst.

10   The change from kingship is into tyranny, since tyranny is baseness of a monarchy, and a vicious king becomes a tyrant. The change from aristocracy is into oligarchy by vice in the rulers, who distribute the things that belong to the city contrary to what is deserved, and all or most of its goods to themselves, and the ruling offices always to the same people, making being rich count for most; so few people rule, and bad ones instead of the most decent. The change from timocracy is into democracy, since they have a common boundary; for timocracy is meant to be rule of a multitude of people, and all those within the
20 property qualification are equal. The least bad of these is democracy, since it deviates to a small extent from the form of constitutional rule. Constitutions, then, most often change in this way, since this is the way they change the smallest amount and the most easily.

One may find likenesses of them, and patterns of a sort, in households. For the relationship of a father to sons has the shape of kingship, since the father's care is for his children; hence Homer's Zeus is addressed as father, for kingship is meant to be fatherly rule. Among the Persians, the rule of the father is tyrannical, since they treat their sons as slaves. The rule of a master over slaves is also tyrannical, since
30 it is the advantage of the master that is active in it. But while this seems right, the Persian way is clearly wrong, for rule over different people is of a different kind. The relationship of a husband to a wife seems aristocratic, since the man rules as a result of worthiness, and over those things which a man ought to rule; as many things as are suited to a woman, he turns over to her. If the husband is in charge of everything, he changes the relationship into an oligarchy, since he does it contrary
1161a to worthiness, and not insofar as he is better suited.[245] Sometimes wives rule, when they are heiresses, but their rule does not come from virtue,

---

[244] Athens had a group of nine ruling officials called archons, from whom one was chosen by lot each year to preside over sacrifices and certain other functions traditionally belonging to kings.

[245] The distribution of authority in a marriage makes it resemble constitutional rule, as Aristotle says in the *Politics* (1259b 1), though of a kind that itself tends to be mis-named as aristocracy (1293b 34-38).

but from wealth and power, just as in oligarchies. The relationship of brothers seems timocratic, for they are equal, except to the extent that they differ in age; for this reason, when they differ greatly in age their friendship is no longer of a brotherly sort. And democracy is present most of all in households without masters (since there everyone is equal), and in those in which the one who rules is weak, and there is license for everyone.

Chapter 11. In each form of constitution friendship shows itself, to   10
the extent that justice does. In a king toward his subjects this is present in a superiority in conferring benefits, since he does good for those over whom he is king, if he is good and pays attention to them, in order for them to do well, like a herdsman with sheep; hence Homer calls Agamemnon the shepherd of the people. Fatherly friendship is also of this sort, but differs in the magnitude of the benefits done, since he is responsible for one's being, which seems greatest, as well as for nurture and education. And these things are also attributed to one's forefathers. And a father is by nature suited to rule sons, and forefathers their descendants, and a king his subjects. These friendships consist in   20
superiority, which is why parents are also honored. So what is just among these people is not the same but is in accord with worth, and so too is the friendship. The friendship of a husband for a wife is the same as in an aristocracy, since it is in accord with virtue, with the greater good going to the better person, and what is fitting going to each; and so too with what is just. The friendship of brothers is like that in a fraternal association,[246] since they are equals and of similar age, and such people are, for the most part, alike in feelings and in character. The friendship that results from timocratic rule seems like this, since the citizens are meant to be equal and to be decent, so that the ruling is done in parts and equally, and so the friendship is that way too.   30

In the deviant constitutions, in the same way that what is just is of small extent, so too is the friendship; and it is least in the worst, since in a tyranny there is little or no friendship. For in those situations in which there is nothing shared by the ruler and the ruled, there is no friendship, since there is no justice either, as in a craftsman in relation to a tool or in a soul in relation to a body or in a master in relation to a slave; while all these things are helped by those who use them, there   1161b
is no friendship toward things without souls, nor anything just. And neither is there toward a horse or a cow, nor toward a slave as a slave. For there is nothing in common, since the slave is an ensouled tool, as a tool is a soulless slave. Insofar, then, as he is a slave, there is no friendship toward him, though there is insofar as he is a human being, for there seems to be something just for every human being toward all those who are capable of sharing in law and contractual agreement,

---

246   See the note to 1157b 23.

and so there is friendship too, to the extent he is a human being.[247] So
friendships and justice are of small extent in tyrannies, but in democra-
10   cies they are of greater extent, since many things are common to people
who are equal.

Chapter 12. Every sort of friendship, then, is in a community,[248] as
was said, though one might separate out that of relatives or in a fraternal
association; but those of fellow citizens or tribesmen or shipmates, and
all those of that sort, seem more like communities, since they seem as
if they result from a certain kind of agreement, and one might rank a
friendship with a foreign guest among these.

Friendship between relatives seems to be of many forms, but they
are all derived from the paternal kind, for parents love their children
as being something that is part of themselves, and children love their
20   parents as being something from which they come. But parents know
what comes from them more than their offspring know that they are
from these parents, and the source feels what it begets as its own more
than the offspring feels the one who produces it; for what comes from
itself is the source's own, as is a tooth or hair or anything else to the one
who has it, but to that, its source is nothing of its own, or only less so.
And parents love more in length of time, since they love their children
as soon as they come into being, but children love their parents after
some time has gone by, when they get understanding or perception. And
from these things it is clear why mothers have greater love.

Parents, then, love children as themselves (for things that come
from themselves, by being separated, are a sort of other selves), while
30   children love their parents as being by nature from them; and brothers
love one another by being by nature from the same parents, since their
sameness with them produces a sameness with one another, for which
reason people speak of the same blood or root and such. So they are in a
certain way the same, in separate selves. And common upbringing and
what goes with similarity of age contribute a great amount to friendship, since it is "age mate with age mate"[249]; and those who are alike in
character are comrades, which is why brotherly friendship resembles
1162a   that of a fraternal association. Cousins and other relatives are bound

---

247   If the slavery rests on force and custom alone, it is wholly unjust and disadvantageous on both sides, but if it has a natural basis there is a friendship
like that of parent and child. (See *Politics* 1255b 12-15 and 1260b 5-7, and note
to 1134b 10 above.)

248   In fact, what was said at 1159b 26-27 was that every sort of community gives
rise to friendship, and at 1160b 22-24, it was added that all these are patterned
after relationships within the household. The kinds of love within the family,
though they bear the same name as friendship (*philia*), and are its ultimate
patterns, are more deeply rooted, and are given a separate discussion in this
chapter.

249   "Age mate gladdens age mate" is quoted as an old saying in Plato's *Phaedrus*,
240C.

together from these causes, since it results from their being descended from the same people. Some are more kin, others more alien, according as the original ancestor is near or far.

And there is a friendship in children for their parents, as in human beings for gods, for something good and superior, since parents have done the greatest good for them; for they are responsible for their being and being raised, and for the being educated of those who become so. And such a friendship has more that is pleasant and useful in it than one between unrelated people, to the extent that life is shared more in common between them. And there are present in brotherly friend- 10 ship the same things as in a fraternal association, and more so among decent people, and generally in those who are alike, to the extent that they are more kin and have already loved one another from birth, and to the extent that those who are from the same parents, and raised and educated alike, are more alike in character, and their testing over time is the most thorough and most certain. The things conducive to friendship are in proportion in the other relatives.

The friendship of a husband and a wife seems to be present by nature, since a human being is by nature disposed to pair off even more than to form a political association, to the extent that a household is prior to and more necessary than a city, and the production of offspring is more common among animals. Among the other animals, then, the 20 community goes that far, but human beings dwell together not only for the sake of producing offspring, but also for the things that go into life, since the work is divided from the start, and is different for a man and for a woman, so that they help one another by placing each's own work into the common supply. For these reasons, there seems to be both use and pleasure in this friendship, and it would be a friendship for virtue as well, if the people are decent, for there is a virtue belonging to each, and each would take delight in such a mate. And children seem to be a bond, which is why couples without children break up more quickly, since children are a good shared by both, and what is shared holds things together. How a husband ought to conduct his life in relation to 30 his wife, and in general a friend in relation to a friend, seems to be no different a thing to look for from how it is just, since what is just does not seem to be the same for a friend in relation to a friend as in relation to a stranger, or a comrade, or someone he goes to school with.

Chapter 13. Since there are three kinds of friendship, as was said at the start, and in each kind there are some who are friends in equality and others in accord with superiority (since people who are similarly good become friends, or a better person with a worse, and likewise with 1162b people who are pleasant or who are friends for use, who are equal or differ in their benefits), the ones who are equal ought, in accord with their equality, to be equal in loving and all the rest, while those who are unequal ought to give what is proportional to the superiority.

And complaints and reproaches arise only, or most of all, in friendship for use, as is reasonable. For those who are friends on account of virtue are eager to do good to one another (since this belongs to virtue and to friendship), and since they are in competition in this way, there are no complaints or fights, for no one scorns someone who loves him

10   and does good for him, but if he is gracious, defends himself by doing good. And the one who outdoes the other in this would not complain to his friend, since he hits what he aims at, for each of them is stretching out toward something good. Nor does this happen very much between those who are friends for pleasure, since what they desire comes to both at the same time if they enjoy passing the time together; it would obviously be ridiculous for one of them to complain that the other doesn't please him, when he has it in his power not to spend his days with him. But friendship for use is full of complaints, since people who use one another for their benefit always want something more, and believe they have less than what is due, and make the reproach that the amount they get is not as much as they want, even

20   though they are entitled to it. Those who do the favors are not capable of supplying all the things the ones who get them want.

And it seems that, in the same way what is just has two sides, one unwritten and the other according to law, there are also two sides to friendship for use, one having to do with character, the other legalistic. Complaints arise, then, most of all when people break up the friendship on grounds that are not the same as those on which they entered into association. The legalistic kind rests on stated conditions, either of a completely commercial sort from handing over to handing back, or more generous about time, but similarly commercial about what is for what. In the latter sort, the benefit is clear and undisputed, but the postponement has something friendly about it, which is why, in some places, there can

30   be no lawsuits for these situations, but they believe that one must put up with the people one has agreed to associate with on trust. The kind that has to do with character is not on stated conditions, but as one gives to, or does anything else whatever for, a friend, but the giver considers that he deserves to get back something equal or greater, as though he had not given something but lent it, and he will complain if the way he began the association is not the same as the way it was dissolved.

This happens because all or most people want what is beautiful but choose what is beneficial, and while it is a beautiful thing to do good

1163a   not in order to be repaid in kind, it is beneficial to have something good done for one. So one who can ought to give back in return the value of what he received, and willingly, and what he would have agreed to give back if he could have.[250] (For one ought not to make someone a friend

---

[250]   The last phrase, from the comma, follows the long parenthesis; it is moved here for clarity and the translation adopts a slight editorial change suggested by Bywater.

who is unwilling. So when one has made a mistake in the beginning and accepted a favor from someone from whom he ought not have, since it was not from a friend or from someone doing it for its own sake, one ought to break off the relationship just as one who has received a benefit on stated conditions.) If he cannot do so, not even the giver would have considered it his due. So if it is possible, something ought to be given back, but one ought to consider at the beginning from whom one is accepting the favor and on what conditions, in order that one might submit to those conditions or not.

But it is a matter of dispute whether one ought to measure the favor   10
by the benefit to the one who receives it, and make the return according to that, or by the service of the one who does it. Those who receive favors say they got from their benefactors the sorts of things that were small to them and that it was possible to get from others, making them seem little, while back the other way, the others say they were the greatest things they had, which could not have come from anyone else, and which were given at a time of danger or some such need. But since it is a friendship for use, is the measure then the benefit to the one who gets it? For he is the one in need, and the other person supplies that need as a way to get back something equal to it; so the sort of aid that comes is the amount by which the former is benefited, and so he ought to give back as   20
much as was gained by him, or even more, since that is a more beautiful thing. But in friendships based on virtue there are no complaints, and the choice of the one who does the favor seems to be the measure, since what governs virtue and character is in the choice.

Chapter 14. There are also differences in friendships that involve superiority, since each person believes he deserves to have more, but when this happens the friendship is dissolved. For the better one thinks it appropriate for him to have more, since more is bestowed upon the good, and it is similar with someone who confers greater benefits, for these people say that someone who is not useful ought not to have an equal amount, since it becomes a charity and not a friendship if the things one gets from the friendship are not going to be in accord with   30
the worth of the work put in. For they assume that, just as, in a partnership for money, those who put in more get more, so too ought it to be in friendship. But with the one in need or the inferior one, it is the other way around; they take it to belong to a good friend to provide for those in need, for what, they ask, is the benefit of being a friend to a person of serious worth or power if one is not going to enjoy anything out of it?

Now it seems that each side is right in what it considers appropri-   1163b
ate, and that one ought to distribute more out of the friendship to each person, though not more of the same thing, but to the superior more honor and to the one in need more gain, since honor is the reward of virtue and of doing good for others, but gain is what is helpful for need.

And this is the way it seems to be in political constitutions, since the one who provides nothing good to the common supply is not honored, for what is held in common is given to the one who benefits the common good, and honor is something held in common. For it is not possible at the same time to be given money out of the common supply and to
10   be honored. For no one puts up with the lesser share in everything, so people allot honor to the one who is diminished in money, and money to the one who takes bribes; for what is in accord with worth equalizes and preserves friendship, as was said.[251]

So this is the way one ought to associate with unequals: the one who is given the benefit of money or virtue ought to give honor in return, giving back what he is capable of giving. For friendship seeks after what is possible, not what is deserved, since there is not even any such thing in all cases, as in the honors given to the gods and to parents; no one could ever give back what they deserve, and one who does them honor as far as possible seems to be a decent person. This is why it would not seem to be permissible for a son to renounce a father, but is permissible
20   for a father to renounce a son; for one ought to repay someone who has benefitted him, but there is nothing a son can do that is worthy of the things that have already been done for him, so that he always owes a debt. But it is permissible for those to whom a debt is owed to release it, and so this is permittted to a father. At the same time, perhaps, it would seem that no one would ever cut off a son who did not go to extremes in viciousness, for apart from the love that is natural, it is not a human sort of thing to reject assistance. But for a son who is vicious, providing assistance would be something avoided or not eagerly sought, since most people want to be treated well, but avoid doing that to others as something unprofitable. About these things, then, let the discussion go this far.

BOOK IX

Chapter 1. In all hybrid[252] friendships, what is proportional equalizes and preserves the friendship, as was said, just as, in the political

---

[251] See 1159a 33-b 2. The extreme case of a mother's selfless love for a child revealed that friendship lies in the act of loving or giving. That conclusion made it possible to look at any friendship from one side at a time, and thus to address cases in which the giving is unequal, extending finally all the way down to the opposite extreme of the most mercenary political arrangements.

[252] Literally "friendships not alike in kind [on the two sides]." Those considered in Bk. VIII were (a) between similar and equal people, (b) between similar and unequal people, and (c) between dissimilar people for different kinds of use or different kinds of pleasure; all were friendships within a single one of the three main varieties. Those taken up now involve mixtures across the kinds, such as friendships for use on one side and pleasure on the other. The

community, a return is made to a leatherworker for shoes according to their worth, as with a weaver and the rest. Here, then, the currency has been provided as a common measure, and all things are referred to it and measured by it. But in sexual relationships, sometimes a lover complains that, despite loving surpassingly, his love is not requited, even if it so happens that he has nothing loveable about him, and often the beloved complains that the lover who previously promised everything now fulfills none of it. Such things result whenever the one loves the beloved for pleasure, while the other loves the lover for something useful, and these are not both present. For when a friendship comes from these reasons, a break-up happens whenever those things for the sake of which they loved one another do not take place, since they were not fond of each other but of attributes that belonged to them and were not lasting, which is why the friendships too are of that sort. But a friendship that comes from their characters does last, since it is for itself, as was said.[253]

But there are differences whenever what comes to them is different and not what they sought, for whenever the thing one aims at is not what one gets, it is like getting nothing; it is like the person who promised to give the harpist more, the better he would sing, but at dawn, when the harpist asked to be paid, said he had already given what he promised in the form of pleasure in return for pleasure. If each of them had wanted that, it would have been sufficient, but if one wants enjoyment and the other wants gain, and the former gets it while the latter does not, the things that come from their relationship would not be well provided; for it is those things which one happens to need that one also expects, and for the sake of which he will give the things he does.

But to which of them does it belong to decide what is deserved, the one who is first to give or the one who is first to receive? For the one who is first to give seems to entrust it to the other person. This is just what people say Protagoras did, for when he taught anything whatever, he used to insist that the learner evaluate how much it seemed to be worth to know it, and used to take that much. But in such matters, it is "wages for a man's hire" that satisfy some people.[254] But people who get the money in advance and then do none of what they claimed because of the excessiveness of their promises, naturally come upon complaints,

1164a

10

20

30

principle applied is again taken from 1159a 33-b 2, where it was derived from considering the one-sided love of a mother separated from her child.
[253] At 1157a 10-12, where it was observed that people who fall in love for pleasure often, as a result of their intimacy, learn to love one another for what they are.
[254] From Hesiod, *Works and Days*, line 368. The story about Protagoras is in Plato's *Protagoras*, 328B-C, with the addition that the learner had to take an oath to the gods that he was paying what he thought right.

since they do not accomplish what they agreed to. No doubt the sophists are forced to do this, since no one would give any money for what they know.[255] And those who do not do what they get fees for are naturally subject to complaints.

But as for those among whom no agreement has been made for services rendered, it was said[256] that those who give freely to one another for their own sake are free of complaints (for friendship in accord with virtue is of this sort), and one ought to make a return in accord with one's choice (since this is characteristic of a friend as well as of virtue), and it seems to be this way too with those who have shared in philosophy, for its worth is not measured in money and no honor could be of equal weight with it, but perhaps it is enough, as with gods and one's parents, to give what is possible. But when the giving is not of this sort but for something, it is perhaps most appropriate for what is given in return to be what seems to both to be what is deserved, but if this does not happen, it would seem to be not only necessary for the one who is first to get something to make the decision, but also just; for one who gets back however much that one was benefited, or whatever the pleasure he got amounted to, will have the value that issues from this. For it seems to happen this way also with things bought and sold, and in some places there are laws that there can be no lawsuits for willing contractual agreements, since it is proper to dissolve relations with a person one has trusted in the same way one entered into partnership. For they believe that it is more just for the one to whom something has been entrusted to decide its value, than it is for the one who entrusted it to him to do so. For many things are not valued at the same amount by those who have them as by those who want to get them, since one's own things and the things one gives seem to each person to be worth a lot; however, the return comes about in accordance with the amount the recipients decide. But perhaps one ought to set the value not at how much it seems worth when he has it, but at how much he estimated it before having it.

Chapter 2. There is also an impasse over things such as whether one ought to turn over all matters to one's father and obey him in all things, or obey a doctor when one is sick and vote for someone skilled at war to be a general; similarly, ought one to assist a friend rather than someone of serious worth, and pay back someone who has done a favor or give to a comrade, if both are not possible? Or is it no easy thing to determine all such matters precisely? For they contain many differences of all sorts in magnitude and smallness, of both what is beautiful

---

[255] It was a standing joke in Plato's dialogues (e.g., *Gorgias*, 519C-D) that the sophists promised to teach virtue and then, having done so, complained that their students cheated them out of their fees.

[256] See 1162b 6-13 and 1163a 21-23.

and what is necessary. But it is not unclear that all things ought not to   30
be given over to the same person; for the most part, one ought return
favors rather than gratify comrades, just as one ought to pay back a loan
to the person to whom one owes the debt rather than give the money
to a comrade. But perhaps even this is not always so; for example, if
one has been ransomed from pirates, ought he to ransom his ransomer
in return, no matter who he might be, or if the ransomer has not been
captured, but demands his money, ought one to pay him back or [in   1165a
either case] ransom one's father?[257] For it would seem that one ought
to ransom one's father even in preference to oneself.

So while, as was said, one ought in general to pay back a debt, if an
act of giving exerts a stronger pull by means of its beauty or necessity,
one ought to incline toward these. For sometimes it is not even equitable
to return what was originally given, when someone would do a favor
for a person he knows to be seriously deserving, but the former, to
whom the return would be made, is someone the latter thinks is vicious.
Sometimes one ought not even make a loan in return to someone who
has lent money to him, if the latter made the loan to a decent person
believing he would be paid back, while the former could not hope to
be paid back by a corrupt person. So if the latter is truly of that sort,   10
his claim to a return is not equitable, while if he is not that way but
people think so, it would not seem out of place to assume it. So just as
has been said repeatedly, discourse concerning feelings and actions has
the definiteness that belongs to the things it is about.[258]

So it is not unclear that one ought not to give the same things in
return to all people, nor all things to one's father, just as one does
not make all sacrifices to Zeus; but since there are different things
for parents and brothers and comrades and those who have done
one favors, one ought to portion out what is appropriate and fitting to each. And people seem to do just that, for they invite their
relatives to weddings, since their family is shared with them and so   20
are the actions that have to do with this, and for this reason people
believe that relatives ought to meet at funerals especially. And as for
sustenance, there would seem to be a need to provide it for parents
especially, since one is in their debt, and it is a more beautiful thing

---

[257] Two cases that are both exceptions to the preceding rule are presented com-
pactly: (a) if one's ransomer and one's father are both captives, the necessity is
equal, and it is more beautiful to rescue one's father, but (b) if one's ransomer
deserves repayment but one's father is a captive, it is more necessary to rescue
the father than to repay the debt. And it is not to be concluded that these are
two new rules that replace an incorrect one; exceptions could be constructed
within them as well. It is judgment that decides where the stronger motive
lies, and character that determines the quality of one's judgment. (Compare
1113a 31-33.)

[258] See 1094b 19-27, 1098a 26-33, 1103b 34-1104a 11, 1112a 34-1112b 11, 1137b
13-24, 1159a 3-5.

to provide this to those who are responsible for one's being than to oneself. One ought to give honor to parents as to gods, but not all honor, since one ought not even to give the same honor to a father as to a mother--nor yet that which belongs to someone wise or that which belongs to a general--but one ought to give the honor suited to a father and similarly the honor suited to a mother. And honor is to be given to all one's elders on account of their age, by standing up and giving them a seat, and things of that sort. To brothers and comrades,

30   in turn, one ought to give frank speech and a sharing of all things. To relatives and distant family members and fellow citizens and all the rest, one ought to try always to apportion what is appropriate, and to take account of what belongs to each sort as a result of closeness as well as of virtue or usefulness. The judgment is easier among people related in the same way, and more troublesome among those of different kinds, but one certainly ought not to give it up on that account, but to determine it as well as possible.

Chapter 3. There is also an impasse about whether or not to dis-

1165b   solve friendships with people who do not remain the same. Or is there nothing strange about breaking off with those who are friends for use or pleasure when they no longer have these attributes? For they were friends of those things, and when they have left those things behind it is reasonable for them not to love. But someone might complain if, while loving him for use or pleasure, one pretended that it was for his character. For as we said in the beginning,[259] most differences between friends come about when they are not friends in the same way they think they are. So whenever someone has been mistaken, and assumed he was loved for his character, though the other person acted in no such

10   manner, he should blame himself, but when he has been deceived by the other person's pretense, it is just to complain about the one who deceived him, even more than about those who counterfeit the currency, to the degree that the wrongdoing has to do with something more valuable.

But if one has accepted someone as good, and he becomes or seems corrupt, should one still love him? Or is this not possible, if not everything is loveable, but only what is good? But what is bad is not loveable and one should not love it, for one ought not to be fond of vice or become like someone base, and it was said that like is a friend to like. Then should one break it off immediately? Or not in all cases, but with those who are incurable in vice? And one ought to help those who can be straightened out, more so with respect to character than

20   with wealth, to the extent that it is a better thing and belongs more to the special nature of friendship. But the one who breaks it off would

---

[259]   At the beginning of the discussion of the break-up of friendship, at 1162a 23-25.

not seem to be doing anything strange, since it was not to that sort of person that he was a friend; so when it is impossible to rescue someone who has changed, one withdraws from him.

But if one person stays the same while the other becomes more decent and differs greatly in virtue, should one treat the former as a friend? Or is this not possible? And this becomes especially clear in a great separation, as in people who were friends as children; for if the one remains a child in his thinking, while the other is a man such as the most powerful, how could they be friends when they are neither satisfied by the same things nor enjoy and feel pain at the same things? For these things will not even be present for them in one another, but without that it would not be possible to be friends, since they would be incapable of living together. So ought one to bear oneself toward him in no other way than if he had not ever been a friend? Rather, one ought to be mindful of the intimacy there has been, and just as we think one ought to show more kindness to friends than to strangers, so too ought one to allot something to those who have been friends on account of the friendship that went before, whenever the break-up has not come from an excess of vice.

Chapter 4. Now the things involved in friendship toward those around us, and by which friendships are defined, seem to come from things related to oneself.[260] For people consider a friend to be someone who wishes for and does good things, or things that seem good, for the sake of the other person, or who wants the friend to be and to live, for the friend's own sake, which is the very thing mothers feel toward their children, and which friends who are in conflict feel. Others consider a friend to be someone with whom one spends time and who prefers the same things, or someone who shares in pain and enjoyment with a friend. This too happens with mothers especially. And friendship is defined by any of these things.

But each of them belongs to a decent person in relation to himself (and to everyone else, insofar as they assume that they are decent people, but it seems, as was said,[261] that virtue and the person of serious worth are the measure of each thing), since he is in agreement with himself and desires the same things with all his soul; and so he wants good things for himself, or those that seem so, and does them (since it belongs to a good person to work hard at good things), and for his

---

[260] In Bk. VIII, where the focus was on the variety of kinds of friendship, a comparison was made to the kinds of political constitutions, which made a friendship seem to be a small version of such a community. Here, Aristotle turns his discussion toward what is central in friendship, and responsible for its unity rather than for its variety. From this standpoint, the life of friendship seems to be an expansion of the soul instead of a contraction of communal life.

[261] See 1113a 29-33.

own sake (since they are for the sake of his thinking part, which seems to *be* each person), and he wants himself to live and be preserved, and especially that in him by which he exercises judgment. For *being* is a good thing for a person of serious worth, and each person wants good things for himself, and no one chooses to have all things by becoming someone else (for even now a god has what is good), but while being whoever he is, and each person would seem to *be* his activity of thinking, or that most of all. And such a person wants to spend time with himself, since he does it pleasantly, for his memories of things he has done are delightful and his expectations of things he is going to do are good, and such things are pleasing. And his thinking is well supplied with things to contemplate. And he most of all is at one with himself in pain and pleasure, since at all times it is the same thing that is painful or pleasant, and not one thing at one time and something else at another, since he is, so to speak, without regrets.

So it is because each of these things is present in a decent person in relation to himself, and because he can be related to a friend as he is to himself (since the friend is another self), that friendship seems to be any of these things, and that friends seem to be those to whom they belong. But let the question whether there *is* friendship toward oneself or not be set aside for the present, though it would seem that there could be friendship in this respect, insofar as each person is two or more, and because a surpassing instance of friendship is like a friendship toward oneself. But it appears that the attributes mentioned are present in most people, even in those who are of low character. But is it insofar as they are pleased with themselves and assume themselves to be decent that they share in them?

Certainly these attributes are not present in any of those who are completely base and do ungodly things, nor do they even seem to be. And they are hardly present in people of low character, for they differ with themselves, and desire some things but wish for others, like unrestrained people; for they prefer things that are pleasant but harmful, instead of what seems to be good for themselves, and they refrain from doing what they believe is best for themselves out of cowardice and laziness. And those by whom many terrible crimes have been committed, who are hated for their viciousness, even flee from living and do away with themselves. And corrupt people look for others to spend their days with, running away from themselves, for when they are by themselves they have many uncomfortable recollections, and anticipate other things of the same kind, but when they are with others they forget. And since they have nothing loveable about them, they feel no friendliness toward themselves. Such people do not even feel joy or pleasure along with themselves, since the soul within them is in a state of civil war, and one part, on account of vice, is pained at refraining from certain things when another part is pleased; one part drags them here and the other part there, as if tearing them apart. But if it is not possible to feel pain and pleasure at the same time, still, after a little while, they are pained because they were pleased, and wish these things had not become pleasant to them, since people of low character are full of regrets.

So it is apparent that a base person is not even disposed in a friendly way toward himself, on account of having nothing loveable about him. Then if being that way is too miserable, one ought to avoid vice with the utmost effort, and try to be a decent person, for in that way one can be in a friendly state with oneself, and also become a friend to someone else.

Chapter 5. Goodwill seems like something that has to do with friendship, though it surely is not friendship, since goodwill arises toward people one does not know, and without their being aware of it, but friendship does not. These things were also mentioned before.[262] And goodwill is not loving either, since there is no intensity or desire in it, but these things go along with loving; and loving involves intimate acquaintance, while goodwill is also of sudden origin, as happens in connection with those engaged in athletic competition, since people become goodwilled toward them and share their wishes, but would not share their action in any way, for as we said, they become good-willed suddenly and like them superficially. So goodwill seems to be a beginning of friendship, in the same way the pleasure of seeing is the beginning of falling in love, for no one falls in love without first being pleased by someone's looks, but someone who delights in those looks is not any the more in love, except when he yearns for the absent person and longs for that person's presence.

So too, it is impossible for those who have not become goodwilled to be friends, but those who are goodwilled do not have a friendship any the more, since they merely wish for good things for those toward whom they are goodwilled, and they might not do anything to help them or go to any trouble over them. Hence, making a metaphor, one might say that goodwill is out-of-work friendship, but when time has passed and it has reached the point of intimate association it can get to be friendship, though not the sort that is for use or pleasure, since no goodwill comes about in those cases.[263] Someone who has had favors done for him does give back goodwill in return for what he has received, as a way of doing what is just; and one who wants someone else to fare well because he has a hope of being favored by that person seems to be

30

1167a

10

---

[262] See 1155b 32-1156a 5.

[263] It is now evident that "friendships" for use or pleasure are not properly friendships at all, even in a reduced or partial way. They are like the false forms of courage discussed in Bk. III, Chap. 8, that share various incidental features with the true form, but lack the thing that makes it courage.

goodwilled not toward that person but rather toward himself, just as he would not be a friend if he paid attentions to him in order to make some use of him. But in general, goodwill arises on account of virtue or some sort of fitness, when someone appears to one as beautiful or courageous or some such thing, as we said about those involved in athletic competition.

Chapter 6. Like-mindedness, too, seems to be something involved in friendship. For this reason it is not sameness of opinion, since this could be present even in people who are ignorant of one another; nor do people speak of those who judge alike about anything whatever, such as about the things in the heavens, as being like-minded (for it is not a friendly thing to think alike about these), but they speak of cities as being like-minded, whenever people judge alike about what is advantageous, and choose the same things, and act on the things they believe in common. So people are like-minded about things that are to be done, and among these, about those that are of magnitude and capable of belonging to both or all of them together; for example, cities are like-minded whenever it seems good to everyone for the offices to be elected, or to make an alliance with the Spartans, or for Pittacus to rule, when he too was willing. And when each of two people wants to rule himself, like those in the *Phoenician Women*,[264] there is civil strife, since it is not being like-minded when each has the same thing in mind, whatever that might be, but has it in mind that the same thing be in the same person, as when both the populace and the decent people think the best people should rule, for in that way what they aim at comes about for everyone. So like-mindedness seems to be friendship in a political sense, just as people mean it,[265] for it has to do with what is advantageous and what relates to life.

And such like-mindedness is present among decent people, since they are of like mind both with themselves and with one another, being on the same terms, so to speak (for the things that such people want stay constant and do not ebb and flow like tidewater), and they want things that are just and advantageous, and aim at these in common. But it is impossible for people of low character to be like-minded except to a small extent, in the same way that it is impossible for them to be friends, since they aim at having more in the way of benefits and come up short in work and public services; and each of them, though he wants these things for himself, watches his neighbor closely to hinder him, since if they are not constantly on guard, the common good is destroyed. So it

---

264 Euripides's *Phoenician Women* involves the conflict of Eteocles and Polyneices in Thebes. Pittacus was an elected dictator who resigned after fourteen years, against popular opinion. See note to 1113b 33.

265 Of the various synonyms for agreement, this seems to be the one commonly chosen in political contexts, e.g., by Plato, *Republic*, 545D, or Thucydides, *The Peloponnesian War*, Bk. VIII, Chap. 93.

turns out that they are in a state of civil strife, compelling one another to do what is just but not wanting to themselves.

Chapter 7. People who do favors seem to love the people they do them for more than those who receive them love those who do them, and this is inquired about as something that happens paradoxically. To most people, it seems that the latter owe a debt and the former have it owed to them, so just as, with loans, those who owe them wish there were no people to whom they owed them, while those who lent them are anxious over the safety of those who owe them, so too, it seems that those who do favors wish for those who receive them to be there to return their favors, while making the return is not something the latter care about. Now perhaps Epicharmus would claim that they say these things from taking a debased point of view, but it seems to be a human one, since most people are forgetful, and aim at getting something good rather than at doing good. But the reason for it would seem to be something more rooted in nature, and not like what has to do with those who make loans, since there is no loving in their case, but a wishing for safety for the sake of a return, but those who have done good love and feel affection for the people for whom they have done it, even if the latter are not useful to them and could not become so later.

And this is the very thing that happens in the case of artisans, for every one of them loves his own work more than he would be loved by the work if it took on a soul. And perhaps this happens most of all with poets, since they are overly fond of their own poems, loving them like children. But what happens with people who do favors seems like such a case, for the one the good is done to is their work, and they love this more than the work loves its maker. The reason for this is that one's *being* is choiceworthy and loveable for everyone, but we *are* by being-at-work (since it is by living and acting), and the work is, in a certain way, its maker at-work; so he loves the work because he also loves to *be*. And this is natural, for that which something is in potency, its work reveals in its being-at-work. At the same time, for the one doing the favor something beautiful comes from the act, so that he delights in the one in whom this is present, but for the one receiving it there is nothing beautiful in the one doing it, but if anything, something advantageous, and this is less pleasing and loveable. And while the being-at-work of what is present, the hope of what is to come, and the memory of what has been are all pleasant, what goes with being-at-work is the most pleasant and is loveable in the same way; so for the one who makes something, his work endures (for what is beautiful is long-lasting), but for the one who receives something, what is useful is used up. And the memory of beautiful things is pleasant, but the memory of useful things is not quite so, or is less so, though the expectation seems to work the opposite way.

20

30

1168a

10

20   And loving seems like making, while being loved seems like receiving, so feeling love and the attributes of friendship go with those who have the greater part in action. Also, everyone loves things more that have come to him with effort, as those who have made money love it more than those who have inherited it; but receiving a favor seems to be without effort, while doing a favor is an exertion. And for these reasons mothers love their children more, for giving birth is great labor, and they know more that they are their own. This too would seem to be particular to people who do favors.

30   **Chapter 8.** But one might raise an impasse whether one ought to love oneself most, or someone else. For people criticize those who show the most fondness for themselves, and, as though they were in disgrace, disparage them as self-lovers; and it seems that a base person does everything for his own sake, and that someone is the more corrupt to the extent that he does so the more—so that people complain about him, for example, that he does nothing apart from his own interest—but a decent person acts on account of what is beautiful, and the better a person he is, the more on account of the beautiful, and for the sake of a friend, while he disregards his own interest. But the facts are not in

1168b   harmony with these claims, and this is not unreasonable. For people say that one ought to love one's best friend most, and a best friend is someone who wishes for good things for the sake of that person for whom he wishes them, even if no one is going to know he does; but this belongs most of all to oneself in relation to oneself, and so too do all the rest of the things by which a friend is defined, for it was said that all the things that have to do with friendship arise out of oneself and extend to others.[266] And all the proverbs agree with this opinion, such as "one soul" and "the things of friends are common" and "friendship is equal relationship" and "the knee is closer than the shin,"[267] since all

10   these would apply most of all to oneself, for one is a friend to oneself most of all, and so what he ought to love most is himself. So there is appropriately an impasse about which side it is right to follow, since both have a certain credibility.

Now perhaps it is necessary to separate these sorts of arguments and to distinguish to what extent and in what way each of them is truthful. So if we were to grasp the sense in which each side means love of self, it would probably become clear. Now those who bring it into reproach call people self-lovers who distribute a greater amount to themselves in the way of money, honors, and bodily pleasures, since most people crave these and zealously chase after them as though they

---

[266] See Chap. 4 above.

[267] For the first of these sayings, see Euripides's *Orestes* (1045-6); the second is mentioned above at 1159b 31-2 and the third at 1157b 36-1158a 1; the fourth, derived from the poet Theocritus, has been compared to "charity begins at home."

were the best things, so that they are also things that are fought over. Those, then, who are greedy for these things gratify their desires and their passions generally, and the irrational part of the soul, and most people are of this kind; hence, from its being bad for the most part, the name has become so as well, and people justly reproach those who love themselves in this way. And it is not unclear that most people are accustomed to mean by self-lovers those who distribute such things to themselves, for if someone were always eager to do what is just or what is temperate himself, most of all, or do anything else whatever that is in accord with the virtues, and in general were to save up for himself what is beautiful to do, no one would say he was a lover of self or blame him.

But it would seem rather that it is such a person who is a lover of self; at least he takes for himself the things that are most beautiful and most good, and gratifies what is most authoritative in himself, and obeys this in all things. And just as a city, or any other organization, seems to be, most of all, its most authoritative part, so too does a human being; and so the person who loves and gratifies this is most a lover of self. And people are called self-restrained and unrestrained according to whether intellect masters them or not, as though this were each person; and the things people seem most of all to have done themselves and willingly are the things they have done with reason. That, then, this is each person, or is so most of all, is not unclear, nor that a decent person loves this most. Hence such a person would be a lover of self most of all, though in a different form from the one that is reproached, differing as much as living by reason does from living by passion, and as much as desiring either the beautiful or what seems advantageous.[268] Everyone, then, approves of and praises those who are exceptionally zealous about beautiful actions, and if they all competed for the beautiful, and strained to the utmost to perform the most beautiful actions, then for all in common there would be what is needful, and for each in particular there would be the greatest of goods, if indeed virtue is that.

Therefore, a good person ought to be a lover of self, since he will both profit himself and benefit the others by performing beautiful actions, and a corrupt person ought not, since he will harm himself and those around him by following base passions. So in a corrupt

---

[268] The combination of things in this sentence is important. Even though the thinking part is most properly oneself, it is only the love of the beautiful that properly satisfies that part. That in turn means that the irrational part of the soul must be brought into its best condition, so that the beautiful can be discerned (1113a 29-33), and the whole human being can be fulfilled. It is from here to the end of this chapter that the beautiful is most directly and extensively discussed. The earlier treatment of virtue of character led up to the beautiful as its only proper aim, but the current question about what makes self-love a good thing converges with that earlier part of the inquiry and extends it.

person, what he ought to do and what he does are out of harmony, but a decent person does what he ought, since every intellect chooses what is best for itself, and the decent person obeys his intellect. But it is also true of a person of serious worth that he does many things for the sake of his friends and his country, and if necessary, dies for them,[269] since he will give up money and honors, and all the goods people fight over, to gain what is beautiful; for he would choose to have an intense pleasure for a short time rather than a mild one for a long time, and to live in a beautiful way for a year rather than in a random way for many years, and to perform one great and beautiful action rather than many small ones. And this no doubt is what happens with those who die for others; they choose something great and beautiful for themselves. Such a person would also give up money in a case in which his friends would get more money, since there would be money for the friend, but a beautiful act for himself, so that he distributes the greater good to himself. And it is the same way with honors and offices, for he will give up all these things to a friend, since this is a beautiful thing for him, and something to be praised. And he seems appropriately to be someone of serious stature, since he prefers the beautiful above all things. And it is possible that he would even give up actions to a friend, and it would be a more beautiful thing to become responsible for the friend's performing them than to perform them himself.[270] So in everything that is praised, a person of serious worth obviously distributes to himself the greater share of the beautiful. In this way, then, one ought to be a lover of self, as was said, but one should not be so in the way most people are.

Chapter 9. It is also a matter of dispute whether someone who is happy needs friends or not. For people say there is no need of friends for those who are blessed and self-sufficient, since good things belong to them already; so since they are sufficient to themselves they lack nothing, while a friend, who is another self, supplies what someone is incapable of supplying by himself. Therefore, "when destiny provides well, why does one need friends?"[271] But it seems absurd, when people assign all good things to the happy person, not to grant him friends,

---

[269] These attributes recall those associated with greatness of soul (1124b 8-10), and the narrative or portrait-like style of this passage is also reminiscent of that discussion. It may be that the aspirations of the great soul find their only fulfillment in friendship, which expands the soul to encompass another self. See note to 1169b 10 below.

[270] A careful reader may see that one further step would allow the friend the still greater satisfaction of giving up the action to oneself, and a sophistical reader might say this led to an infinite regress. A thoughtful reader will see that the equality and commonality sought in friendship have here been realized, and that the pleasure is the same for both in either case.

[271] Euripides, *Orestes*, 667.

which seem to be the greatest of external goods.[272] And if it belongs to   10
a friend to do good more than to receive it, and doing good for others
belongs to a good person and to virtue, and it is a more beautiful thing
to do good for friends than for strangers, a person of serious worth will
need people to do good to. Hence it is inquired even whether one needs
friends more in good fortune than in bad fortune, since the unfortunate
person needs those who will do good for him, and those who are fortunate need people to do good for.

And perhaps it is absurd to make the blessed person solitary, since
no one would choose to have all good things by himself, for a human
being is meant for a city and is of such a nature as to live with others.
So this belongs to the happy person too, since he has the things that   20
are good by nature, and it is clear that it is a better thing to spend one's
days with friends and decent people rather than with strangers and
anyone at random. Therefore it is necessary for the happy person to
have friends. What then is meant by the people referred to first, and
in what sense are they right? Is it that most people think of friends as
being for use? Of such friends, then, a blessed person will have no need,
since the good things already belong to him. And he has no need of
friends for pleasure either, or only to a small extent (for since his life
is pleasant he does not need pleasure that is brought in from outside
it), and since he has no need for friends of those kinds, he does not
seem to need friends.

Nonetheless, this is not true. For it was said at the beginning that
happiness is a certain way of being-at-work,[273] and it is clear that
being-at-work is something that happens, and not something that is   30
present like some possession. But if being happy consists in living and
being-at-work, and the being-at-work of a good person is serious and
pleasant in itself, as was said at the beginning, and if what is one's own
also belongs among things that are pleasant, and we are better able to
contemplate those around us than ourselves, and their actions better
than our own, and the actions of serious people who are their friends
are pleasant to those who are good (since they have both the attributes   1170a
of things that are pleasant by nature), then a blessed person will have
need of friends of this sort, if indeed he chooses to contemplate actions
that are decent and his own, and the actions of a good person who is a
friend are of that kind. And people believe that a happy person must
live pleasantly. Well then, life is difficult for one who is alone, since
it is not easy by oneself to be at work continuously, but it is easier to
be so among and in relation to others; so the being-at-work, which is

---

[272] At 1123b 20-21, in the discussion of greatness of soul, this was said to be
honor, but the argument made at 1159a 25-27 showed why that conclusion
was inadequate.
[273] See 1098a 16-18. For the argument that this way of being-at-work is pleasant
in itself, see 1099a 13-21.

pleasant in itself, will be more continuous, which it needs to be in the case of a blessed person, since a person of serious stature, insofar as he is of serious stature, enjoys actions in accord with virtue and disdains those that result from vice, just as a musical person is pleased by beautiful melodies and pained by bad ones. And a certain training in virtue would come from living among good people, as Theognis also says.[274]

And to those who examine it from a standpoint having more to do with nature, it appears that a serious friend is naturally choiceworthy to a serious person. For it was said that what is good by nature is good and pleasant in itself to a serious person. And living is defined, for animals, by the potency for sense-perception, and for human beings by the potencies for sense-perception and thinking; but a potency leads back to its being-at-work, and what governs it is in its being-at-work, so that living in its governing sense appears to be perceiving and thinking. And living is among the things that are good and pleasant in themselves, since it is determinate, and what is determinate belongs to the nature of the good; and what is good by nature is also good for a decent person, and consequently seems to everyone to be pleasant. And one ought not to take the case of a vicious and corrupt life, or a life spent in pain, since such a life is indeterminate, as are the attributes that belong to it.[275] In the next sections, what has to do with pain will be clearer.

Now if living itself is good and pleasant (and it seems to be so from the fact that all desire it, and those who are decent and blessed most of all, since the life they lead is the most choiceworthy and their living is most blessed), and if one who sees is aware that he sees, and one who hears is aware that he hears, and one who walks is aware that he walks, and similarly in the other cases there is something in us that is aware that we are at-work, so that whenever we perceive we are aware that we perceive and whenever we think we are aware that we think, and if being aware that we are perceiving or thinking is being aware that we *are* (since our *being* is perceiving or thinking), and being aware that we are alive is something pleasant in itself (since life is a good thing by nature, and it is pleasant to be aware of the good that is present in oneself), and if being alive is choiceworthy, and especially so for good people, because their *being* is good and pleasant for them (since people are pleased by being additionally aware of something that is good in itself), and if a serious person is the same way toward

---

274 The quotation is given in part at 1172a 13-14.
275 This simply means that there are many different ways to go wrong or to be ill, a point made at 1106b 28-33, while the good of anything is what promotes and preserves the determinate nature that makes it what it is. The "next sections" that clarify pain as well as pleasure are Chaps. 1-5 of Bk. X.

a friend as he is toward himself (since the friend is another self), then just as one's own *being* is choiceworthy for each person, so too, or very nearly so, is that of a friend. But one's *being* is choiceworthy on account of the awareness of oneself as being good, and such an   10 awareness is pleasant in itself. Therefore one also ought to share in a friend's awareness that he *is*, and this would come about through living together and sharing conversation and thinking; for this would seem to be what living together means in the case of human beings, not feeding in the same place like fatted cattle. So if being is choiceworthy in itself to a blessed person, since it is good and pleasant by nature, and that of one's friend is very nearly the same, then a friend would also be something choiceworthy. But that which is choiceworthy for him ought to be present to him, or he will be deficient in that respect. Therefore, for someone who is going to be happy, there will be a need for friends of serious worth.[276]

Chapter 10. Ought one then to make as many friends as possible?   20 Or, as in the case of foreign guests, where "neither a host to many nor a host to none"[277] seems to have been harmoniously said, will it also be fitting in the case of friendship to be neither a friend of none nor yet a friend of excessively many? The saying seems to fit very well with those who are friends for use, since helping out many people in return is wearisome, and a lifetime is not enough to do it. More such friends than are sufficient for one's own life are superfluous, and are obstacles to living beautifully, so there is no need for them. And also with those who are friends for pleasure, a few are enough, as is a little sweetening in one's food. But should friends of serious worth be greatest in   30 number, or is there also some measure of a group that is conducive to friendship, as there is of a city?[278] For neither could there be a city made of ten people, nor would it still be a city when made of ten times ten thousand. The amount is perhaps not some one number, but anything

---

[276] The argument of the last two paragraphs is one of the two main places in which the *Nicomachean Ethics* ascends to, and finds its place within, Aristotle's study of the things that are higher than human beings. The other is in Bk. X. The vast bulk of evidence from which the inquiry takes its source comes from ordinary experience and opinion, but it is a confirmation of its conclusions that they are continuous with those of other inquiries concerned with the soul, the natural world, and being as a whole. Moral goodness, friendship, and happiness are inseparable ultimately because a human being has a nature as a living thing and a constituent of the whole of things.

[277] See Hesiod, *Works and Days*, 715.

[2/8] This is discussed in the *Politics*, Bk. VII, Chap. 4. The main point is that everyone needs to know enough about everyone else to serve on a jury or deliberate about laws, or at least vote for others intelligently. In Plato's *Republic* (422E-423C), the limit is that beyond which factions or classes play a larger role than the common bond of unity. Both authors are thinking of a population on the order of a few thousand people.

between certain limits.

1171a   So too, the number of friends is limited, and is perhaps the most with whom one is able to share a life (since this seemed to be the thing most characteristic of friendship); it is not unclear that it is impossible to share a life with many people and spread oneself out among them. And it is also necessary for them to be friends of one another, if they are all going to spend their days in one another's company, and for this to be the case among many people is hard work. It also becomes difficult to share joy and pain intimately with many people, since it is likely to fall to one's lot at the same time to rejoice with one person and grieve with another. Perhaps, then, it is a good idea not to seek to be a friend to as many people as possible, but with however many people are suf-
10   ficient for sharing a life. It would not even seem possible to be much of a friend to many people, and for the same reason that it is impossible to be in love with more than one person, since that is meant to be an extreme form of friendship, directed toward one person; so to be very much of a friend is possible only toward a few.

And it also seems to be this way in fact, since there do not come to be many friends in the friendship of a fraternal association, and the celebrated friendships that are spoken of are pairs. People who are friendly toward many and fall into familiarity with everybody, seem to be friends to no one, except as fellow citizens--they are called obsequious. As fellow citizens, it is possible to be a friend of many people and not be obsequious, but decent in the true sense; but it is not possible to be a friend to many people on account of virtue and
20   for themselves, and one should be well satisfied to find even a few such friends.

Chapter 11. Does one need friends more in good fortune or in misfortune? For people seek them out in both circumstances, since those who are unfortunate need help, and those who are fortunate need companions and people for whom they may do good, since they want to do so. While, then, it is more necessary amid misfortunes—which is why one needs useful friends at those times—it is more beautiful amid good fortunes—which is why people seek out friends who are also decent, since it is preferable to do favors for them and to spend time with them. For also, the very presence of friends is pleasant both in good fortune and in misfortune, since those in distress have
30   their cares lightened by sharing them with friends. Hence one might raise the question whether friends take up a portion of them as of a weight, or it is not this, but their presence, which is pleasant, and one's mindfulness of their feeling one's grief that make the pain less. Now whether it is for this reason or for some other that their cares are lightened, let the question be put aside, but what is described does appear to happen.

But the presence of friends seems to be something of a mixed

blessing, for while the very seeing of friends is pleasant, both on other   1171b
occasions and when one is in misfortune, and becomes a help toward
not feeling pain (since a friend is a source of consolation both by sight
and by word, if he is adroit, for he knows one's character and the things
by which one is pleased and pained), seeing the friend pained at one's
own misfortunes is something painful, since everyone avoids being a
cause of pain to his friends. This is why someone of a manly nature,
even if he is not exceptionally resistant to pain, is reluctant to make his
friends share it, and does not stand by while the pain comes to them; in
general, he does not permit others to express grief with him because he
himself is not apt to express grief. But girlish women and womanish men   10
enjoy having people lament with them, and love them as friends and
partners in grief. But it is clear that, in all things, one ought to imitate
the person who is better.

But the presence of friends amid good fortunes combines a pleasant
way of passing the time with a mindfulness that they are given pleasure
by one's own good things. Hence it would seem that one ought to be
eager to invite friends into one's good fortunes (since it is a beautiful thing to do good for others), but hesitant to invite them into one's
misfortunes. For one ought to pass along as little as possible of what is
bad, which is the source of the saying "I unfortunate am enough." One
ought to call upon friends for help most of all when they will benefit
one greatly while being put to little trouble. Conversely, it is perhaps   20
fitting to go uninvited to friends who are in misfortune, and to do so
with good cheer (for it belongs to a friend to do a good turn, and especially to those who are in need and do not expect help, since this is
more beautiful and more pleasant for them both), but to those who are
in good fortune, while it is appropriate to be eager to lend one's effort
(since even in those circumstances there is need of friends), one ought
to be slow to take favors, since it is not a beautiful thing to be eager to
get benefits. But perhaps one ought to be careful not to seem rude by
rejecting them, since this happens sometimes. So the presence of friends
is plainly something to be chosen in all circumstances.

Chapter 12. Is it then the same way with friends as with lovers,
for whom seeing the beloved is their greatest contentment, and the   30
thing they choose over the other senses, since it is especially through
seeing that love is present and comes to be present, so that for friends
too, living together is the most choiceworthy thing? For friendship is
a sharing in common, and one has the same relation to a friend as to
oneself, while in relation to oneself, the awareness that one *is* is something choiceworthy, and thus it is so in relation to the friend as well;
but the being-at-work of this awareness comes about in living together,
and so, naturally, friends aim at this. And whatever *being* consists in for   1172a
any sort of people—whatever it is for the sake of which they choose to
be alive—this is what they want to be engaged in with their friends.

This is why some friends drink together, others play dice together, and still others engage in athletic exercise together and go hunting together, or engage in philosophy together, each sort spending their days together in whatever it is, out of all the things in life, that they are most contented by; for since they want to share their lives with their friends, they do those things and share those things that they believe living together consists in.

So the friendship of people of low character becomes corrupt (for they share in base activities, not even being constant in these, and become corrupt in becoming like one another); but the friendship of decent people is decent, and grows along with their association, and they seem to become even better people by putting the friendship to work and by straightening one another out, for they have their rough edges knocked off by the things they like in one another. Hence the saying "[you will learn] from what is good in the good."[279]

So let the things that have to do with friendship be discussed to this extent. The next thing would be to go over what has to do with pleasure.

BOOK X

Chapter 1. After these things, perhaps it comes next to go over what has to do with pleasure.[280] For this seems to be something especially indwelling in our kind, which is why people educate the young by steering them by means of pleasure and pain; and it seems that what is most conducive to virtue of character is to enjoy what one ought and hate what one ought. For these feelings extend through the whole of life, having in them a weight and a power that tend toward virtue and toward a happy life, since people choose things that are pleasant and

---

279   Theognis, line 35. The next line is "but by mingling among the bad, you will lose what sense you have."

280   In Bk. VII, Chaps. 11-14, Aristotle worked through the philosophic opinions about pleasure, and gave his own account of it, but the end of that discussion was unresolved, since it left open the possibility that there is no happy life for a human being, but only trade-offs among the pleasures that fulfill various parts of our complex nature. This review of pleasure leads to a final assessment of all the things that have withstood scrutiny and been found to have a plausible claim to contribute to happiness. It is noteworthy that, while Bks. I and II looked at the popular opinions about pleasure, and Bk. VII examined philosophic opinions, the present discussion singles out two philosophic opinions whose merits are entwined with the examples set by the lives of the people who argued them. The extreme teaching about pleasure in this chapter is associated with Speusippus, Plato's successor as head of the Academy. Eudoxus, the defender of the opposite extreme presented in the next chapter, was also in the Academy with Aristotle, Speusippus, and Plato, and was a distinguished mathematician and astronomer.

avoid things that are painful. And it would seem that one ought least of all to bypass such things, both for other reasons and because they involve a great dispute. For some people say that pleasure is the good, while others at the opposite extreme say it is completely base, some of them perhaps being convinced that it is that way, but others believing that it is better for our life to make pleasure appear to be something base, even if it is not, on the grounds that most people are heavily inclined toward it and are enslaved to their pleasures, on account of which they need to be led to the opposite side, since in that way they would come to the mean.   30

But it may well be that this is not a good thing to say. For words that concern things in the realm of feelings and actions are less believable than deeds are, and when they are discordant with what is perceived, those who say them are despised and discredit the truth along with themselves. For if someone who condemns pleasure is seen sometimes going after it, he seems to incline toward it because all of it is good, since making distinctions is not something most people do. So true statements seem to be the most useful ones, not only for knowing but also for life; for since they are in tune with one's deeds they are believed, and they encourage those who understand them to live by them. Enough, then, of such things; let us go on to the things that have been said about pleasure.   1172b

Chapter 2. Now Eudoxus believed that pleasure is the good, because one sees that all beings, both rational and irrational, aim at it, while in all things what is choiceworthy is good and what is most choiceworthy is best; so the fact that all things are carried to the same goal reveals that this is the best thing for them all (for each thing discovers what is good for itself, just as it discovers its food), and what is good for all things, and at which all things aim, is the good. His arguments were convincing on account of the virtue of his character, more than on their own account, since he seemed to be an exceptionally temperate man, so that he seemed to be saying these things not as a lover of pleasure but because that is the way things are in truth. And he believed that the same thing is no less evident from the opposite side, since pain is in itself something avoided by all things, so likewise its opposite is something choiceworthy. But what is most choiceworthy is what we choose neither on account of anything else nor for the sake of anything else; and such, by general agreement, is pleasure, since no one asks for what purpose one feels pleasure, because pleasure is chosen for itself. And when pleasure is added to any good thing whatever, such as to acting justly or being temperate, it makes it more choiceworthy, but it is by itself that the good is augmented.   10

But surely the latter argument, at any rate, seems to show that pleasure is among the things that are good, but no more so than any other, since every one of them is more choiceworthy along with another   20 good thing than when it is alone. Indeed, Plato argues in rebuttal by that sort of argument that pleasure is not the good, since a pleasant life is more choiceworthy along with intelligence than apart from it, but if the mixture is better, then pleasure is not the good, for the good does not become any more choiceworthy when something is added to it.[281] And it is clear that nothing else that becomes more choiceworthy along with any of the things that are good in themselves would be the good either. But what is of that sort, that we have any share in? For that is the sort of thing being sought. On the other hand, those who argue in opposition that what all things aim at is not good are not saying anything; for those things that seem so to all people, we declare to be so, and someone who destroys that trust will not very likely say anything that is more to be trusted. For if it were only things without intelligence that desire pleasant things, there would be something in what they say, but if beings with judgment desire them as well, how could they be saying anything? And perhaps even in the lower animals there is something naturally good that is stronger than they themselves are, that aims at their proper good.

And what has to do with the contrary of pleasure does not seem to be well reasoned either. For they claim that it does not follow, if pain is something bad, that pleasure is something good, since a bad thing can also be the opposite of a bad thing, and both of them can be opposed to something neutral; the reason they give is not wrong, but it is surely not true in the case of the things they are speaking of. For if both pleasure and pain were among bad things, both of them ought to be avoided, while if they were among neutral things, neither of them ought to be avoided, or both of them in a similar way. But as things are, it is obvious that people avoid one of them as bad and choose the other as good; hence it is in that way that they are opposed.[282]

Chapter 3. Nor is it the case that, if pleasure is not classed among qualities, it is for that reason not among good things either; for the ways of being-at-work that belong to virtue are not qualities, and neither is happiness. And they say that the good is definite, while pleasure is indefinite because it admits of being more and less. Now if they judge this from the experience of being pleased, then the same conclusions would also have to apply to justice and the other virtues, in relation to which people plainly speak of those who are of that sort, and who act

---

281   The argument is in Plato's *Philebus*, 60D. The claim that pleasure is the good, rather than merely something good, implies that pleasure is the one and only thing for the sake of which anything else is chosen. See 1096b 8-1097a 3.

282   At 1153b 4-7, the analogy was made to greater, lesser, and equal. Two opposite extremes can together be opposed to a mean only if they are alike in some respect that differentiates the pair of them from the mean.

in accord with the virtues, more and less. For people are more just or more courageous, and it is possible to act justly or be temperate more or less.[283] If, however, they judge by the pleasures, then it may be that they do not state the reason, if there are unmixed as well as mixed pleasures. And what prevents pleasure from being the same way health is, which, though it is definite, admits of being more and less? For the same proportion of things is not present in everyone, nor is a certain one always present in the same person, but while it slackens, it stays present up to a certain point, and differs as more and less. So what has to do with pleasure also admits of being of that sort.

And having set it down that the good is complete, while motions and processes of coming into being are incomplete, they try to show   30 that pleasure is a motion and a process of coming into being. But they do not seem to be right in arguing even that it is a motion. For swiftness and slowness seem to be properties of every motion, if not in themselves, as with the motion of the cosmos, then in relation to another motion; but these do not belong to pleasure in either way. For it is possible to become pleased quickly, just as it possible to get angry   1173b quickly, but it is not possible to be pleased quickly, even in relation to someone else, as it is possible to walk and to grow and all such things. So it is possible to change into pleasure quickly or slowly, but it is not possible to be at-work in accord with it—I mean to be pleased—quickly. And how could it be a process of coming into being? For it does not seem that a thing happens to come into being out of any chance thing, but that it comes into being out of that into which it is dissolved; and pain would be the destruction of that of which pleasure is the coming-into-being.

They say that pain is a deficiency of what is natural, and pleasure a restoration of it, but these are things that happen to the body. So if pleasure is a restoration of what is natural, that in which the restoration   10 takes place would also feel the pleasure; therefore, this would be the body, but that does not seem to be the case. Therefore the restoration is not the pleasure, but when a restoration comes about one would feel pleasure, as one would feel pain when being wounded. Their opinion seems to have come from the pains and pleasures involved with food, for when people have come to be in need of it and have first felt pain, they feel pleasure at being filled up again. But this does not happen with all pleasures, since the pleasures of mathematics are free of pain,

---

[283]   The virtues are settled conditions that do not themselves have gradations, but people who are acquiring them, or have stopped short of acquiring them, can have more or less of what belongs to them. Aristotle said in Bk. VII that most of us fall into the middle ground of restraint and unrestraint (see 1150a 15-16 and 1152a 14-17), and in Bk. VIII he used the capacity for friendship as a measure of the goodness of one's character (see 1156b 8-9).

and among the pleasures that come from the senses, so are those that come by smell, and also many things that are heard and seen, as well as memories and hopes. So of what will these be the processes of coming
20   into being? For no lack of anything has come about of which there could be a restoration.

To those who bring up the pleasures that are matters of reproach, one might say that these are not pleasant (for just because they are pleasant to people who are in a bad condition, one ought not to suppose that they would also be pleasant to anyone except these, just as in the case of things that are healthy, or sweet or bitter, to people who are sick, or things that appear white to people who have a disease of the eyes), or one might say something along the lines that the pleasures are choiceworthy, but not when they come from those things, just as it is choiceworthy to get rich, but not by betraying someone, or to be healthy, but not by eating just anything; or else pleasures differ in kind, for the ones that come from beautiful things are different from the ones that come from shameful things, for it is not possible to feel the pleasure
30   that comes from something just without being a just person, or the pleasure that comes from something musical without being a musical person, and similarly in the other cases. And the fact that a friend is different from a flatterer seems to make it clear that pleasure is either not good or varies in kind, since the former seems to associate with others with a view to the good, and the latter with a view to pleasure,
1174a   and people reproach the latter and praise the former as associating with a view to different things.

Also, no one would choose to live throughout life having the thinking of a child, even while having as much as possible the pleasures by which children are pleased, nor to enjoy something of the most shameful kind, even if one is never going to feel any pain from it. And we would eagerly exert ourselves for many things even if they were to bring no pleasure, such as seeing, remembering, knowing, and having the virtues. And if pleasures necessarily follow along with these things, that makes no difference, since we would choose them even if no pleasure were to come from them. It seems to be clear, then, that pleasure is not the good and that not every pleasure is choiceworthy, and that there are
10   some pleasures that are choiceworthy in themselves, differing in kind or in the things they come from. So let this be a sufficient discussion of the things that are said about pleasure and pain.

Chapter 4. But what pleasure is, or what sort of thing it is, would become more evident to those who take it up again from its source. Now the activity of seeing seems to be complete over any time whatever, for there is nothing it lacks which would complete its form by coming about at a later time; pleasure too is like something of this sort.[284] For

---

[284]   This is equivalent to Aristotle's assertion at 1153a 10 that pleasure is a way

it is something whole, and there is no time at which one could take a pleasure, the form of which would become complete after it went on for a longer time. Hence pleasure is not a motion, since every motion is in time and directed at some end, as housebuilding is, and is com- 20
plete when it brings about that at which it aims—that is, in the whole of the time, or at that time. But all the motions that are in parts of the time are incomplete, and are different in form from the whole and from one another. For setting stones together is different from making grooves in a column, and these motions differ from the making of the temple; the making of the temple is something complete (for it is lack-ing nothing in relation to what was intended), but the making of the foundation or of a decorative tablet is incomplete, since each of these is the making of a part. They are different in form, then, and it is not possible to find a motion complete in its form in any time whatever except in the whole.

And it is similar in the case of walking and the rest of the motions. For if change of place is a motion from somewhere to somewhere, there 30
are also differences of form within this: flying, walking, jumping, and such. But not only are there differences in that way, but also within walk-ing itself, since the from-which-to-which is not the same in a racetrack as in a part of it, or in one part as in another, nor is traversing this line here the same as traversing that one there, for not only does one pass 1174b
through a line, but a line that is in a place, and this one is in a different place from that one. What has to do with motion has been discussed with precision in other writings, but it seems that it is not complete in every stretch of time, but the many motions within it are incomplete and differ in form, if the from-where-to-where defines the form. But the form of a pleasure is complete in any time whatever. It is clear, then, that they must be different from one another, and that pleasure is one of the things that are whole and complete.[285] This would be apparent also from the fact that it is not possible to be in motion except in a stretch of time, but it is possible to feel pleasure, for what is in the *now* is something whole. And it is clear from these things that they are not right even in saying that there is a motion or coming-into-being with 10

---

of being-at-work (*energeia*). There the question was whether pleasures have ends outside themselves; here the question is whether pleasure has the tem-porally progressive structure of a motion, or the structure of an activity that is completely itself at every instant. The present discussion goes back to the source of the distinction between motion and being-at-work, as discussed in the *Metaphysics*, especially at 1048b 18-36.

[285] One could, of course, subdivide any pleasant activity into parts that differ from one another, but that does not mean that the pleasure is similarly divided. The distinction is like that between extensive and intensive mag-nitudes; cutting a red cube in half bisects its volume and its weight, but not its redness.

respect to pleasure. For these are spoken of as belonging not to all things, but only to those that have parts and are not wholes, since there is no coming-into-being of seeing, or of a point, or of a numerical unit, nor does any kind of motion or becoming belong to these; neither, then, do they belong to pleasure, for it is something whole.[286]

Now since every one of the senses is at work in relation to something perceptible, and is completely at work when it is in its best condition and directed toward the most beautiful of the things perceptible by that sense (for it seems that its complete being-at-work is of this sort most of all, and let it make no difference to speak of the sense itself, or of the organ in which it is present, as being at-work), for each sense, that way of being-at-work is best that belongs to what is in its best condition, directed toward the best of what is perceptible by it. This would be most complete and most pleasant; for there is a pleasure that goes with each of the senses, and similarly with thinking and contemplation, and its most complete activity is most pleasant, and it is most complete when it belongs to a power that is in good condition directed toward that which is of most serious worth among the things apprehended by it, and the pleasure brings the activity to completion. But the pleasure does not complete it in the same manner that the perceptible thing and the power of perceiving do when they are of serious worth, just as health and a doctor are not responsible in similar ways for one's being healthy.[287] And it is clear that pleasure comes with each of the senses (since we speak even of things seen and heard as being pleasant), and it is clear too that this is greatest whenever the sense is at its best and is at-work upon something of the same sort. When the thing perceiving and the thing perceived are at their best, there will always be pleasure when what acts and what is acted upon are present to one another. But the pleasure brings the activity to completion not as an active condition present within it all along, but as something

---

[286] Pleasure is one of the examples Aristotle gives in Bk. VII, Chap. 3, of the *Physics* of things that come to be present when something else changes. With an embryo, for example, there is a continuous change in material from the two parents, which pre-exists and passes over into a new condition, but the baby is a whole and is not an attribute of its underlying material. Likewise with pleasure, the body alters, or one's attention turns from one thing to another, and the pleasure is felt. This is important since it helps one re-interpret the restorative pleasures involved in things like eating and drinking. See 1154a 25-b 20.

[287] This comparison was used at 1144a 3-5 for the relation of wisdom to happiness, as something that constitutes it, in part, from within, rather than finding external means to it. But a further distinction is about to be made, three sentences below; pleasure is not a part of an activity of perceiving or thinking, but something that comes over its totality when it is complete. This should be contrasted, from the opposite side, to the kind of pleasure that is not inherently connected with an activity but a mere appendage (see 1099a 15-16) to it.

that comes over it, like the bloom of well-being in people who are at the peak of their powers.

So as long as the intelligible or perceptible thing, and the power that discerns or contemplates it, are such as they ought to be, there will be pleasure in their being-at-work, for while the thing acted upon and the thing acting remain as they are and have the same relation to one another, the same thing naturally comes about. How is it, then, that no one feels pleasure continuously? Does one get tired? For it is impossible for anything belonging to human beings to be at-work continuously, so that pleasure does not come to be continuous either, since it follows the activity. Some things give delight when they are new, but not to a similar extent later, for this same reason; for at first one's thinking is excited and is at work upon them with full concentration, as, in the case of sight, when people look intently at something, but afterward the activity is not that way but is negligent, and hence the pleasure grows dim.

But one might assume that all beings reach out for pleasure because they all desire to live.[288] Life is a certain kind of being-at-work, and each person is at-work in connection with those things and by means of those capacities that satisfy him most: a musical person by hearing and with melodies, a lover of learning by thinking and with topics of contemplation, and so too with each of the rest. The pleasure brings the activities to completion and hence brings living to completion, which is what they all strive for. It is reasonable, then, that they also aim at pleasure, since it brings living to fulfillment for each of them, which is worthy of choice. For the present, let the question be dismissed whether we choose to live for the sake of pleasure, or choose pleasure for the sake of living, for these appear to be joined together and incapable of separation. For without being-at-work, no pleasure comes about, and pleasure brings every way of being-at-work to completion.

Chapter 5. This is also why pleasures seem to differ in kind, since we believe that things that are different in kind are brought to completion by different means. (For this is obviously so with natural things and those made by art, such as animals, trees, a picture, a statue, a house, and a utensil.) Similarly, ways of being-at-work that are different in kind are brought to completion by means that differ in kind. But the activities of thinking differ in kind from those of perceiving, and these differ in kind from one another, and so too with the pleasures that

1175a

10

20

---

[288] This assumption offers a point of view from which practically everything that has preceded it may be brought together. The following sentence echoes the culmination of the friendship books (1172a 1-8); the one after that suggests a way of looking at the active life of virtue as a whole; and the next one unites the rationally choosing and irrationally desiring parts of the soul. Pleasure rightly understood is not in conflict with reason, with the discipline of the virtues, or with the self-forgetting of friends.

complete them. This would be apparent also from the way in which
each of the pleasures is bound up with the activity it completes, since
the appropriate pleasure contributes to the growth of the activity. For
those who are at-work with pleasure discern each sort of thing better
and are more precise about it; for example, people who enjoy doing
geometry become skilled at geometry, and understand each part of it
more, and likewise those who love music or architecture or each of the
other pursuits become better at their particular work because they enjoy
it. The pleasures make the activities grow, and what makes something
grow is of its own kind; but things that are alike in kind with activities
different in kind are themselves different in kind.

And this might be still more clear from the fact that pleasures from
different sources are impediments to activities. For people who are passionately devoted to the flute are unable to pay attention to arguments
if they hear someone playing a flute, since they enjoy the flute-playing
more than the activity that presently occupies them; so the pleasure
derived from the flute-playing ruins the activity that involves argument.
And this happens in a similar way in other cases as well, whenever one
is at work at two things at the same time, since the one that is more
pleasant knocks the other aside, and more so whenever it greatly surpasses it in pleasure, with the result that one stops being at work at the
other. For this reason, when we are enjoying anything at all intensely,
we hardly do anything else at all, but when we are mildly pleased with
things of one sort, we do things of other sorts; for instance, people who
eat snacks in theaters do this most when the actors are bad. And since
their own particular pleasures add precision to ways of being-at-work,
and make them longer lasting and better, while pleasures of different
kinds wreck them, it is clear that there is great difference among them.
For the pleasures that differ from those of the activities do just about the
same thing as their own particular pains; for their own pains ruin activities, as in a case when writing or calculating is unpleasant or painful to
someone, since the one does not write and the other does not calculate
when the activity is painful. So opposite things happen to activities as
a result of their own pleasures and pains, and those that are their own
are the ones that come about in the course of the activity itself. And it
was said that the pleasures that differ from those of the activities do
something very much like the pain, since they ruin the activities, though
not in the same manner.

Now since ways of being-at-work differ in decency and baseness,
and since some are to be chosen, others are to be avoided, and still
others are neutral, their pleasures also differ similarly, since a special
pleasure goes with each activity. The special pleasure in an activity of
serious worth is decent, and the special pleasure in a base activity is
corrupt, since even the desires for beautiful things are praised, while
those for shameful things are blamed. But the pleasures that are in them

are more closely akin to activities than are the appetites for them, since the appetites are distinct from them in both time and nature, while the pleasures are close together with the activities, and so inseparable that there is dispute whether the being-at-work is the same thing as the pleasure. However, it does not seem likely that the pleasure is the thinking or the perceiving (since that would be absurd), but because they are not separated they appear the same to some people.

Just as the ways of being-at-work are different, then, so too are the pleasures. Sight surpasses touch in purity, and hearing and smell   **1176a** surpass taste, and their pleasures differ in a similar way; and the pleasures that have to do with thinking surpass these, and those of each sort have differences one from another. And there seems to be a particular pleasure for each sort of animal, just as there is also a particular kind of work, since the pleasure is in accord with the way of being-at-work. And this will be apparent to one who considers each kind, since different sorts of pleasure belong to a horse, a dog, and a human being; as Heracleitus says, donkeys would rather have garbage than gold,[289] since food is more pleasant than gold to donkeys. So the pleasures of different species of animals are themselves different in species, and it would be reasonable for those belonging to the same species to be undifferentiated; but in the case of human beings at least,   **10** they differ by no small amount. For the same things delight some and give pain to others, and things that are painful and hateful to some are pleasant and loveable to others. This also applies to things that are sweet, since the same things do not seem sweet to someone with a fever and to someone healthy; nor does the same thing seem hot to a sickly person and to someone in good shape, and this happens similarly in other cases.

But in all such matters, it seems that a thing is what it shows itself to be to a person of serious moral stature. And if this is beautifully said, as it seems to be, then the measure of each thing is virtue, or a good person, insofar as he is good, and what appear to be pleasures to this person would be pleasures, and the things he enjoys would be pleasant. And if some things that are hard for this person to endure appear pleas-   **20** ant to someone, that is nothing to be wondered at, since many kinds of corruption and damage happen to human beings, and these things are not pleasant except to those people and others with that disposition. So it is clear that one ought not say that things that are agreed to be shameful are pleasures, except for those who are corrupt; but among the pleasures that seem to be decent, which sort or which one ought one to say is that of a human being? Or is this clear from the ways of being-at-work, since the pleasures follow upon these? So if there is one or more than one activity belonging to the man who is fulfilled and blessed, the

---

[289] Fragment 9 in the Diels numbering.

pleasures that bring them to completion should be spoken of, in the governing sense, as the pleasures of a human being, while the rest are pleasures in a secondary and greatly diminished sense, corresponding to their activities.

30   **Chapter 6.** Now that the things having to do with the virtues, with friendships, and with pleasures have been discussed, what remains is to go through in outline what has to do with happiness, since we set this down as the end at which human things aim. And the account of it would be shorter for those who take up again what has been said before. Now we said that happiness is not an active condition,[290] since it could then be present in someone who was asleep throughout life, living the life of a vegetable, or in someone suffering the greatest misfortunes. So 1176b   if these consequences are not satisfactory, but one ought instead to place happiness in some form of being-at-work, as in what was said before, and among ways of being-at-work, some are necessary and are chosen for the sake of something else while others are for their own sake, it is clear that one ought to place happiness as one of those that are chosen for their own sake and not among those that are for the sake of something else, since happiness stands in need of nothing but is self-sufficient. And those activities are chosen for their own sake from which nothing is sought beyond the being-at-work; and actions in accord with virtue seem to be of this sort, since performing actions that are beautiful and serious is something chosen for its own sake.

But so are the pleasures that come from playing, since they are not 10   chosen for the sake of any other things; people are harmed by them more than they are benefitted, since they neglect their bodies and their property. But many of those who are considered happy escape into pastimes of this sort, and for this reason people who are charming in such ways of passing the time are highly regarded around tyrants, for they display themselves to the latter as pleasing in those things which they aim at, and the people tyrants need are of that sort. It seems, then, that these pastimes are conducive to happiness because those who are in power spend their leisure in them, but perhaps such people are no indication, since virtue does not consist in having power, nor does intelligence, and the activities that are of serious worth come from these; and 20   if those people run off to bodily pleasures because they have no taste for pleasure that is pure and suited to people who are free, one ought not to believe, on that account, that those pleasures are more worthy of choice. Even children believe that the things valued by themselves are the best things. So it is reasonable that, just as different things appear worthwhile to children and to men, so too do different things appear worthwhile to people of a low sort and to decent people. As has been

---

[290] See 1098b 31-1099a 7, where happiness is compared to a prize at the Olympic games, which goes not to the best trained athlete but to the one who performs best.

said repeatedly,[291] the things that are worthwhile and pleasant to a person of serious moral stature are the ones that are so; to each person, the way of being-at-work that results from his own active condition is the most choiceworthy, and to a person of serious worth that is the activity that results from virtue.

Therefore, happiness does not consist in play, for it would even be absurd for our end to be play, and to work hard and undergo troubles all through one's life for the sake of playing. For we choose everything, 30 so to speak, for the sake of something else, except happiness, since this is the end. But to be earnest and to labor for the sake of play seems foolish and too childish. But to play in order that one might be serious, as Anacharsis says, seems to be right, since play seems like relaxation, and since people are incapable of laboring continuously, they need relaxation. So relaxation is not the end, since it comes about for the 1177a sake of being-at-work. And the happy life seems to be in accord with virtue, and this involves seriousness and does not consist in play. And we speak of serious things as better than those that bring laughter and involve play, and say that the activity of the better part or of the better person is always the more serious, and the activity of what is better is more powerful and more conducive to happiness from the start. And any random person, or a slave, might enjoy bodily pleasures no less than the best person, but no one would grant a share of happiness to a slave, if he does not even have a share in his life. For happiness does not consist in such pastimes, but in activities in accord with virtue, as 10 was said before.

Chapter 7. But if happiness is being-at-work in accord with virtue, it is reasonable that it would be in accord with the most powerful virtue, and this would belong to the best part. Now whether this is intellect or some other part that seems by nature to rule and lead and have a conception about things that are beautiful and divine, and to be either divine itself or the most divine of the things in us, the being-at-work of this part in accord with its own proper virtue would be complete happiness. That this way of being-at-work is contemplative has been said.[292] And this would seem to be in agreement with the things said before and with the truth. For this way of being-at-work is the most 20 powerful (since the intellect is the most powerful of the things in us, and the things with which the intellect is concerned are the most pow-

---

291   See 1099a 22-24, 1113a 25-33, 1166a 12-13, 1170a 14-16.

292   This is the first time Aristotle has said this so explicitly, but it was clearly implied twice: at 1095b 14-1096a 5, by a reductio argument that rejects the claims of lives devoted to enjoyment or action to be the highest lives and leaves the contemplative life as the only candidate, and at 1143b 33-1144a 6, where contemplative wisdom was said to be dominant among those activities that constitute happiness not as a consequence of what they understand but by their mere being-at-work.

erful of the things that can be known); it is also the most continuous, for we are more able to contemplate continuously than to act in any way whatever.

And we believe that pleasure must be mixed in with happiness, and by general agreement the most pleasant of the ways of being-at-work in accord with virtue is that which goes along with wisdom; at any rate, philosophy seems to have pleasures that are wonderful in their purity and stability, and it is reasonable that the way of life of those who have knowledge is more pleasant than that of those who are seeking it. And what is referred to as self-sufficiency would be present most of all in the contemplative life, for while the wise and the just person, and the

30   rest, are in need of the things that are necessary for living, when they are sufficiently equipped with such things, a just person still needs people toward whom and with whom he will act justly, and similarly with the temperate and the courageous person and each of the others, but the wise person is able to contemplate even when he is by himself, and more so to the extent that he is the more wise. He will contemplate

1177b   better, no doubt, when he has people to work with, but he is still the most self-sufficient person. And contemplation seems to be the only activity loved for its own sake, for nothing comes from it beyond the contemplating, while from things involving action we gain something for ourselves, to a greater or lesser extent, beyond the action. And happiness seems to be present in leisure, for we engage in unleisured pursuits in order that we may be at leisure, and we make war in order that we may stay at peace.

Now the activity of the virtues that involve action is present in political pursuits and in things that pertain to war, and the actions that have to do with these things seem to be unleisured—completely so with the actions involved in war (for no one chooses to make war for the sake of

10   making war, or even prepares for war in that way, since anyone would seem to be completely bloodthirsty if he were to make friends into enemies so that battles and killings might come about). But the activity of the person engaged in politics is also unleisured, and political activity achieves, beyond itself, positions of power and honors and happiness for oneself and one's fellow citizens that is different from their political life, and which it is clear that we seek as something different from it. So if, among actions in accord with the virtues, those that pertain to politics and war are pre-eminent in beauty and magnitude, but they are unleisured and aim at some end and are not chosen for their own sake, while the being-at-work of the intellect seems to excel in serious-

20   ness, and to be contemplative and aim at no end beyond itself, and to have its own pleasure (which increases its activity), so that what is as self-sufficient, leisured, and unwearied as possible for a human being, and all the other things that are attributed to a blessed person, show themselves as the things that result from this way of being-at-work, then

this would be the complete happiness of a human being, if it takes in a complete span of life, for none of the things that belong to happiness is incomplete.

But such a life would be greater than what accords with a human being, for it is not insofar as one is a human being that he will live in this way, but insofar as something divine is present in him, and to the extent that this surpasses the compound being,[293] to that extent also the being-at-work of it surpasses that which results from the rest of virtue. So if the intellect is something divine as compared with a human being, the life that is in accord with the intellect is divine as compared with a human life. But one should not follow those who advise us to think human thoughts, since we are human, and mortal thoughts, since we are mortal, but as far as possible one ought to be immortal and to do all things with a view toward living in accord with the most powerful thing in oneself,[294] for even if it is small in bulk, it rises much more above everything else in power and worth. And each person would even seem to *be* this part, if it is the governing and better part; it would be strange, then, if anyone were to choose not his own life but that of something else. What was said before[295] will be fitting now too: what is appropriate by nature to each being is best and most pleasant for each, and so, for a human being, this is the life in accord with the intellect, if that most of all is a human being. Therefore this life is also the happiest.

Chapter 8. The life in accord with the rest of virtue is happy in a secondary way, since the activities that result from it are human ones. For we act toward one another in ways that are just and courageous and in accord with the virtues in other respects in our dealings and necessary services and actions of all sorts, as well as in our feelings, by observing what is suitable to each, and all these appear to be human concerns. Some of them even seem to derive from the body, and in many respects virtue of character is bound up together with our feelings. And practical judgment is linked together with virtue of character, and it with practical judgment, if the sources of practical judgment are dependent upon virtues of character, while the right thing belonging to virtues of character is dependent upon practical judgment. These may also be entangled with the passions that have to do with the compound being, but the virtues of the compound are of a human sort, so that the life and the happiness that are in accord with these are human as well.

30

1178a

10

20

---

293   Our compound nature is discussed most directly at 1154b 20-31, as the source of our desire for change, even when it is for the worse, since we experience more than one kind of pleasure.

294   At 1153b 31-32, Aristotle suggests that all desire for pleasure is ultimately directed toward this highest activity; the contrary advice is given widely by poets, who include Euripides, Sophocles, and Pindar.

295   See 1170a 16-b 19, where Aristotle argues that the life most appropriate to a human being must be one shared in friendship.

But the happiness that belongs to the intellect is separate; let this much be said about it, for to be precise about it is something greater than the topic at hand.[296] And it would seem to have little need of external props, or less than virtue of character has. For both there is a need for necessary things, and let it be equal, even if someone involved in politics goes to more trouble about his body and things of that sort, since it would differ to some small extent, but for their activities there will be a great difference. For the generous person will need money

30   for performing generous acts, and so will a just person, for paying back what is due (since wishes are unseen, and even people who are not just pretend to wish to act justly), and a courageous person will need strength, if he is to accomplish any of the things that go with his virtue, and a temperate person will need opportunity—for how else will he or any of the others be manifest? It is also a matter of dispute whether the choice or the actions are more determining of virtue, since

1178b   it is present in both; it is clear that the completeness of it would consist in both together, but for the actions many things are needed, and more of them to the extent that the actions are of greater magnitude and more beautiful. But for someone who contemplates there is no need of such things for his being-at-work; rather, one might say they get in the way of his contemplating. But insofar as he is a human being and lives in company with a number of people, he chooses to do the things that have to do with virtue, and thus will have need of such things in order to live a human life.

That complete happiness is a contemplative activity would also be made clear by the following consideration: we assume that the gods

10   most of all are blessed and happy, but what sort of actions will it be right to attribute to them? Acts of justice? Or will it appear ridiculous if they make contracts and return items held in trust and all that sort of thing? How about courageous acts, enduring frightening things and taking risks because that is a beautiful thing? Or generous acts? To whom will they give? And it will be absurd if they were to have a currency or any such thing. And what would their temperate acts be? Or will praising them for not having base desires be impertinent? And for someone who goes through them all, it would be obvious that the things involved in actions are small and unworthy of the gods. But surely everyone supposes that they are alive at any rate, and are

20   therefore at-work, for they are surely not asleep like Endymion.[297] But

---

[296] See *Metaphysics* 1072b 14-30, and *On the Soul* 408b 1-32 and 430a 10-25. By a concentration of attention, the whole of one's life may be withdrawn, for a time, from all concerns of our compound nature, into the act of contemplation.

[297] A young shepherd given the gift of perpetual sleep, either by Selene so that he could never resist her love, or by Zeus so that he would never grow old.

when someone who is living is deprived of acting, and still more of making anything, what remains except contemplation? So the being-at-work of a god, surpassing in blessedness, would be contemplative, and so among human activities, the one most akin to this would be the most happy.

A sign of this as well is that the rest of the animals do not participate in happiness, since they are completely deprived of such an activity. For the gods, the whole of life is blessed, and for human beings it is so to the extent that there is in it some likeness to such a way of being-at-work; but none of the other animals is happy since they do not share in contemplation at all. So happiness extends as far as contemplation does, and the more it belongs to any beings to contemplate, the more it belongs to them to be happy, not incidentally but as a result   30 of contemplating, since this is worthwhile in itself. And so happiness would be some sort of contemplation. But there will also be a need of external prosperity for one who is a human being, since nature is not self-sufficient for contemplating, but there is also a need for the body to be healthy and for food and other attentions to be present. But one   1179a certainly ought not to suppose that someone who is going to be happy will need many things or grand ones, if it is not possible to be blessed without external goods; for self-sufficiency does not consist in excess any more than action does, and it is possible for one who is not a ruler of land and sea to perform beautiful actions. For one would be capable of acting in accord with virtue from moderate means (and it is possible to see this plainly, since private people seem to perform decent actions not less than powerful people but even more), and it is sufficient if that much is present, since the life of someone who is at-work in accord with virtue will be happy.

And Solon perhaps beautifully revealed those who are happy,   10 saying they are those who have been supplied with external things in measure, who have performed the most beautiful deeds, as he supposed them, and who have lived temperately, for someone with moderate possessions is capable of acting as one ought.[298] And Anaxagoras, too, seems to have believed that the happy person is neither rich nor powerful, when he said that it would be nothing to wonder at if such a person would appear strange to most people, since they judge by externals, perceiving these alone. So the opinions of the wise seem to be in harmony with our arguments. Now such things have some trust-worthiness, but the truth in matters of action is discerned from deeds and from life, since they are the determining thing in these matters.   20 So we ought to examine the things that have been said by applying

---

[298] This is what Solon told Croesus, who wanted to be congratulated for his riches, in Book I, Chap. 30, of Herodotus's *History*.

them to deeds and to life, and if they are in harmony with the deeds one ought to accept them, while if they are out of tune one ought to consider them just words.

But the person who is at-work with the intellect and takes care of this and is disposed in the best way toward it seems also to be most dear to the gods. For if some care for human beings comes from the gods, as is believed, then it would also be reasonable for them to delight in what is best and most akin to them (and this would be the intellect), and to do good in return to those who love and honor this most, since such people care for the things that are dear to them, and also act rightly
30   and beautifully. And it is not unclear that all these things belong most of all to one who is wise. Therefore he is most dear to the gods, and it is likely that the same person is the happiest. So in this way too, a wise person would be the most happy.

Chapter 9. Now if what has to do with happiness as well as with the virtues, and also with friendship and pleasure, has been sufficiently discussed in outline, ought one to assume that our chosen task has its
1179b   end? Or, as has been said,[299] is the end in matters of action not contemplating and knowing each of them but rather doing them? Then it is not sufficient to know about virtue, but one must try to have it and use it, unless there is some other way that we become good. Now if discourses by themselves were sufficient for making people decent, then justly "they would take many large fees," as Theognis says,[300] and one would need to provide them, but as things are, discourses appear to have the power to encourage and stimulate open-natured young people, and would make a well-born character that loves what is truly beautiful
10   be inspired with virtue, but they are unable to encourage most people toward what is beautiful and good. For they are naturally obedient not to respect but to fear, and refrain from base actions not on account of shame but on account of penalties. For since they live by feelings, they pursue the pleasures that they are comfortable with and the things by means of which these will come about, and avoid the pains opposed to these pleasures, while they have no notion of what is beautiful and truly pleasant, having had no taste of it. What sort of discourse, then,

---

[299]   The reference is to the beginning of Bk. II, Chap. 2. There is a mutual interdependence involved here that has given rise to extensive debate. Contemplative activity is identified as our highest and most complete happiness, but it is insufficient for anything that depends upon action. The life of action is called a happy life in only a secondary way, but it appears to be an indispensable foundation for a contemplative life, since wisdom is not mere cleverness, but requires good character and right choices. At the end of Bk. VII, Aristotle focused on the difficulty of satisfying a complex nature; here he seems to be emphasizing the complex conditions that permit such satisfaction.

[300]   In verses 432-434, the fees Theognis imagines are those doctors could get if they could cure the human heart of vice and blindly self-destructive passion.

could reform such people? For it is not possible, or not easy, to change by words things that have been bound up in people's characters since long ago; perhaps one should be content if, when everything is present by which we seem to become decent, we might gain a share of virtue.   20

Now some people think one becomes good by nature, others think it is by habit, and still others think it is by teaching. As for what comes from nature, it is clear that it is not up to us that it is present, but by some divine cause it belongs to those who are fortunate in the true sense; and argument and teaching are perhaps not powerful in all people, but it is necessary for the soul of the listener to have been worked on beforehand by means of habits, with a view to enjoying and hating in a beautiful way, like ground that is going to nourish the seed.[301] For someone who lives by feeling could not hear words that would turn him away, nor could he even understand them; when someone is in that condition, how is it possible to change his mind? And in general, feeling seems to yield not to reasoned speech but to force. So it is necessary for a character to be present in advance that is in some way appropri-   30
ate for virtue, loving what is beautiful and scorning what is shameful. But it is difficult to hit upon a right training toward virtue from youth when one has not been brought up under laws of that sort, for living temperately and with endurance is not pleasant to most people, and especially not to the young.

Hence it is necessary to arrange for rearing and exercises by laws, since they will not be painful when they have become habitual. And   1180a
no doubt it is not enough for people to hit upon the right rearing and discipline when they are young, but also afterward, when they have reached adulthood, they must practice these things and habituate themselves, and we would need laws about these things as well, and so, generally, about the whole of life; for most people are more obedient to compulsion than to argument, and are persuaded more by penalties than by what is beautiful. This is why some people think the lawmakers ought to exhort people to virtue and encourage them to act for the sake of what is beautiful, since those who have been guided decently in their habits will be responsive, but must also impose punishments and penalties on those who are disobedient or lacking in natural capacity, and banish altogether from among them those who are incurable. For a   10
decent person who lives with a view to what is beautiful is obedient to argument, but a corrupt person who strives for pleasure is disciplined by pain like a beast of burden. Hence these thinkers also say that the pains inflicted ought to be of the sort that are most opposed to the pleasures people like.

---

[301] Note that habits belong only to the preparation of the soil, and are neither the seed nor the crop. Habituation is a necessary but early education, that is superseded by argument and understanding. See above, 1104b 8-13.

So if, as was said, someone who is going to be good needs to have been raised and habituated in a beautiful way, and if he needs to live in that way amid decent practices and not do things that are base either unwillingly or willingly, these things would happen to people whose lives are conducted with some intelligence and right ordering, so long as it has strength. So while a father's orders do not have strength or compulsion, nor in general do those of any man who is not a king or something of the sort, the law has a compulsory power, while being speech that comes from a certain thoughtfulness and intelligence. Now among human beings, those who oppose people's impulses are hated, even when they do so rightly, but the law is not hated when it orders what is decent. But in the city of the Spartans alone, or among few others, does the lawgiver seem to have taken care for upbringing and exercises, while in most cities they have been utterly careless about such things, and each person lives the way he wants, "laying down the law for his children and wife" in the manner of a Cyclops.[302]

The best thing, then, is for there to be a public concern that is right and has the power to do this, but when there is a lack of concern in public, it would seem appropriate for each person to make some contribution to the virtue of his own children and friends, or at least to choose to do so. And it would seem from what has been said that he would be more capable of doing this if he became knowledgeable about lawmaking. For it is clear that public concerns are brought about by means of laws, and that decent ones are brought about by laws of serious merit, and it would seem to make no difference whether they are written or unwritten or whether one or many people will be educated by means of them, any more than in the case of music or gymnastics or other exercises. For just as legal regulations and national characters have strength in cities, so too in households, the father's words and habits have strength, and still more so on account of kinship and the good that is done, since his family members are already loving and obedient to him by nature.

And further, educations tailored to each person are better than those that are given in common, just as in the case of medical treatment, for in general rest and fasting are beneficial for someone with a fever, but perhaps not for some particular person, and a boxing instructor probably does not impose the same way of fighting on all people. So it would seem that what is applied to each is more precise when private care is given, since each person gets more of what is suited to him. But a doctor, a gymnastic trainer, or anyone else in general would give the best care in one case by knowing what applies to everyone, or to people of a certain sort (for the kinds of knowledge are spoken of as, and are, about what is common); however, no doubt, nothing prevents even someone who is without knowledge from giving care beautifully to

---

[302] See Homer, *Odyssey*, Bk. IX, lines 112-115.

some one person, if he has by experience observed with precision what happens in each instance, just as some people also seem to be their own best doctors, but would be incapable of giving any help to anyone else.   20
Nonetheless, no doubt, for someone who wants to become skilled and able to contemplate, it would seem to be the case that he must go on to what is universal, and be as well acquainted as possible with that, too, for it was said that the kinds of knowledge are concerned with that. Presumably then also, for someone who wants to make people better by giving care, whether to many people or to few, what one ought to do is try to become knowledgeable about lawmaking, if we might become good by means of laws. For it is surely not in the power of just anyone to get whoever is put in front of him into a beautiful condition, but if it is in anyone's power it is in that of the one who knows, just as in the case of medical skill, or of the other areas about which there is some caregiving and practical judgment.

After this, then, ought one not to consider from what source and in what manner one might become knowledgeable about lawmaking? Is it not, as in other cases, from the politicians? For this did seem to be   30
a part of politics. Or does it seem to be dissimilar in the case of politics and in those of the other capacities and kinds of knowledge? For in the other cases, as with doctors and painters, it is obviously the same people who transmit the capacities and are at-work at them; but the sophists profess to teach the things that have to do with politics,[303] while none of   1181a
them practices them, but instead those who engage in politics do, who would appear to do so by some capacity and experience rather than by thinking things through. For they obviously neither write nor speak about such things (even though that would perhaps be a more beautiful thing than writing speeches for lawcourts and popular assemblies), nor in turn have they made their sons or any of their other friends politicians. But that would have been reasonable, if they were capable of it. For they could not have left anything better to their cities, nor would they have chosen for anything greater to belong to themselves, or to those dearest to them, than such a capacity.

Experience seems to contribute no small amount to it though,   10
for otherwise people would not have become politicians by means of political dealings with one another. Hence, for those who aim at knowing about politics, it would seem that there is an additional need for experience. And those of the sophists who profess that art seem to be very far from teaching it. For they do not even know at all what sort of

---

[303] In Plato's *Gorgias*, 464B-466A, sophistry is identified as a counterfeit of the lawmaking part of the political art, and later in the dialogue, beginning at 513C, it is argued that the politicians too lack art or knowledge. Recall (see note to 1094a 27) that throughout the *Nicomachean Ethics*, Aristotle too leaves open the question of whether politics is informed by art by never specifying a noun for the substantive adjective *hê politikê*.

thing it is or what sorts of things it is concerned with; otherwise they would not class it as the same as, or even inferior to, rhetoric, nor would they think it is an easy thing for someone to make laws by collecting the laws that are well thought of, since he would be able to pick out the best ones, as if picking them out did not require understanding, and judging them rightly were not a very great task, as it would be in matters pertaining to music. For it is those who have experience with each sort of thing who judge its works rightly, and understand by what means and in what manner they are achieved, and what sorts of things harmonize with what others; for those who lack experience, it is good enough if they do not fail to notice whether the work is well or badly made, as in the case of painting.

The laws seem to be the works of the political art. How then could anyone become skilled in lawmaking from these, or judge the best ones? For it is manifest that people do not even become medical doctors from textbooks, even though these attempt to state not only the treatments, but also the manner in which one might cure people and how one needs to treat each sort, distinguishing them by their conditions; while these writings seem to be of benefit to people with experience, to those who have no knowledge they are useless. So perhaps collections of laws and constitutions would be useful to those who are capable of examining them and judging what is good or the contrary, and what sorts of things harmonize with what; but for those who, lacking that active capacity, go through such things, it would not be possible to judge them well except spontaneously, though perhaps one might become more astute about them. Since, then, what has to do with lawmaking has been left undiscovered by those who have gone before, perhaps it would be better to examine it ourselves instead, and to examine what has to do with a political constitution as a whole, in order that the philosophic inquiry about human things might be brought to completion as far as is in our power.

First, then, if anything partial has been well said by our predecessors, let us try to go through it, and then, on the basis of the collection of constitutions, to look at what sorts of things preserve and destroy cities, and what sorts do so for each sort of constitution, and for what reasons some are governed well and others are the reverse. For when these things have been examined, perhaps we might also have more insight into what sort of constitution is best, and how each sort is best arranged, and by using what laws and customs. So having made a beginning, let us discuss it.[304]

---

[304] This paragraph is a rough description of Aristotle's *Politics*. He is believed to have had descriptions of 158 constitutions, all of which were lost until a copy of his *Constitution of Athens* was discovered in Egypt in 1890. It is worth noting that, while this last sentence links the two works, the *Nicomachean Ethics* is one of the most polished writings of Aristotle that we possess, while the *Politics* is one of the least.

GLOSSARY

Note: This is not a complete glossary, but an explanation of some of the words used in the *Nicomachean Ethics* that are most important or most easily misunderstood. The same Greek word is not always translated in the same way; the range of meanings of a Greek word is never matched exactly by that of any English word, and different contexts bring different parts of such a range to the foreground. In some rare cases, as with "active condition" and "temperance," a word is translated in a rigidly consistent way to avoid confusion with a related, but importantly distinct, word. More often, even if complete consistency were possible, it would itself be misleading by suggesting that connotations of the English words could be attributed to Aristotle. In general, then, the English word given in bold type is only the predominant translation used, and in one case ("speech") it is a translation used only once, but for the meaning that is at the root of all the rest.

active condition (*hexis*) Any way in which one deliberately holds oneself in relation to feelings and desires (1105b 25-26), once it becomes a constant part of oneself. For example, fear is a feeling, and lack of confidence is a predisposition to feel fear; both are passive conditions. Cowardice or courage are active conditions one may develop toward them. One's character is made up of active conditions. Hence this is one of the most important words in the *Nicomachean Ethics*, and the foundation of Aristotle's understanding of human responsibility (1114b 21-23). It is sometimes mistranslated as "habit" because, in the thirteenth century, Thomas Aquinas read a Latin translation of Aristotle that used *habitus* for *hexis* and *mos* for habit (*ethos*). The confusion that has resulted persists even when *hexis* is translated as "disposition" or "state," words that are too general since they can mean something passively present as well as something actively achieved. A habit is a necessary precondition for the formation of an active condition (1104b 8-13, 1179b 24-26), but there is all the difference in the world between the two.

base (*phaulos*) Of low or corrupt character, or having a shallow and flighty attitude toward things that deserve respect; opposite to anyone or anything of serious worth (*spoudaios*).

beautiful, the (*to kalon*) The good that is chosen for its own sake (1176b 8-9), and hence the highest form of good, taking precedence over the advantageous and the pleasant; the end that determines all virtue of character (1115b 12-13, 1122b 6-7). The word is usually translated elsewhere as "the noble" to avoid "aesthetic" implications, but the Greek uses the word in exactly the way we might say "that was a beautiful thing you did," and Aristotle is emphatic that such a thing can be recognized only by sense-perception (*aisthêsis*; 1109b

23, 1126b 4). The beautiful is what makes an action right, in the same sense in which a painting or poem or musical composition might get everything exactly right. Aristotle considers the recognition of things well made by the arts to be a special case of the more precise and primary recognition of work well accomplished and action well performed (1106b 8-18), in which the quality of what is done is not separable from that of the person doing it (1105a 26-31). See also the entry for *the good*.

being-at-work (*energeia*) The central notion in all of Aristotle's philosophy, the activity by which anything is what it is. To understand any of Aristotle's inquiries is to grasp the centrality in it of being-at-work. In the *Metaphysics*, everything that is derives from and depends upon the things that have their being only by constant activity. In the *Physics*, nature is not explainable by material but only by the formative activities always at-work in material. In *On the Soul*, a soul is not a detachable being but the being-at-work-staying-itself of an organized body. In the *Nicomachean Ethics*, everything depends upon the idea of an active condition (*hexis*) that can be formed by a deliberately repeated way of being-at-work, and that can in turn set free the being-at-work of all the human powers for the act of choice (Bk. II, Chaps. 2-3). For example, actions that belong to courage must be performed before one can become courageous; after the active condition is formed, actions that belong to courage spring from it, not as dead habit but from the full and unimpeded presence of active thinking and desiring.

blessed (*makarios*) Happy to the maximum extent, for which all the external goods of fortune, such as health, riches, and a flourishing family, are necessary but not sufficient conditions (1099a 29-b 8).

character (*êthos*) A stable condition of the soul that makes someone apt to choose in a consistent way (1111b 5-6, 1139a 33-35; compare 1105a 29-33). The word refers only to active conditions determined by deliberate choices to form oneself in particular ways, and never to a mere temperament or natural disposition. Since feelings arise spontaneously, and desires are influenced by habits formed early in life, before one is in a position to choose, character involves taking hold of the things toward which one has been passive, and forming the rational and irrational parts of the soul into a single whole. Particular states of character may be either virtues or vices.

charm (*eutrapelia*) A flexible capacity to speak gracefully and appropriately to others on occasions of relaxation (Bk. IV, Chap. 8), a minor virtue of character. The word is usually translated elsewhere as wit, but the emphasis is not on the content of one's speech, but on one's adroitness at suiting it to the occasion and to the pleasure of those who are at hand.

choice (*proairesis*) Desire informed by deliberation, or thinking infused with desire, and hence an act of the whole human being, in which neither the rational nor the irrational part is superior (1139b 4-5). If desire predominates, one merely takes one thing in preference to others, as an animal or small child might, but deliberation allows one to take a course in the light of alternatives not immediately present and of long-term consequences not obvious at the moment. If rationally determined principles or rules predominate, desires may be left unsatisfied; hence the only "rule" that can make choice be right is the judgment of a person of good character, whose desires are neither excessive nor corrupted (1113a 29-33).

cleverness (*deinotês*) The ability to reason well from ends to means. Mere cleverness, ungoverned by clarity about ends, is therefore no advantage to its possessor, since it can bring about ruin more effectively. It is one component of practical judgment (1144a 23-29).

contemplation (*theôria*) The being-at-work of the intellect, a thinking that is like seeing, complete at every instant. In contemplation a human being is most fully active, in that the power underlying all thinking and perceiving has emerged, but also most at rest in what is knowable. Contemplation is discussed in detail in the *Metaphysics* (1072b 14-30) and in *On the Soul* (408b 1-32, 430a 10-25); in the *Nicomachean Ethics* it is painstakingly uncovered as the most complete human happiness (1177b 19-1179a 30). The relation between contemplation and the virtues of character is best explained in the *Physics* (247b 1-248a 6); to come to rest in contemplation, a human being must overcome the disorder of the soul native to it from childhood.

courage (*andreia*) An achieved condition by which one is apt to choose to endure frightening things, and even the risk of death, when it is a beautiful thing to do so (1115b 7-13). It is not a lack of fear but a capacity to keep fear in proportion and not be ruled by it. Aristotle's careful distinction of courage, in Bk. III, Chap. 8, from the many things that resemble it, provides a model of what constitutes a virtue of character.

decency (*epieikeia*) A sense for what is appropriate. In Bk. V, Chap. 10, Aristotle focuses on decency as the attribute by which people recognize when particular circumstances call for a departure from strict justice, or from any general rules. In that chapter, the word is often translated elsewhere as "equity" in the technical legal sense of that word, but this is misleading, since Aristotle is describing something that goes beyond what is equitable (*to ison*). Decency is one of Aristotle's most frequent ways of naming human goodness.

dissipation (*akolasia*) The vice by which one deliberately chooses to be, or acquiesces in being, someone who indulges in the pleasures of eating, drinking, and sex whenever they are available (1146b 22-23). It differs from mere weakness or lack of restraint (*akrasia*) by being an active condition and part of one's character. The word is related to the meaning of a "spoiled" child (1119a 33-b 7). Desires not brought under control by choice beginning in childhood become the foundation of a slavish kind of life (1118a 23-25), ruled by irrational impulses. "Dissipation" is not an ideal translation, but it seems better than the usual alternatives, which are either obsolete (profligacy), quaint (licentiousness), or too weak (intemperance). It is used consistently here to distinguish the vice from the state of weakness; it captures something of the way in which the vice of deliberate overindulgence puts a human soul at variance with itself (1166b 19-22).

end (*telos*) That for the sake of which anything comes to be or is done, frequently connected with the metaphor of an archer's target, but most importantly, by the root sense of the word, the wholeness in which something comes to completion. In the non-human world, anything that maintains itself in wholeness has its end in being itself. For human beings, ends may also appear as purposes, things chosen in advance that, when accomplished, bring actions to completion. The *Nicomachean Ethics* begins by identifying the meaning of the good, in its broadest sense, with the end at which anything aims.

equality (*isotês*) A governing notion for both justice and friendship. It is used in a broader sense than mere sameness of quantity, to include sameness of ratios. In the case of justice, numerical equality is the standard only for judicial penalties, which seek to undo harm (1132a 2-6); distributive justice, which governs the awarding by a community of honors and of goods from the common supply, goes by proportional equality, apportioning the distribution in accord with what is deserved (1131a 25-32), and the justice that gets things straight in voluntary exchange looks to reciprocal equality, in which quantity is inversely proportional to the worth of what is exchanged (1132b 31-33). In the case of friendship, equality as sameness of character is the aim of friendships based on virtue (1159b 2-5), while friendships of people in inherently unequal conditions are preserved by proportional equality, in which benefits on one side are matched by affection, gratitude, and honor on the other (1158b 23-28, 1163b 1-12). In all human things, measurement is a bringing of qualitative differences under quantitative metaphors (1132b 10-20, 1133b 18-20), where the greatest precision comes from the judgment of a decent and experienced person (1137b 26-32).

forgiveness (*sun-gnomê*) A judgment, made by putting oneself in another's place in imagination, that the other person's action was wrong, but only for reasons that no human being could be expected to overcome (1110a 23-26), appropriate when the other person indicates by remorse and regret that the action was unwilling (1110b 18-19, 1111a 1-2). The word is translated as compassion in Bk. VI, Chap. 11, where it is used more broadly for the thoughtful discernment involved in all decent treatment of others.

fraternal association (*hetairikê*) A social club of young rich men. At the time of the Peloponnesian War, these groups in Athens were antidemocratic political parties that took part in oligarchic governments, and one of which was suspected of sacrilegious vandalism in a major scandal. In Aristotle's time they were banned from political activity, and he treats them as outgrowths of the bond between brothers, friendships for pleasure of leisured young men alike in age and tastes. "Comrade" (*hetairos*), a general word for a fellow worker or fellow soldier or sailor, is most often used in Bk. VIII to refer to a fellow member of such a club.

friendship (*philia*) Any association of people who spend time and do things together, share in pains and pleasures, and wish for each other's good (1166a 1-10). The Greek word takes in all love felt and practiced toward family members, fellow countrymen, and generally those like oneself. Aristotle finds its highest form in the attachment between people of good character, present in each for the sake of the being and well-being of the other, while friendships for the sake of pleasure or usefulness are partial and less enduring. The treatment of friendship in the *Nicomachean Ethics* is longer than that of any other topic, and comes just before the conclusion of the whole inquiry. Books VIII and IX are continuous, but the break makes the first book focus on friendship as a small version of the political community, in which a bond stronger than justice holds people together, while the second treats it as an expansion of the self, through which all one's powers can approach their highest development. Friendship thus provides a bridge between the virtues of character and those of intellect.

good, the (*to agathon*) That at which anything aims, and by which it becomes fully and properly itself. The good of a changeable thing other than a human being is achieved by natural development, when all suitable conditions are present and nothing impedes it. The good of a human being must be secured by intelligence, choice, and effort. The question whether there is a single human good that governs and determines all subordinate goods is dismissed at 1096b 26-31 as an explicit topic, but the whole of the *Nicomachean Ethics* is a gradual ascent to its discovery. The kinds of good chosen are distinguished at 1104b 30-31 as the advantageous, the pleasant, and the beautiful. At 1110b 9-11, the advantageous drops out as subordinate to the other two. At 1148a 22-25, pleasures are ranked as better and worse in accord with the beautiful. At 1169a 8-11, it is said that the greatest of goods is achieved by aiming at the beautiful in action, and throughout the inquiry the beautiful is present in the guise of that which is simply for its own sake. In the *Metaphysics* (1072a 19-b 4), the beautiful that is beyond appearance is identified with the divine intellect, which is responsible for the formative identities that make each thing what it is.

greatness of soul (*megalopsuchia*) The well-founded attitude that one is worthy of great things. It is variously translated elsewhere as "pride," "magnanimity," or "high-mindedness," but these words all miss part of its meaning, which applies both to people like Achilles who do not tolerate insults and people like Socrates who do not care about good or bad fortune (*Posterior Analytics*, 97b 14-26). Book IV, Chap. 3, in which Aristotle discusses greatness of soul, is a model of his dialectical approach to ethics, disentangling what is worthwhile in what might otherwise be a merely contemptuous attitude toward others held by an aristocrat or "elitist." In the course of the chapter, Aristotle shows that those who are greatly concerned with honor ought to consider honor itself something small (1124a 4-19), and that those who are genuinely serious must take few things seriously (1125a 9-16). The lengthy treatment Aristotle gives it elevates greatness of soul to the status of a fifth cardinal virtue, alongside courage, temperance, justice, and wisdom, but its position in the inquiry makes it the lowest of four kinds of active lives that organize all the virtues around one center (1123b 33-1124a 3), superceded successively by justice (1129b 25-27), practical judgment (1144b 30-1145a 2), and friendship (1157a 18-19, 29-31).

habit (*ethos*) Anything that is done because it has been done many times before (1103a 19-23). The study of ethics is about the things that have to do with character (*êthos*), not about socially approved habits, or habits of any kind. Character consists of active conditions, which are not habits, though they require habits as preconditions (1179b 23-26) before they can be brought about by thinking, understanding, and choice. Hence virtues are never habits, and the habits that lead to them are not arbitrarily variable, but require a natural foundation (1103a 23-26). For example, acts that are naturally just (Bk. V, Chap. 7) must be performed in particular ways that vary with local habits and customs, giving rise to the mistaken opinion that justice is merely relative or conventional.

happiness (*eudaimonia*) The condition at which any human being aims, generally taken to result from something obvious such as pleasure, wealth, or honor (1095a 22-23), but argued by Aristotle to be some being-at-work of the soul in accordance with all the virtues, or with the best and most complete of them, that endures throughout life (1098a 16-18), and that fulfills our characteristic capacity as thinking beings (1098a 3-4). The best and most complete virtue is finally discovered to be contemplative wisdom (1177a 12-18), but as part of a human life it is inseparable from friendship and from all the virtues of character (1170b 8-14, 1178b 5-7).

honor (*timê*) The good opinion of others and the display of it in prizes, awards, and political offices. In Bk. I, Chap. 12, Aristotle distinguishes honor, which is bestowed upon the highest goods and those who embody them, and always looks upward, from praise, which is given to those who measure up to some standard, and always implies one's own superior fitness to judge. Honor is the highest aim sought in competitive athletics and in political life, and by people who regard success in life as a competition. Aristotle considers the desire for honor a sign that one has risen above the shallowest belief in happiness as bodily enjoyment, but still as a secondary good, since it is unstable and is always given on account of some perceived excellence, which would be the more primary good even if it were unrecognized by others (1095b 22-31). The Greek word does not have the meaning we sometimes intend by speaking of a sense of honor as an internal standard for self-respect. The sense of one's own worth, when this is both accurate and considerable, is called greatness of soul. The word honor always implies something external; at 1123b 20-21 it is called the greatest of external goods, but this conclusion is overturned at 1159a 25-26 and 1169b 8-10.

impasse (*aporia*) A logical stalemate or paradox that brings one's thinking to a stop. Sophistical reasoning seeks to produce impasses as a display of cleverness, but they are necessary starting points for genuine inquiry; when one is stuck at an impasse, the only way forward is a new perspective or deeper formulation (1146a 21-27, b 6-8). In Aristotle's *Physics*, the definition of motion is a powerful achievement that resolves the impasses of Zeno's paradoxes. In Bk. VII of the *Nicomachean Ethics*, impasses about unrestraint lead to a deeper understanding of vice; in Bks. VIII and IX, impasses about friendship (1155b 8-13, 1168a 28-29) lead to a distinction of its kinds, and a deepened understanding of virtue.

intellect (*nous*) The direct contemplative beholding of the sources of knowledge (1141a 7-8), that gets hold of the universal within any particular perception (1139b 28-29). Hence, as grasping the highest unarticulated sources of thinking, intellect is at the opposite extreme from the perception of ultimate particulars (1142a 25-27), but since this grasping is not abstraction but an openness to that which organizes those very particulars into wholes, intellect unites those extremes (1143a 35-b 5). Grasping the particular as an example of the universal (*epagôgê*), usually mistranslated elsewhere as "induction," is not a gathering of instances but a contemplative act by which intellect stands at the root of both theoretical and practical knowing, being at once the starting point of wisdom's reasoned knowledge (1141b 2-3) and the experienced eye for particulars of someone with practical judgment (1143b 13-14).

irony (*eirôneia*) The gracious vice, associated especially with Socrates, of understating one's own merits; if those merits are small and obvious, understating them becomes ludicrous (1127b 22-31). The profound meaning of the word, for the various ways of speaking on more than one level at once, is a later development; the vague use of the word for anything from coincidence to paradox is a recent degeneration.

justice (*dikaiosunê*) Most properly, an active condition of the soul by which one chooses neither more nor less than one's fair share of those goods that one can have only by depriving others of them; this is the justice that is a part of virtue, but the word is also used for the whole of virtue, regarded as a relation toward other people (1129b 26-27). In the latter sense, justice is a willing acceptance of the laws of the community as governing one's own life (1129b 12-19). In the former sense, justice is again subdivided into its various manifestations: in the distribution of honor and of a community's common supply of possessions in proportion to what people deserve (1130b 30-33, 1131a 25-29); in the equitable judgment of penalties for those who wrong others in any way and thus gain undeserved advantage (1132a 6-14); and in the equitable reciprocal exchange of commodities and services (1132b 31-34). All the forms of justice in its particular sense are opposed to greed (*pleonexia*), the desire to have more of some good thing than one deserves (1129b 1-10), and hence justice involves quantitative judgments, even when the things judged are not strictly measurable. (See the entry for *equality*.) This quasi-mathematical aspect of justice means that the judgments that govern choices of what is just do not look to what is beautiful (compare 1133b 32-33), even though Aristotle calls that the end aimed at by all virtue of character. What is just is superceded in particular cases by what is decent (Bk. V, Chap. 10), and justice itself, as the necessary foundation of shared life, is superceded by friendship, which does look toward the beautiful (1155a 22-30).

knowledge (*epistêmê*) An active condition of the soul by which one is convinced, by explicit reasoning from some source of evidence, that something is invariably the case (Bk. VI, Chap. 3). There are kinds of knowledge (*epistêmai*) concerned with various topics, but the usual translation "sciences" carries connotations that are not part of Aristotle's meaning, of an experimental method of discovery, or that precision is possible only by means of mathematics, or that a body of propositions as opposed to an active condition of the soul can contain knowledge (1147a 10-24). Knowledge becomes wisdom (*sophia*) when its sources are grasped by the contemplative intellect (*nous*, 1141a 18-20); it is a necessary component of skilled making (*technê*) and of deliberate choice, since both depend in part on a rational understanding of something invariable within their material or circumstances (1139a 27-b 1), but these capacities work with things that can be other than they are, and require a know-how that comes from experience, while the latter also requires a judgment that depends on good character.

mean (*meson*) The balanced choice that precisely achieves its end (1106b 8-16). In matters of feeling and action its precision is not quantitative, or subject to calculation, but a judgment made directly by sense-perception (1109b 23, 1126b 3-4), looking to what is beautiful (1115b 12-13, 1122b 6-7). Every virtue of character is a reliable capacity to discern and choose the mean in connection with some kind of feelings and actions, and is therefore itself a mean condition (*mesotês*) between vices of excess and deficiency, but the virtue is never something middling, mediocre, or moderated, but a maximum condition (1106b 36-1107a 8, 22-23) in which all the human powers of thinking and desire are present and free to work together (1139a 22-26, b 4-5). The balanced or whole human being is therefore not a slave to pleasure, fear, or greed, nor one who must hold all desires and aversions rigidly in control, but one who is free to choose what is truly desirable by seeing things as they are (1113a 29-b 2).

ought (*dei*) An impersonal verb signifying what is needed in any situation or circumstances. What one ought to do is never a duty imposed by reason, society, or any external authority, but is rooted in human nature, and the demands imposed by its own need to put to work the capacities within it (1097b 22-34). It does not imply moral obligation, since the vices are based upon opinions of what anyone ought to do to be happy (1152a 4-6). What ought to be done is spoken of impersonally because there are natural consequences in all human beings of actions involving pleasure and pain (1104b 18-24), but it cannot be prescribed by any general rules since it is always dependent upon particulars (1106b 36-1107a 2, 1126b 2-4).

politics (*hê politikê*) The aptitude, skill, knowledge, or other capacity that makes someone suited to arrange and carry out the things that pertain to a city. Aristotle never specifies the noun implicit in the phrase "the political _____," and at the very end of the *Nicomachean Ethics* he raises the question whether any of those who lay claim to this capacity are worthy of the name; his partial identification of it with practical judgment (1141b 23-24) suggests that it should be an art, a skilled know-how directed at producing a successful city. The city (*polis*) is a sovereign and self-sufficient human community, small enough that all citizens can take part in ruling it, that comes into being for the sake of mere life but secures the conditions for good life or well-being (*Politics* 1275b 18-21, 1252b 29-30); since the city aims at the human good, and a human being is by nature meant for life in a city (1097b 11), a necessary part of the political study is ethics, the inquiry about human character and happiness, while the rest of its study and practice have to do with means to that end.

practical judgment (*phronêsis*) The active condition by which someone discerns the right means to the right end in particular circumstances (1144a 6-9). Hence the intellectual virtue of practical judgment and the whole of virtue of character are mutually dependent and must develop together, since the right end is apparent only to someone of good character, while the formation of good character requires the repeated choice of the right action, which is impossible without practical judgment (1144b 18-32, 1145a 4-6). Apart from virtue of character, the capacity to reason from ends to means is mere cleverness (1144a 23-29); practical judgment involves skill in making distinctions and seeing connections, but if one does not recognize that such thinking imposes upon oneself an obligation to act, that skill is merely astuteness (1143a 4-15). Practical judgment is acquired primarily by experience of particulars, but also involves a knowledge of things that are universal and unvarying within those particulars (1141b 14-24), the things studied by Aristotle in his inquiries into politics and ethics. The word *phronêsis* is generally translated elsewhere as "practical wisdom" or "prudence." The latter now has connotations of caution that Aristotle does not intend, and that contribute to the misunderstanding of choosing the mean as playing it safe. The former is used by those who believe that Aristotle is imposing a distinction between *phronêsis* and *sophia* that was not present before his time, but this is a dubious assumption; in earlier writings as diverse as the *Odyssey* and Plato's *Philebus*, *phronêsis* has a general sense of thoughtfulness or intelligence (clearly intended at 1172b

28-30), while *sophia* always carries some implication of excelling in precision (1141a 9-17). The translation "practical judgment" is chosen here as the best way of conveying Aristotle's central understanding that ethical choices can never be deductions from any rules, principles, or general duties, but always require a weighing of particular circumstances and balancing of conflicting principles in a direct recognition of the mean.

praise (*epainos*) The expressed approval given to those who measure up to some standard, implying the superior fitness of those who bestow it to recognize that standard; Aristotle distinguishes praise from the more humble attitude of honor, which is given to those who display the highest good (Bk. I, Chap. 12). Throughout the *Nicomachean Ethics*, Aristotle takes the things that are customarily praised as starting points for inquiry, but only as starting points. He argues that any widespread and enduring belief must have something true about it (1098b 27-29), and that the truth is confirmed when it explains why a false opinion seems plausible (1154a 22-25). Aristotle characteristically moves from what is in fact praised to what is worthy of such praise, as the aim of an implicit and imprecise recognition of the good (1095b 25-26, 1153b 31-32). For example, out of the commonplace admiration for the ostentatious display of wealth, Aristotle uncovers a genuine virtue of putting great private wealth to appropriate public use (Bk. IV, Chap. 2).

rule (*kanôn*) Literally a ruler or straightedge, the word comes to signify any standard by which other things are measured or to which they must conform. Aristotle uses the word only to deny that there are any such things in ethics, apart from the flexible judgment of a serious and decent human being (1113a 31-33, 1137b 29-32). At 1109a 30-b 13 Aristotle gives three general pieces of advice for hitting the mean, which commentators and even some translators have called "rules," but he says clearly that the right thing to do is always something particular that must be perceived (1109b 20-23). From the beginning of the inquiry, Aristotle warns against looking for the precision of formulations and deductions in ethics (1194b 11-27), and his central metaphor of hitting the mean is taken from the skilled eye of the productive artist rather than from the deductive procedure of the mathematician (1106b 5-16).

serious (*spoudaios*) Deserving respect. This is the word that Aristotle reserves for people of the highest human excellence, who see things as they are and know which of them are worth taking seriously (1113a 29-33), thus providing, by their own judgment and choices, the standard for the rest of us to look to. To distinguish the meaning of the word from a mere grave attitude, which could be assumed by anyone, this translation always renders it by a phrase such as "of serious stature," or "of serious worth." The root sense of the word implies haste and urgency, or even anxiety (connotations which Aristotle reserves for the related word *speustikos*), but Aristotle decisively transforms the meaning of the word by arguing that a truly serious person takes few things seriously (1125a 12-16). In Bk. X, Chap. 6, as Aristotle's inquiry takes the next-to-last step toward the discovery of happiness, seriousness (*spoudê*) becomes the ultimate criterion that makes an activity worthy of choice.

shame, a sense of (*aidôs*) A respectful attitude that holds one back from inappropriate behavior (Bk. IV, Chap. 9). It involves both feeling and thinking, but Aristotle regards it as something less than a virtue and appropriate only to the young, a restraint that is unnecessary when a mature active condition has been formed. What is shameful (*aischros*), the extreme opposite of what is beautiful, is recognized by a decent person hypothetically, as that which one ought to be ashamed to do.

speech (*logos*) The power of rational articulation, the characteristic capacity of a human being, by which we think things through and understand what is said or written by others (1098a 3-5). Since *logos* applies to anything in which that power is embodied, it can mean word, sentence, proposition, argument, reasoning, rational understanding, talk, a discourse, a story, a chapter, or a book. A human being is a unity of reason and desire, and suffers if either side gets the upper hand (1111b 1-2, 1139b 4-5). In a good human being, reason and desire are in harmony (1102b 23-28). Since the mathematical meaning of *logos* is ratio, a human life or a choice that is *kata logon* may be understood equally well as "in accord with reason" and "in proportion."

temperance (*sôphrosunê*) The active condition by which one chooses bodily pleasures in the ways and to the extent that they enhance life, not by an effort of self-control but by a harmony of desire with reason (1119a 11-20). "Moderation" is a more contemporary translation of the word, but it is too broad, and it is inaccurate if it implies that desires must be given less than full satisfaction; in a temperate person, the desires themselves are appropriate and can be trusted. Along with courage, temperance is a fundamental virtue of the irrational part of the soul, a stable state of character which, in any mature human being, replaces the overgrown impulses of childhood (1179b 29-1180a 1).

unrestraint (*akrasia*) An active condition so feeble that Aristotle more often calls it a passive experience (see note to 1146b 22), in which a good choice is made (1152a 17), but cannot be carried out in action because no character has been formed by habituation (1147a 14-24, 34-35). The word is properly used of a weakness for the bodily pleasures chosen by a dissipated person, but by analogy for being overpowered even by one's zeal for good and desirable things (Bk. VII, Chaps. 4, 6). Unrestraint is not vice, and self-restraint is not virtue; the need for restraint of each new impulse that arises is an immature and unstable condition, but one beyond which most human beings never get (1150a 9-16).

unwilling (*akôn*) Acting as a result of external force, or in ignorance of some important particular circumstance, and afterward feeling regret because of the pain of remorse (1109b 35-1110a 1, 1110b 18-19, 1110b 30-1111a 2). Anything one does while knowing the circumstances, that is up to oneself, is a willing act, even if it is not deliberately chosen (1111a 22-24). Hence Aristotle does not posit a separate human faculty of will to explain perverse and self-destructive acts, as St. Paul (*Romans*, 7.15) and St. Augustine (*Confessions*, Bk. VIII, Chap. 9) do (compare *Gospel of John*, 1.13), but assigns such behavior to unrestraint in one's desires; his primary example is *hubris*, understood as gratuitously insulting speech or action indulged in for the mere pleasure of feeling the power to cause pain (1149b 20-26). The display of *hubris* is a willing act, not a willful departure from rational choice.

vice (*kakia, ponêria, mochthêria*) A stable active condition of the soul by which one consistently chooses extremes of feeling and action knowingly and for their own sake (1105a 30-33, 1107a 2-6, 1152a 4-6). Vice is a formed state of character, deliberately chosen, blameable finally because it prevents all the powers within the human soul from coming into any sort of internal harmony (1166b 11-29).

virtue (*aretê*) The excellence that makes anything an outstanding specimen of its kind, especially well fitted to its ends. When applied to human beings, the word has no necessary moral implications, though it carries them conventionally. For example Meno, in the Platonic dialogue bearing his name, identifies virtue with power and money (73C-D, 78C-D), but even he, when pressed, is uncomfortable about excluding justice and temperance. This mixture of incompatible opinions is part of the ordinary human heritage, out of which philosophic inquiry may and must begin. The English word "virtue" is an apt translation, just because of its own fruitful ambiguity, combining durable moral connotations with amoral uses such as "the virtue of this tax-avoidance scheme..." Aristotle distinguishes virtue of intellect from virtue of character, but uses the word primarily for the latter, which he defines as a stable active condition of the soul, by which one consistently chooses the mean in matters of feeling and action knowingly and for its own sake (1105a 30-33, 1106b 36-1107a 2). The standard lexicon of ancient Greek derives the word *aretê* from the name of Ares, the war god, but it is more likely related to the verb *arariskein*, meaning to fit together or be fitting. Aristotle's account of virtue finds it displayed especially in the decent person (*epieikês*) who recognizes and chooses what is appropriate, and in the well-balanced person in whom all the parts of the soul are in harmony with one another (1102b 27-28). This human mean does not, in Aristotle's view, require the sacrifice or holding back of any of our powers, but sets free the full being-at-work of them all.

wisdom (*sophia*) The combination of a reasoned knowledge of conclusions (*epistêmê*) with an immediate knowing of their sources by means of the contemplative intellect (*nous*), about things that are everlasting and unchanging (1141a 18-20, 1139b 19-24). Each component of wisdom is an active condition (*hexis*), the live attentive beholding of what is known along with the evidence that makes it convincing (1139b 31-35).

INDEX

References are to the Bekker page and column numbers appearing in the margins throughout the text, and may include the footnotes to those pages. Titles in italics not followed by an author's name are works of Aristotle. This is by no means intended to be a complete index, but is a guide to some of the occurrences of some of the more important names and topics. Discussions of many of those topics may be found also in the glossary.